A Tropical Fish Yearns for Snow

A Tropical Fish
Yearns for Snow

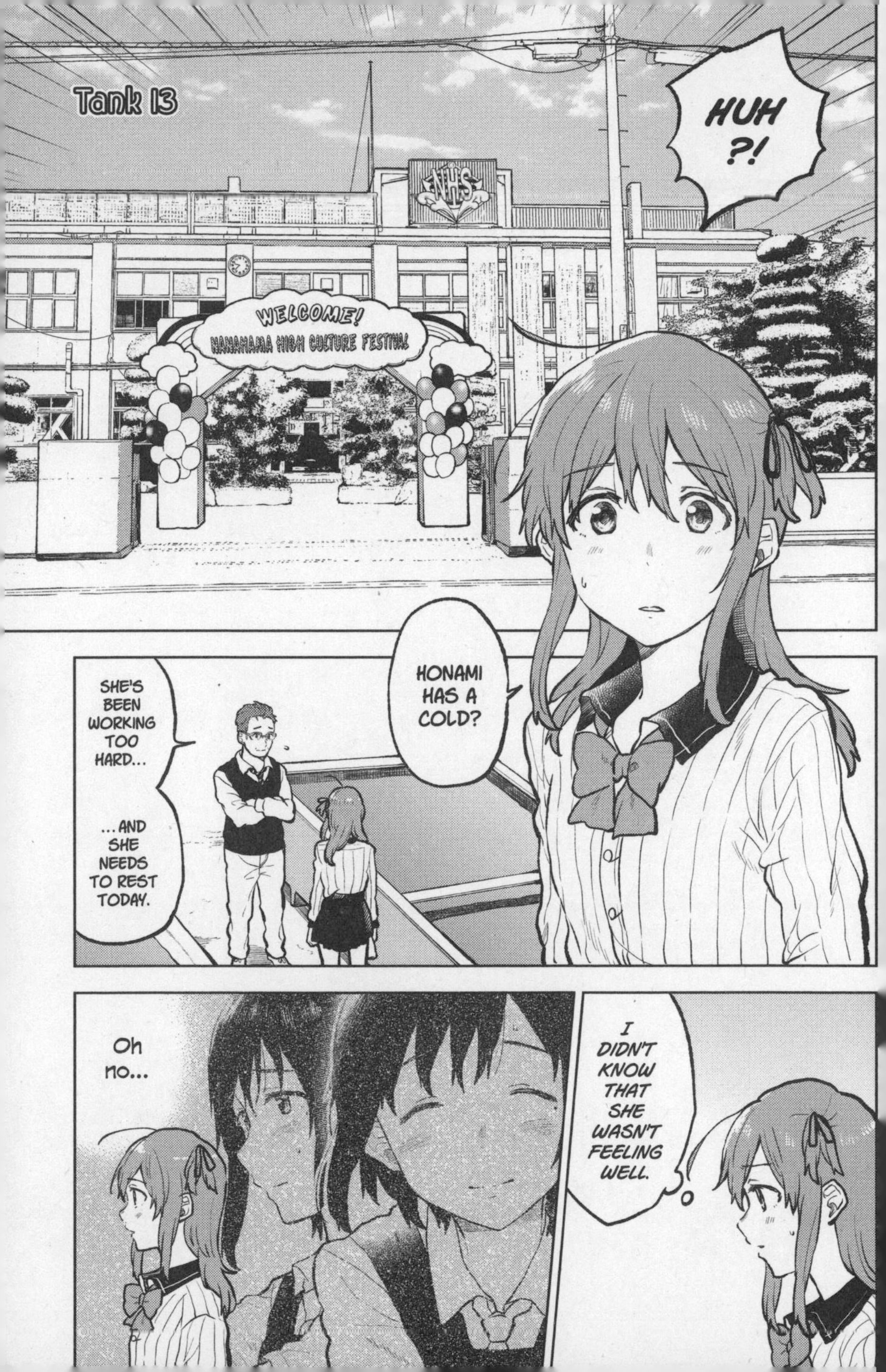
HUH ?!
Tank 13
NHS
WELCOME! NANAHAMA HIGH CULTURE FESTIVAL
HONAMI HAS A COLD?
SHE'S BEEN WORKING TOO HARD...
...AND SHE NEEDS TO REST TODAY.
I DIDN'T KNOW THAT SHE WASN'T FEELING WELL.
Oh no...

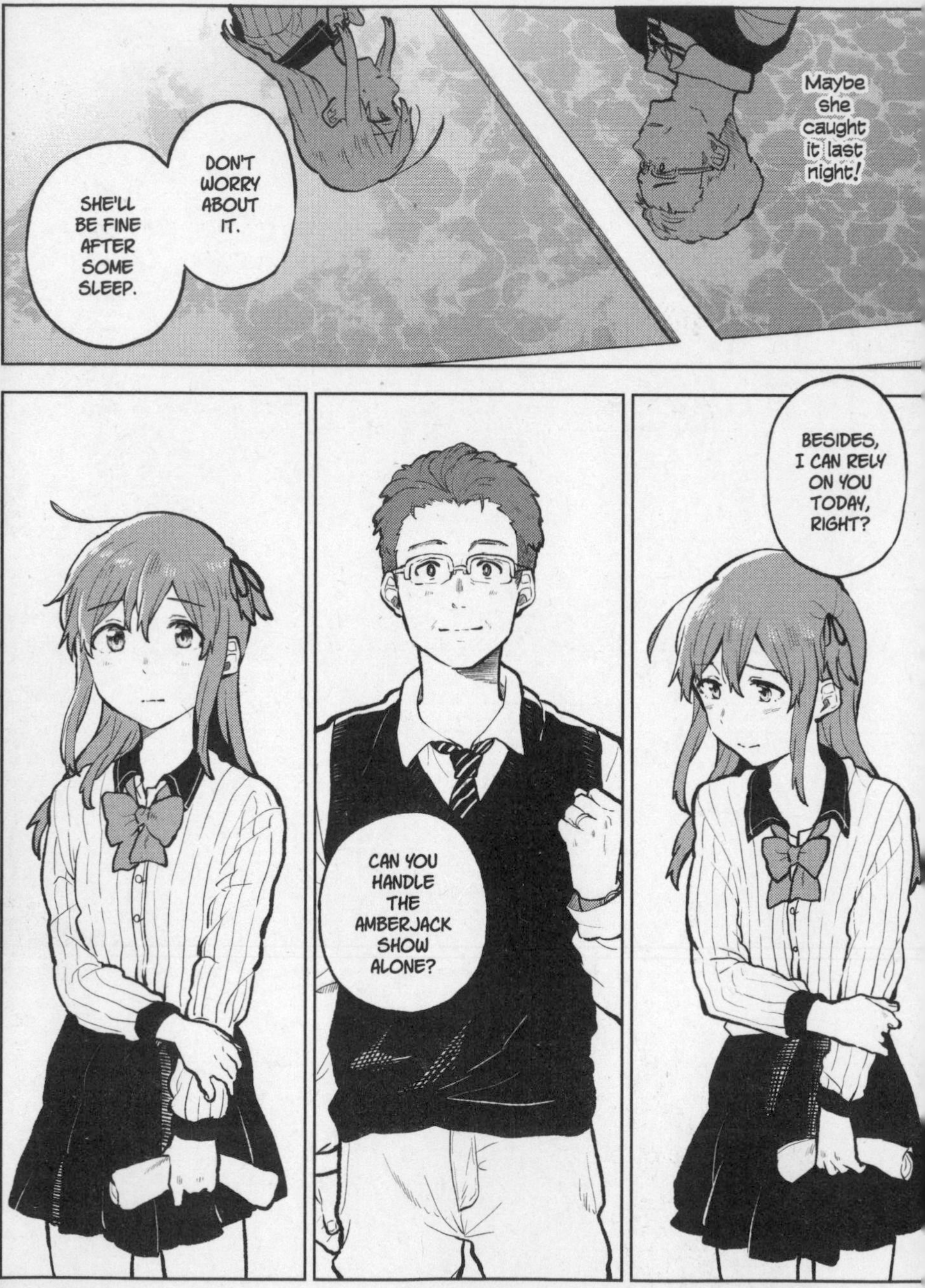
Maybe she caught it last night!
DON'T WORRY ABOUT IT.
SHE'LL BE FINE AFTER SOME SLEEP.
BESIDES, I CAN RELY ON YOU TODAY, RIGHT?
CAN YOU HANDLE THE AMBERJACK SHOW ALONE?

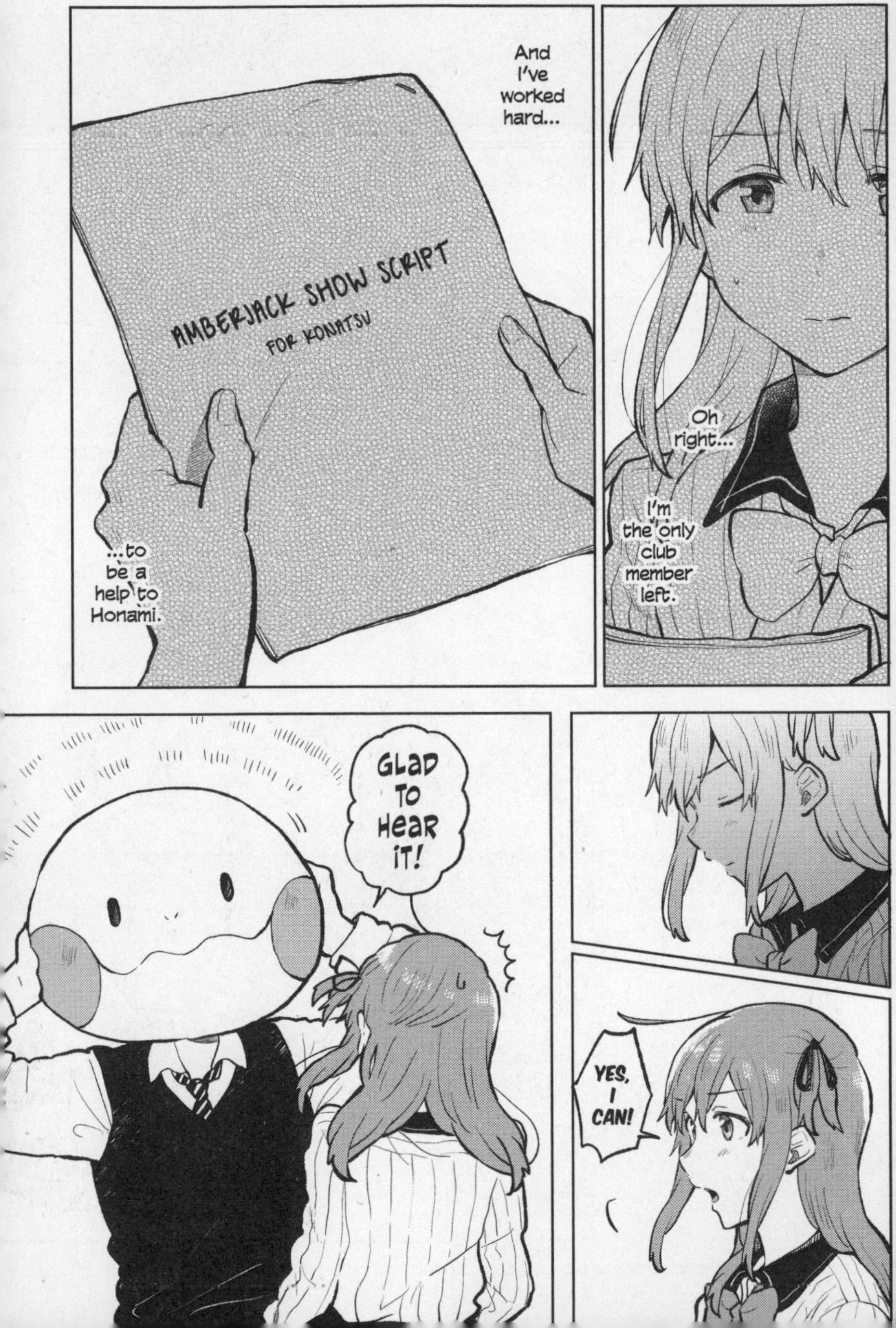
Oh right...
I'm the only club member left.
And I've worked hard...
AMBERJACK SHOW SCRIPT
FOR KONATSU
...to be a help to Honami.
YES, I CAN!
GLAD TO HEAR IT!

MR. HONAMI!

ARE YOU WEARING THAT AGAIN TODAY?

YEAH! I'LL GATHER A BIG CROWD FOR YOUR FIRST SHOW!

LET'S DO OUR BEST!

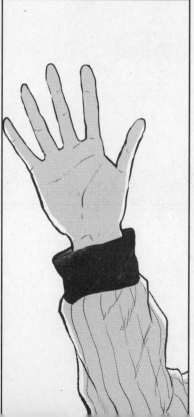

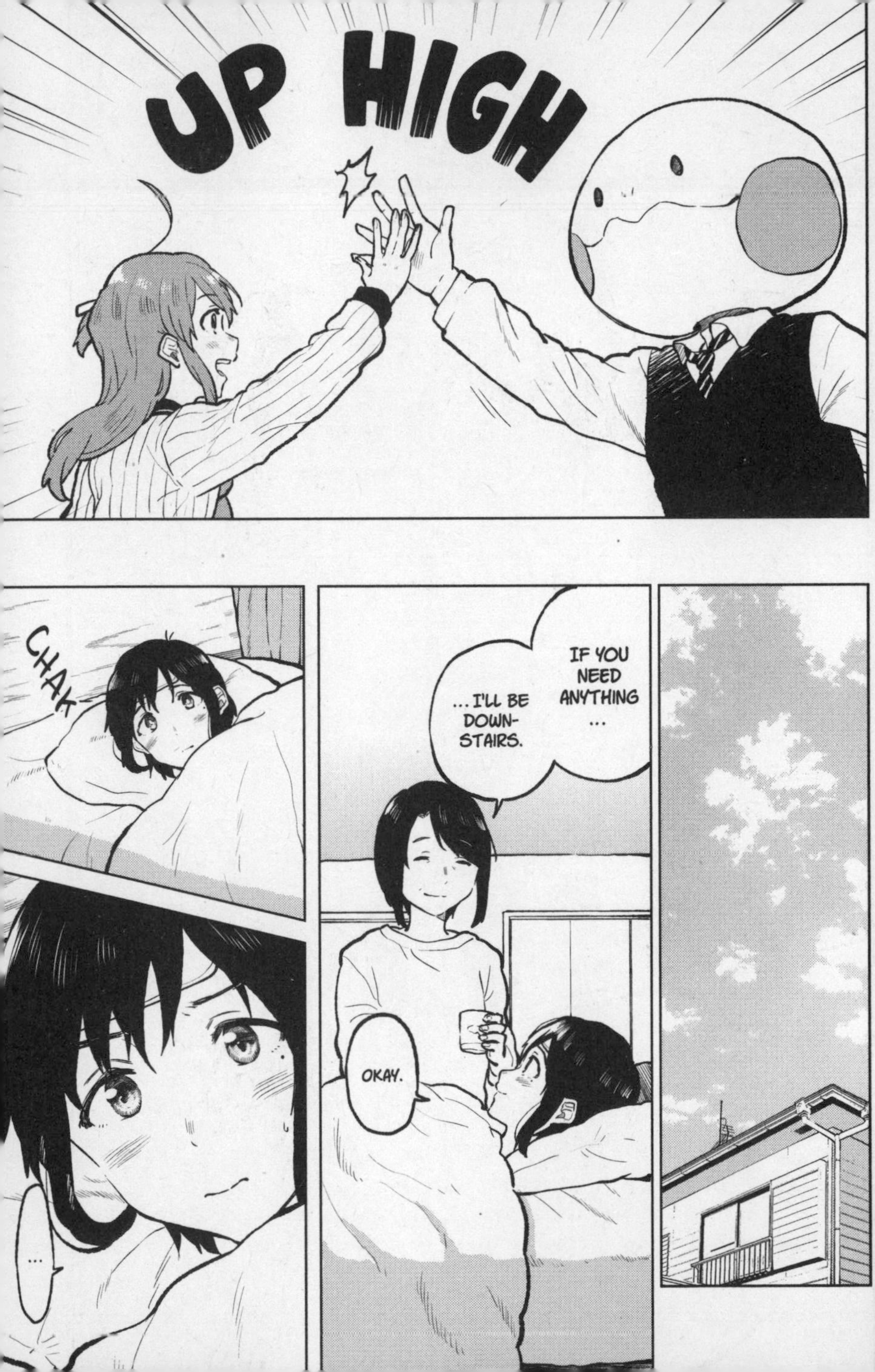
UP HIGH
IF YOU NEED ANYTHING ...
...I'LL BE DOWN-STAIRS.
OKAY.
CHAK
...

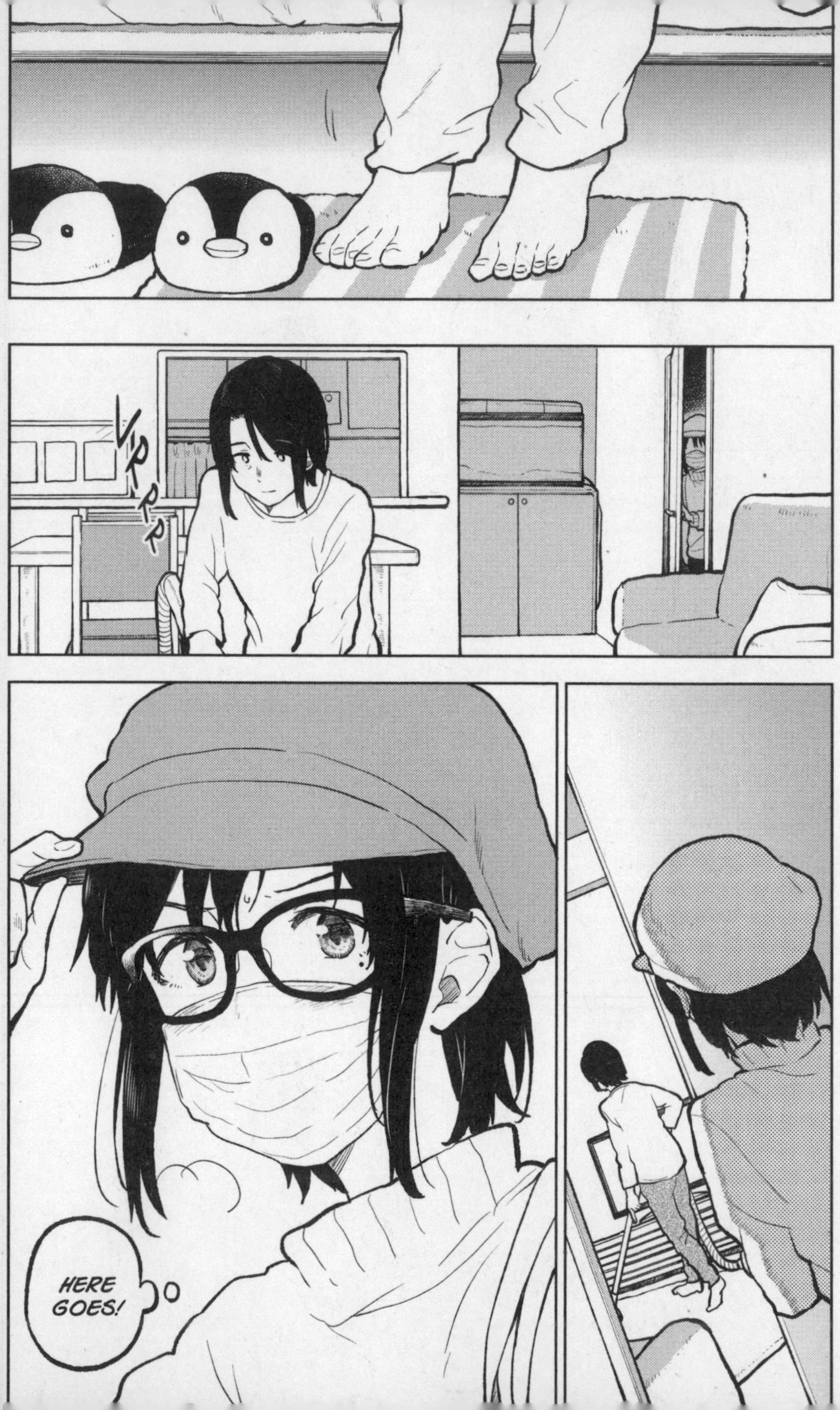
VRRRR
HERE GOES!

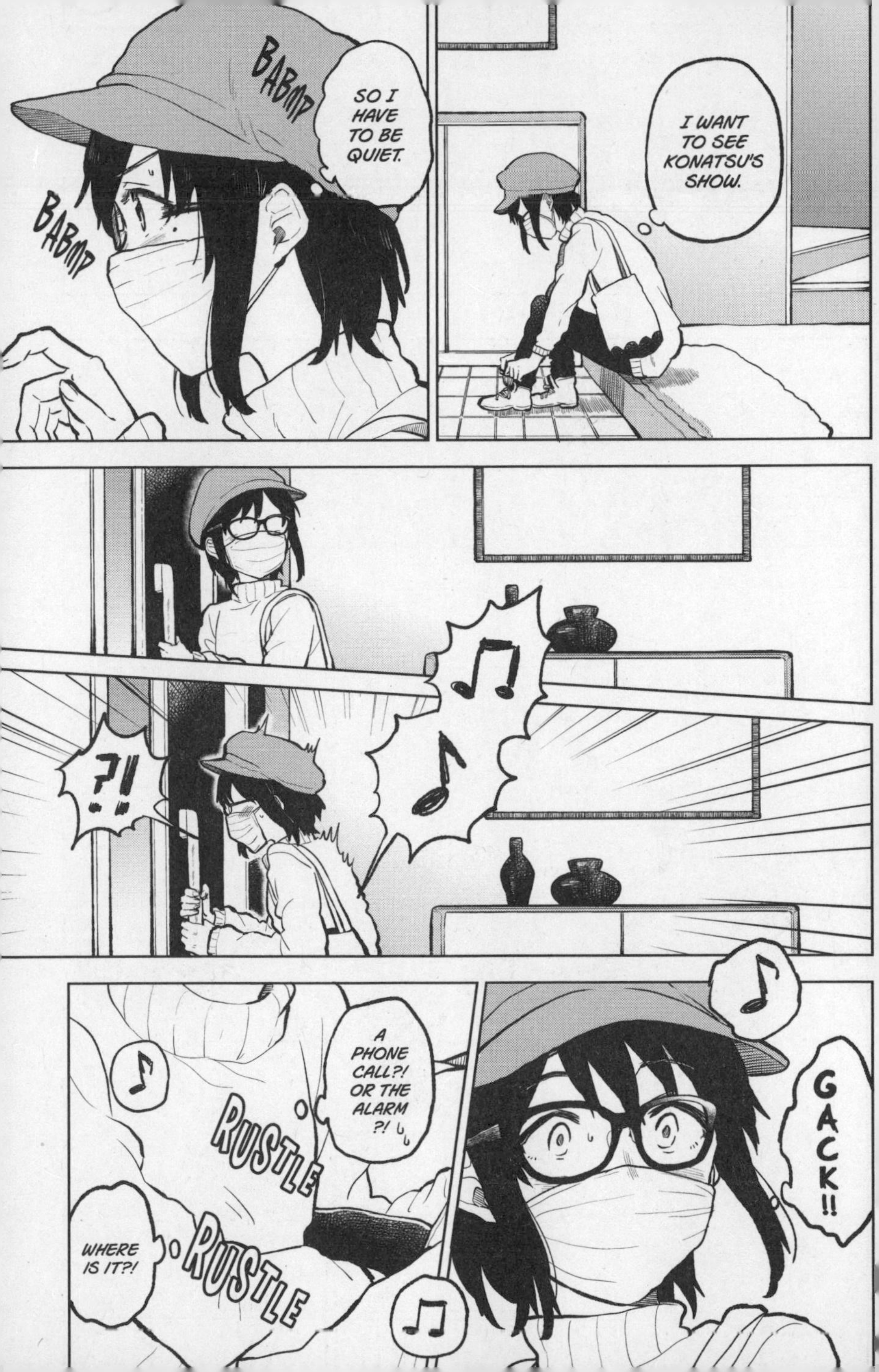
I WANT TO SEE KONATSU'S SHOW.
SO I HAVE TO BE QUIET.
BABMP
BABMP
?!
GACK!!
A PHONE CALL?! OR THE ALARM?!
RUSTLE
WHERE IS IT?!
RUSTLE

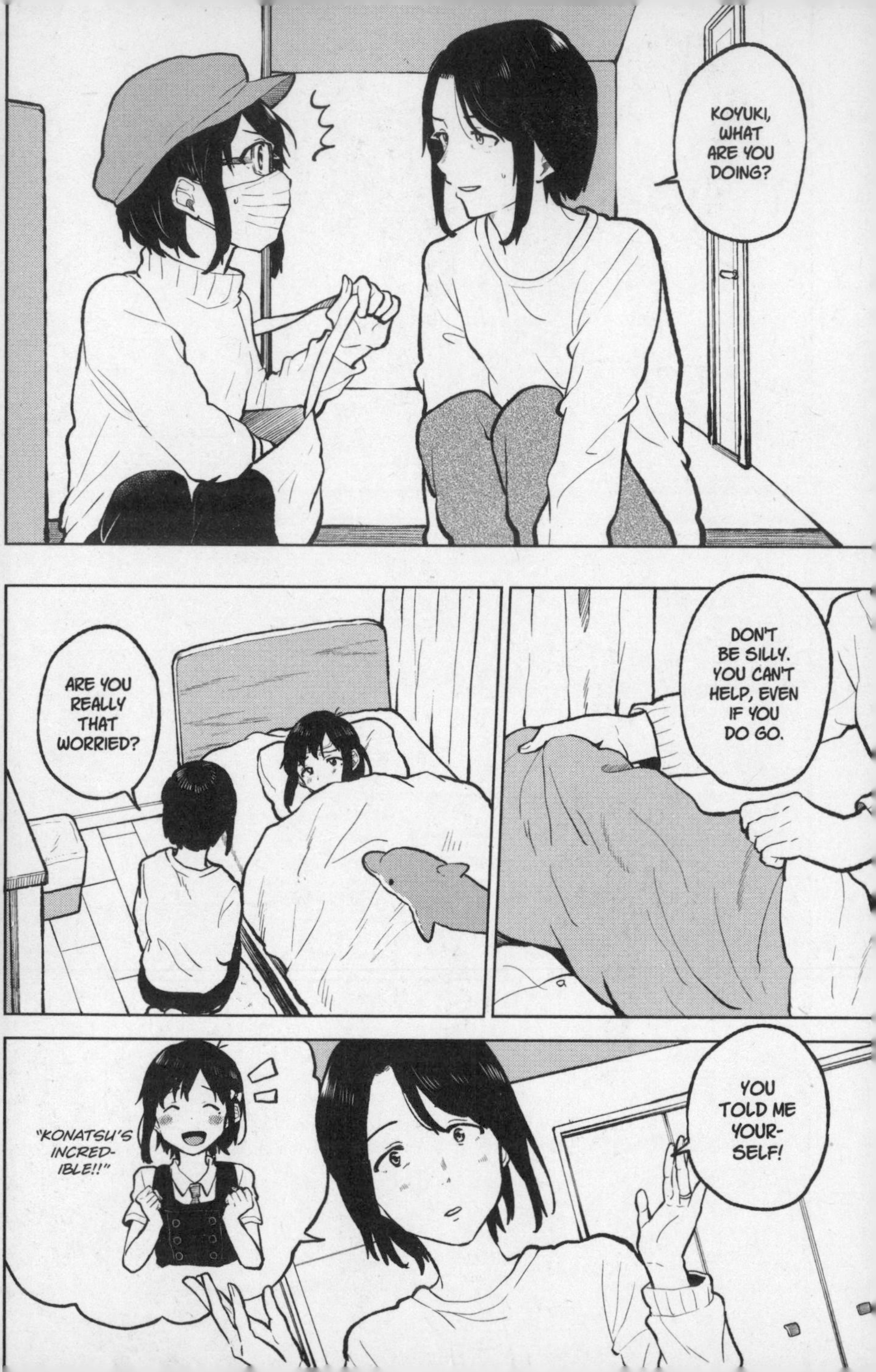
KOYUKI, WHAT ARE YOU DOING?
DON'T BE SILLY. YOU CAN'T HELP, EVEN IF YOU DO GO.
ARE YOU REALLY THAT WORRIED?
YOU TOLD ME YOUR-SELF!
"KONATSU'S INCRED-IBLE!!"

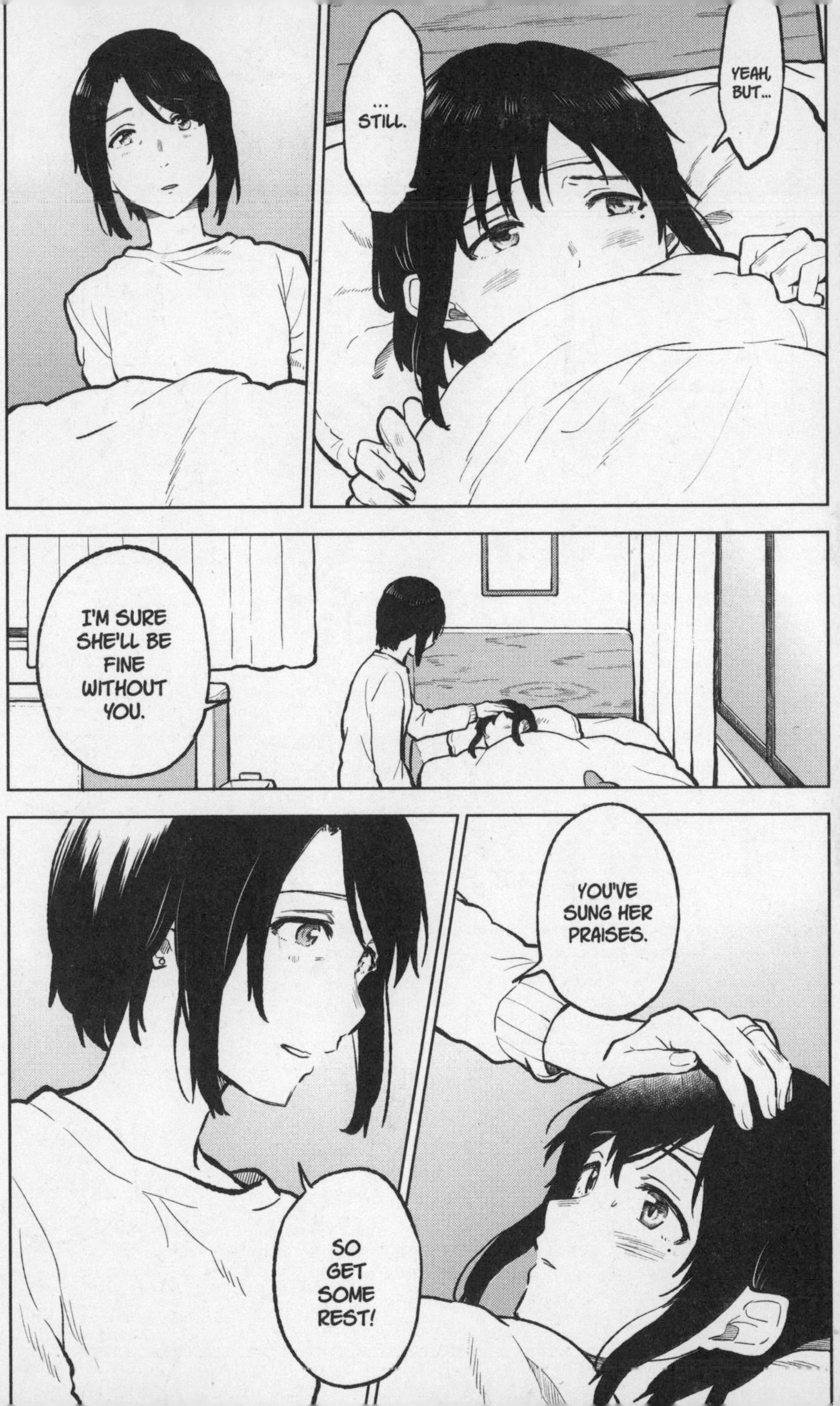
YEAH, BUT...
... STILL.
I'M SURE SHE'LL BE FINE WITHOUT YOU.
YOU'VE SUNG HER PRAISES.
SO GET SOME REST!

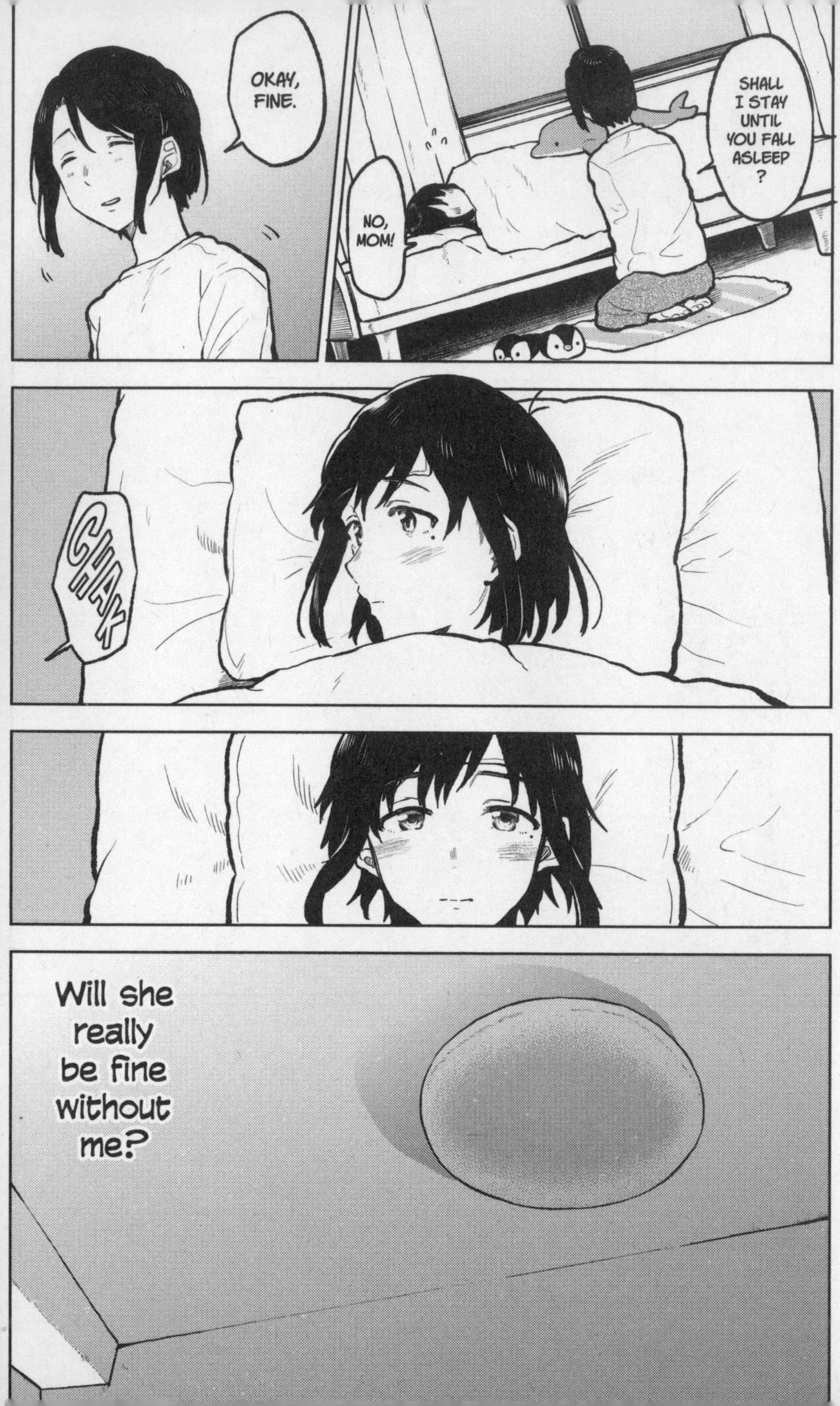
SHALL I STAY UNTIL YOU FALL ASLEEP?
NO, MOM!
OKAY, FINE.
CHAK
Will she really be fine without me?

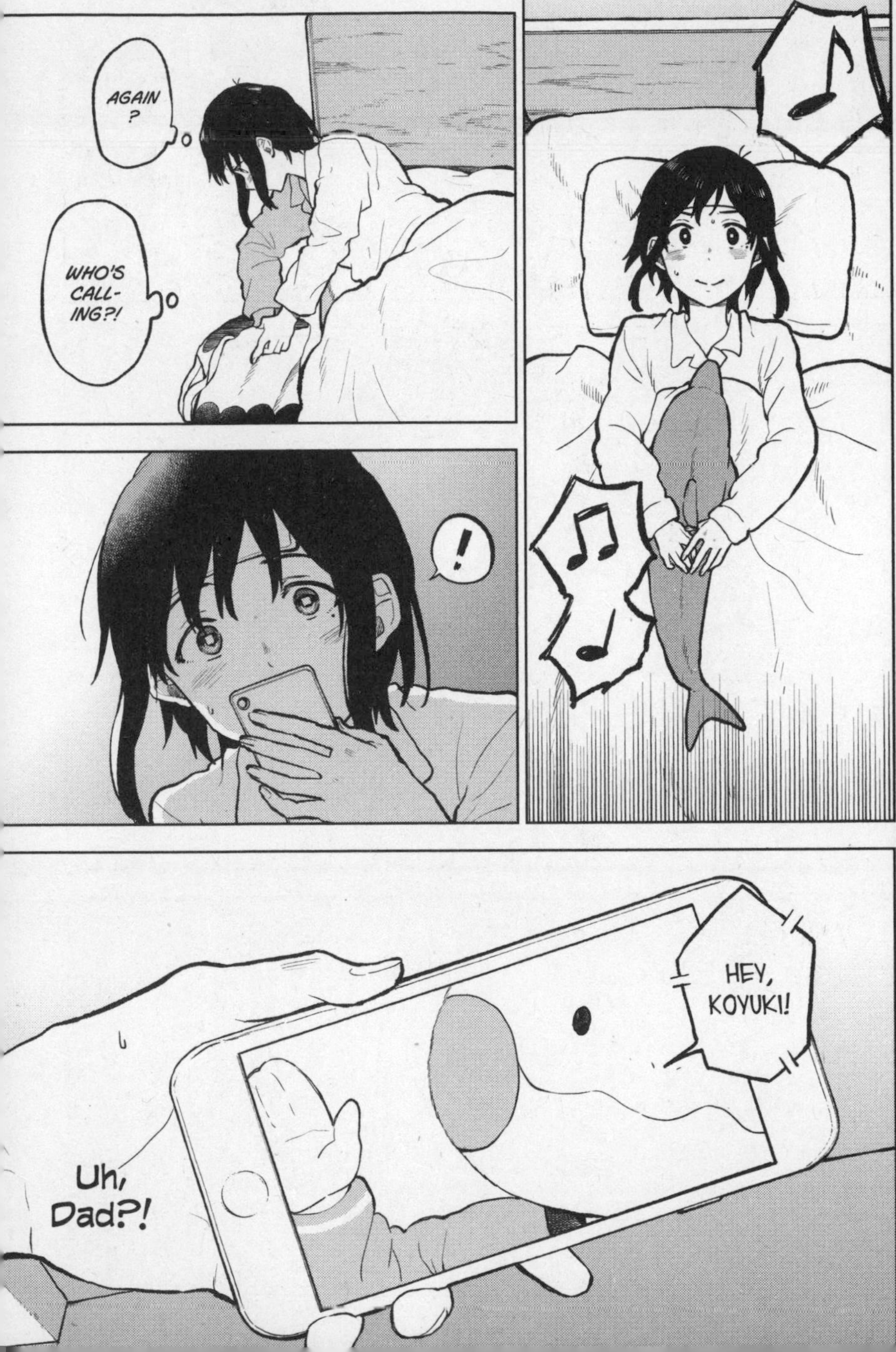
AGAIN?
WHO'S CALLING?!
!
HEY, KOYUKI!
Uh, Dad?!

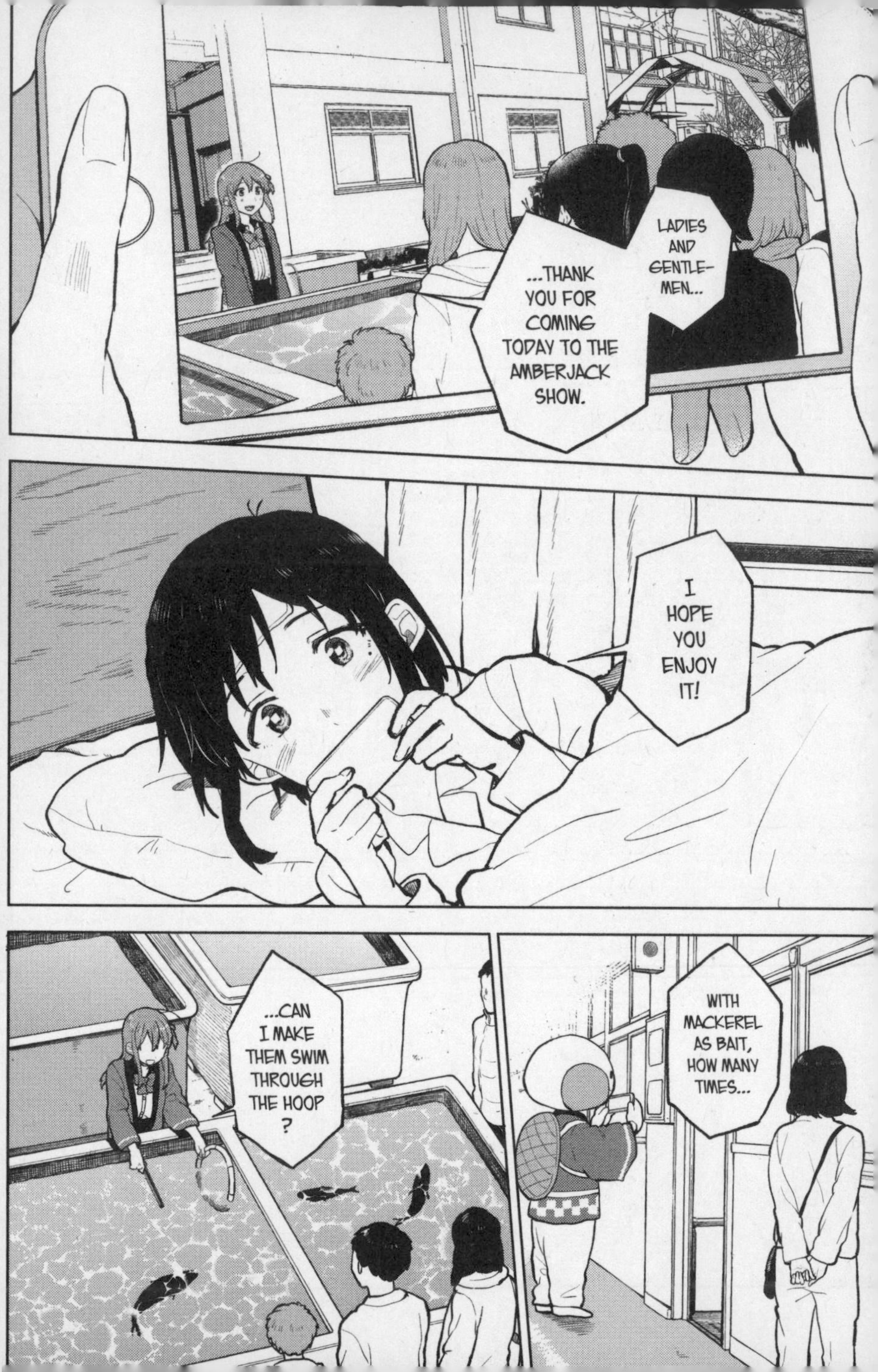
LADIES AND GENTLE-MEN...
...THANK YOU FOR COMING TODAY TO THE AMBERJACK SHOW.
I HOPE YOU ENJOY IT!
WITH MACKEREL AS BAIT, HOW MANY TIMES...
...CAN I MAKE THEM SWIM THROUGH THE HOOP ?

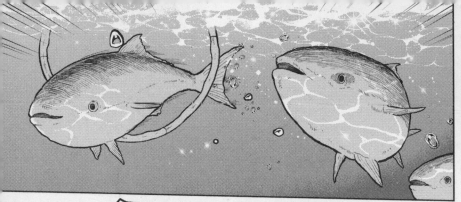

CLAP

EIGHT TIMES IN A ROW!

CLAP

CLAP

...TWO...

...THREE...

...EIGHT!

TMP

TMP

ME!!

NOW I NEED A VOLUNTEER!

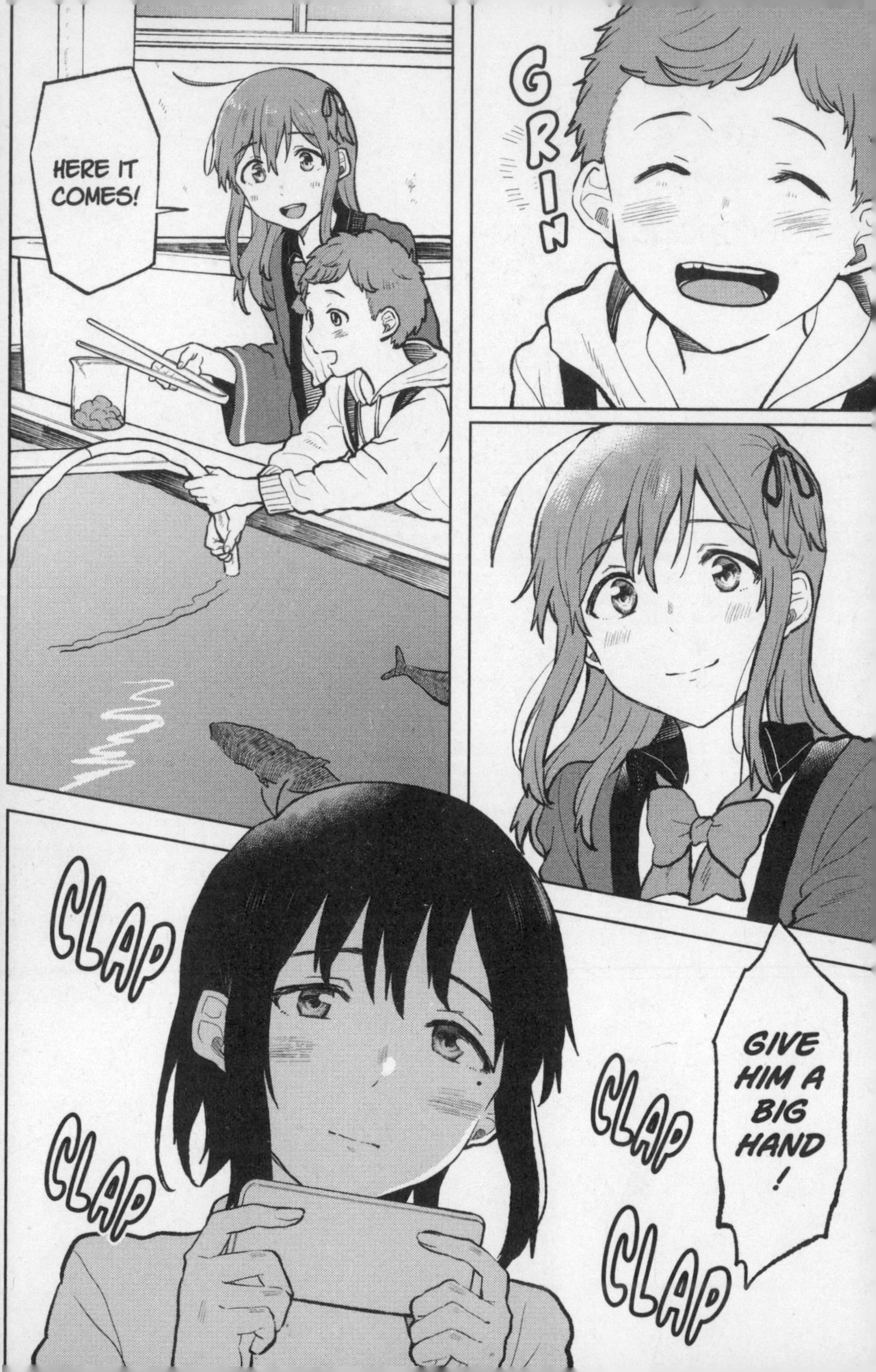
GRIN
HERE IT COMES!
GIVE HIM A BIG HAND!
CLAP
CLAP
CLAP
CLAP

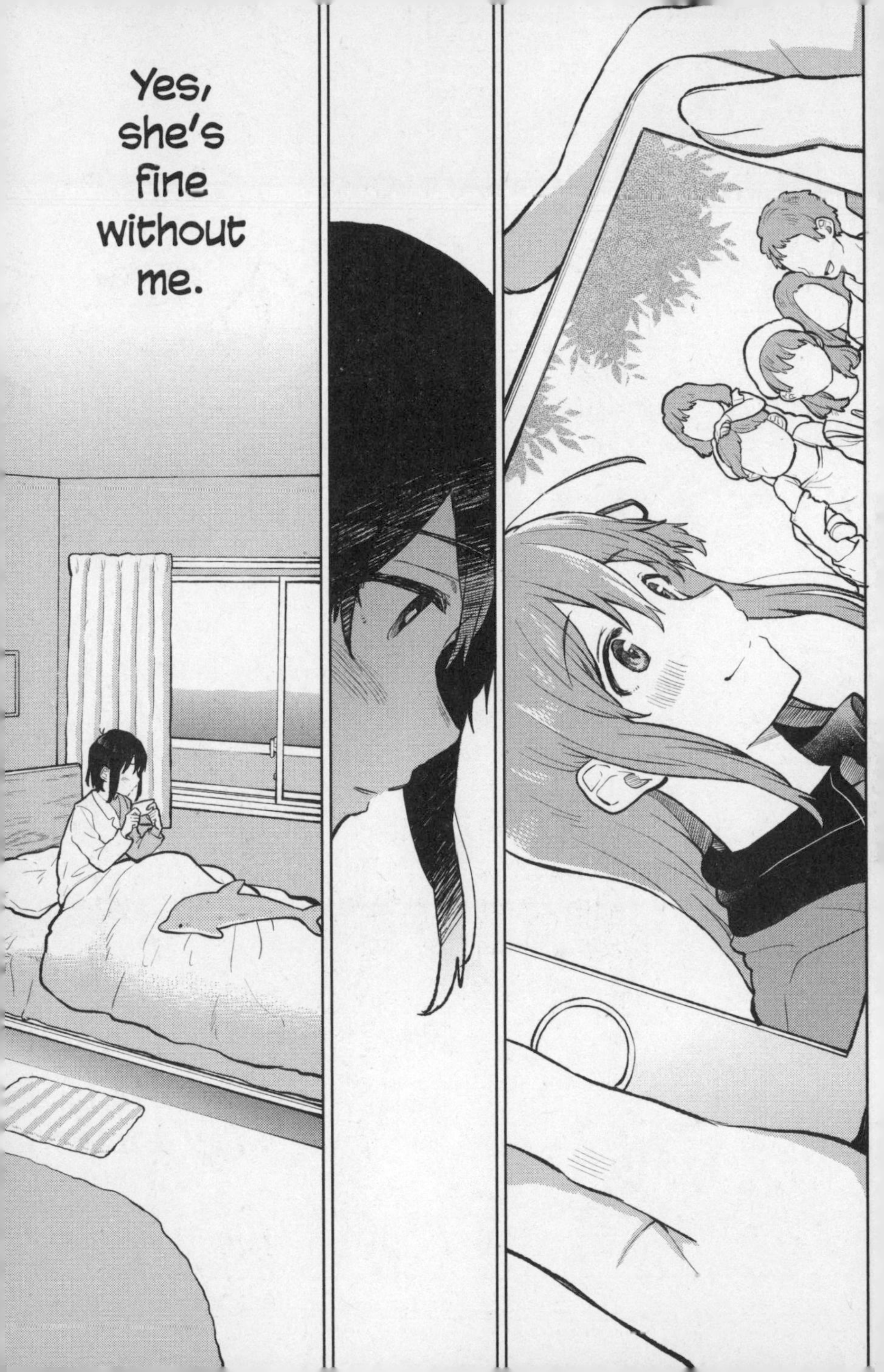
Yes, she's fine without me.

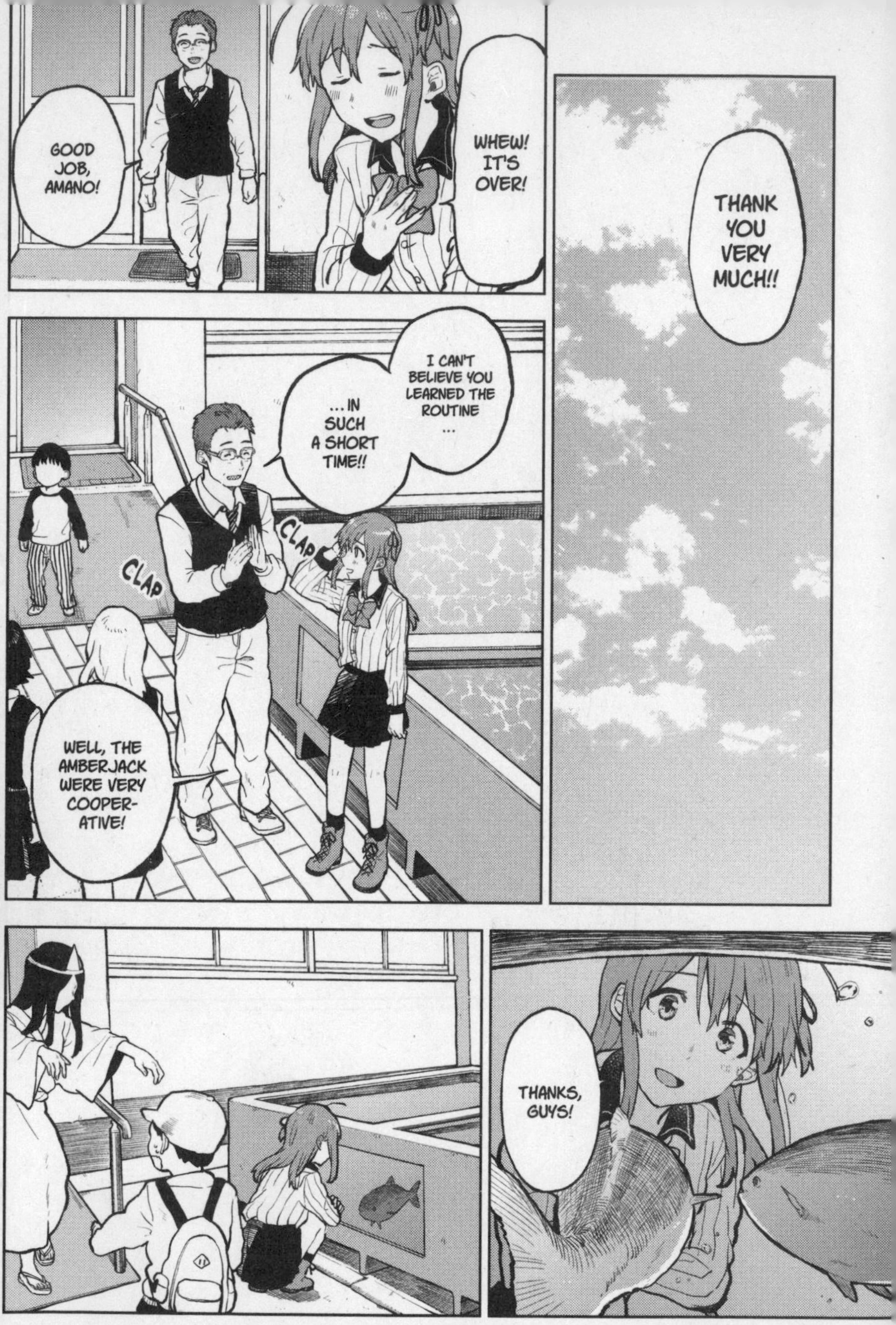
THANK YOU VERY MUCH!!
WHEW! IT'S OVER!
GOOD JOB, AMANO!
I CAN'T BELIEVE YOU LEARNED THE ROUTINE ...
...IN SUCH A SHORT TIME!!
CLAP
CLAP
WELL, THE AMBERJACK WERE VERY COOPER-ATIVE!
THANKS, GUYS!

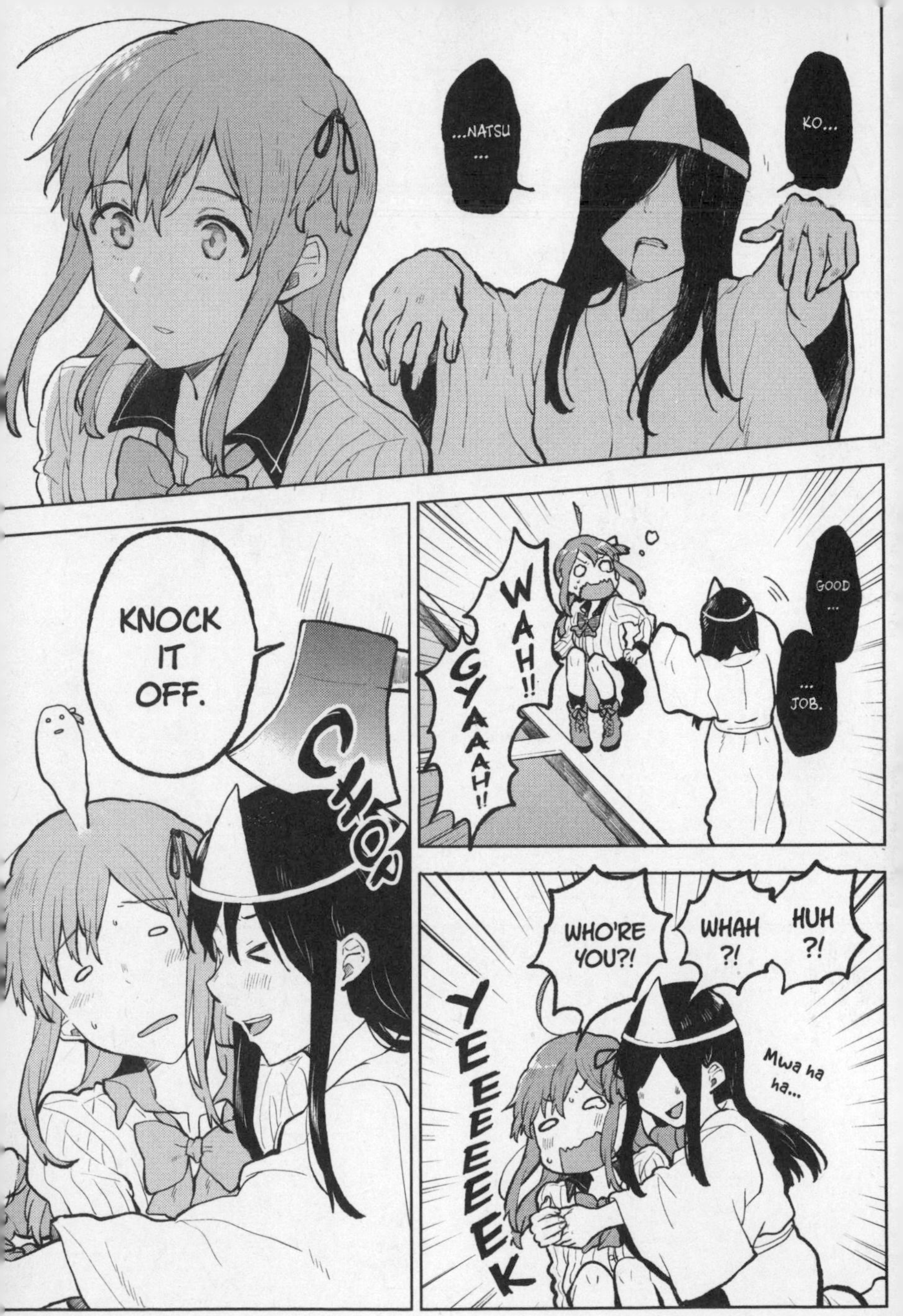
KO...
...NATSU ...
GOOD ... ... JOB.
WAH!!
GYAAAH!!
HUH ?!
WHAH ?!
WHO'RE YOU?!
YEEEEEEK
Mwa ha ha...
KNOCK IT OFF.
CHOP

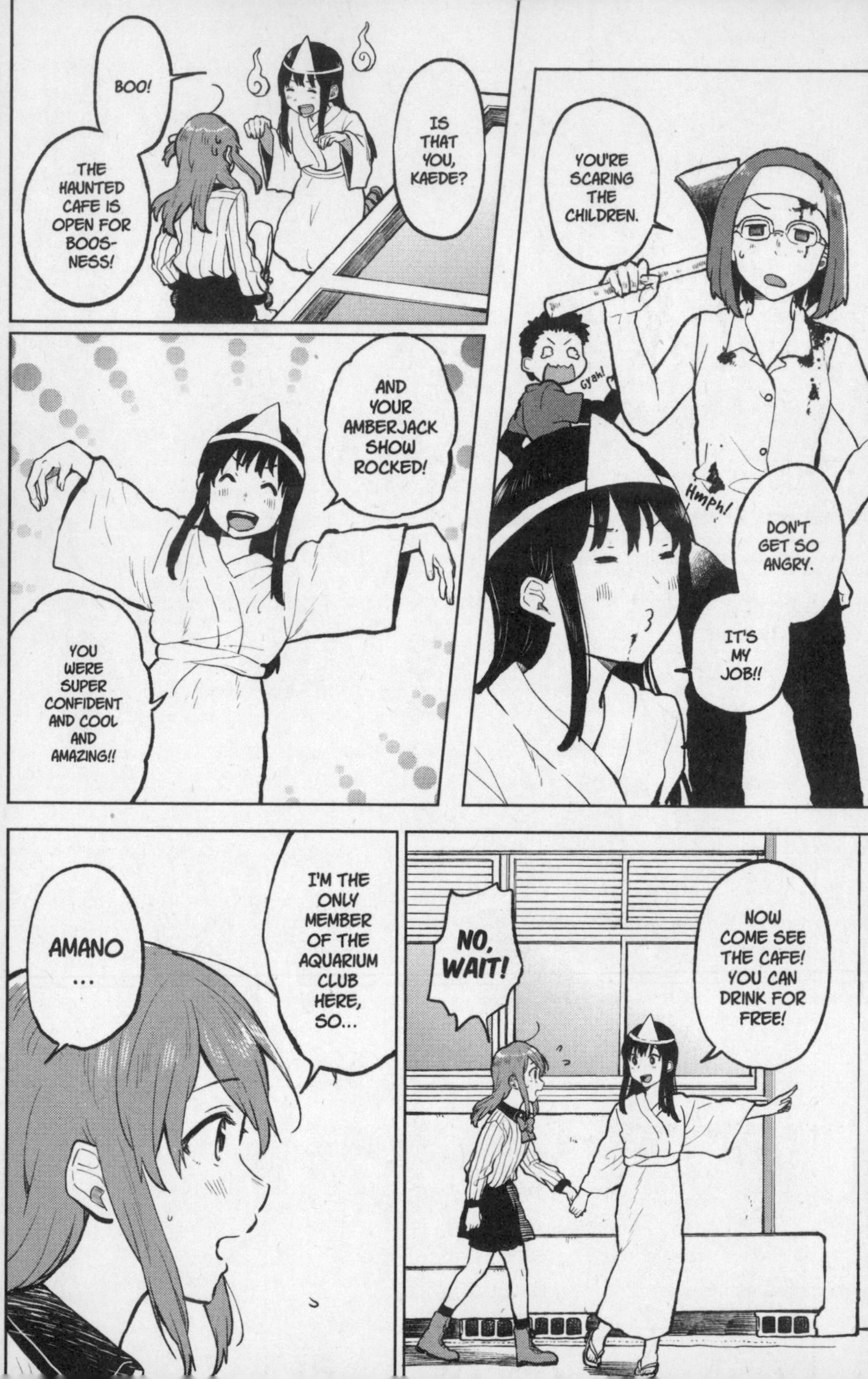
YOU'RE SCARING THE CHILDREN.
Gyah!
Hmph!
DON'T GET SO ANGRY.
IT'S MY JOB!!
BOO!
THE HAUNTED CAFE IS OPEN FOR BOOS-NESS!
IS THAT YOU, KAEDE?
AND YOUR AMBERJACK SHOW ROCKED!
YOU WERE SUPER CONFIDENT AND COOL AND AMAZING!!
NOW COME SEE THE CAFE! YOU CAN DRINK FOR FREE!
NO, WAIT!
I'M THE ONLY MEMBER OF THE AQUARIUM CLUB HERE, SO...
AMANO ...

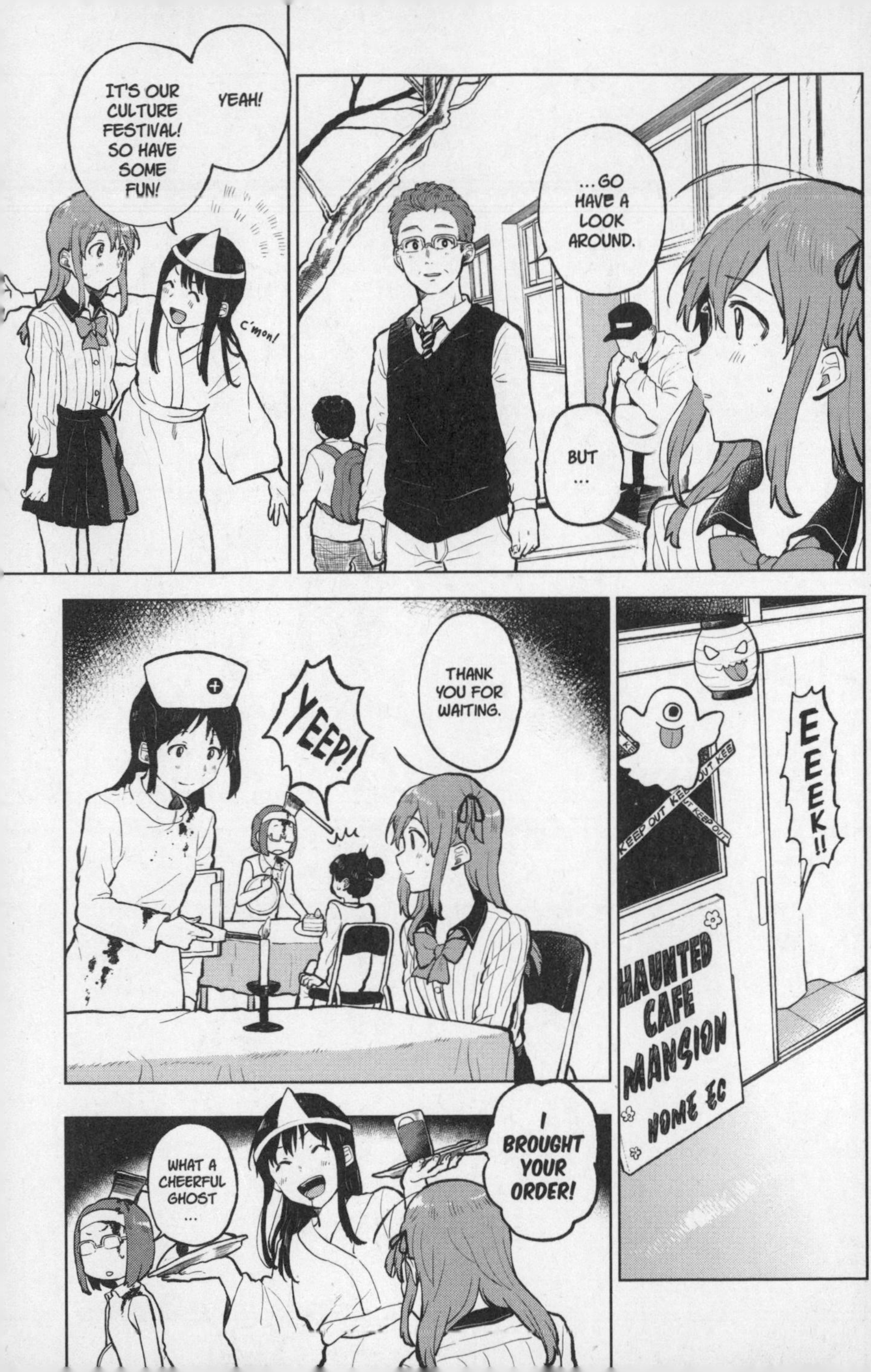
...GO HAVE A LOOK AROUND.
BUT ...
IT'S OUR CULTURE FESTIVAL! SO HAVE SOME FUN!
YEAH!
C'mon!
EEEK!!
KEEP OUT
HAUNTED CAFE MANSION
HOME EC
THANK YOU FOR WAITING.
YEEP!
I BROUGHT YOUR ORDER!
WHAT A CHEERFUL GHOST ...

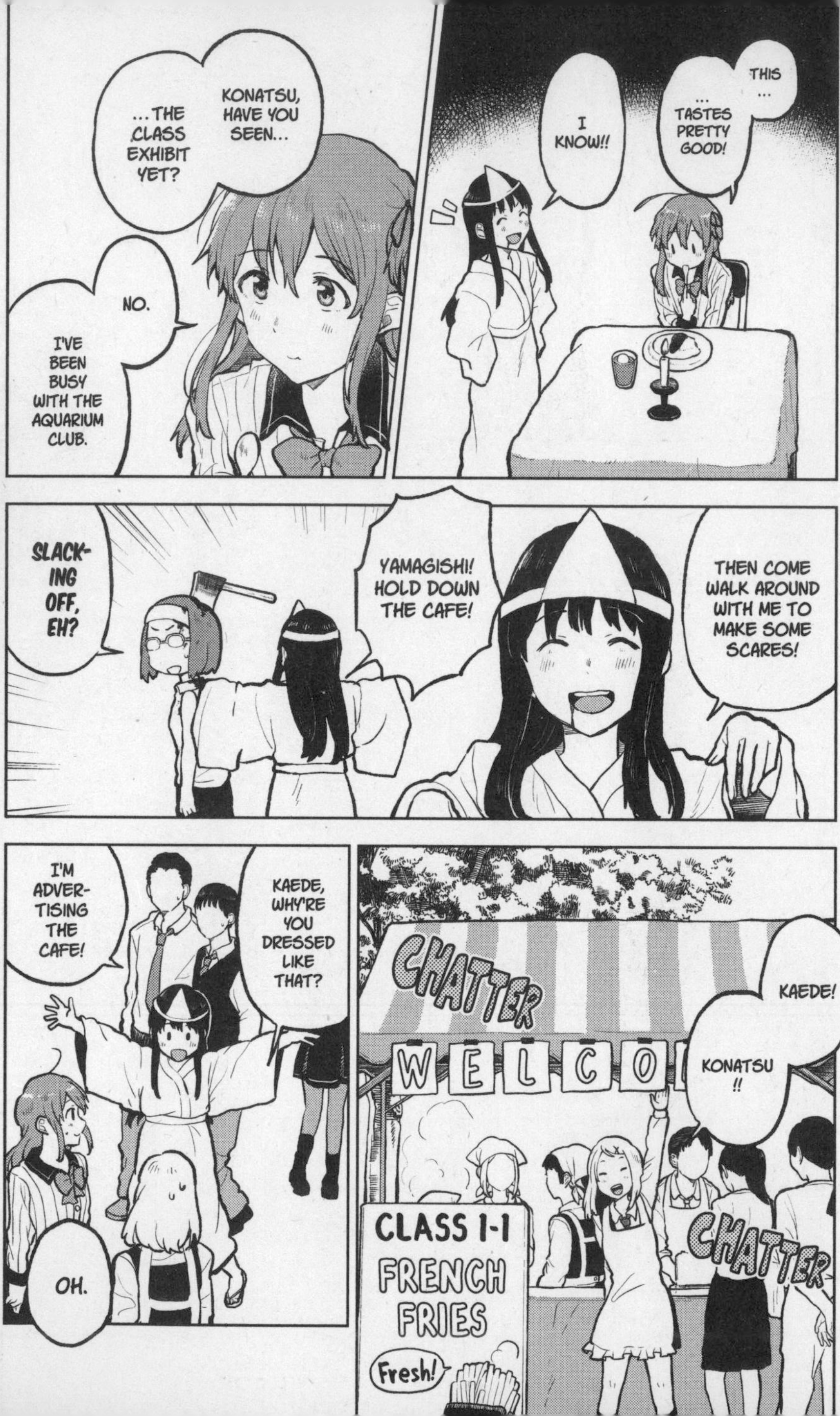
THIS ...
... TASTES PRETTY GOOD!
I KNOW!!
KONATSU, HAVE YOU SEEN...
...THE CLASS EXHIBIT YET?
NO.
I'VE BEEN BUSY WITH THE AQUARIUM CLUB.
THEN COME WALK AROUND WITH ME TO MAKE SOME SCARES!
YAMAGISHI! HOLD DOWN THE CAFE!
SLACKING OFF, EH?
KAEDE!
KONATSU !!
CHATTER
WELCO
CLASS 1-1 FRENCH FRIES
Fresh!
CHATTER
KAEDE, WHY'RE YOU DRESSED LIKE THAT?
I'M ADVERTISING THE CAFE!
OH.

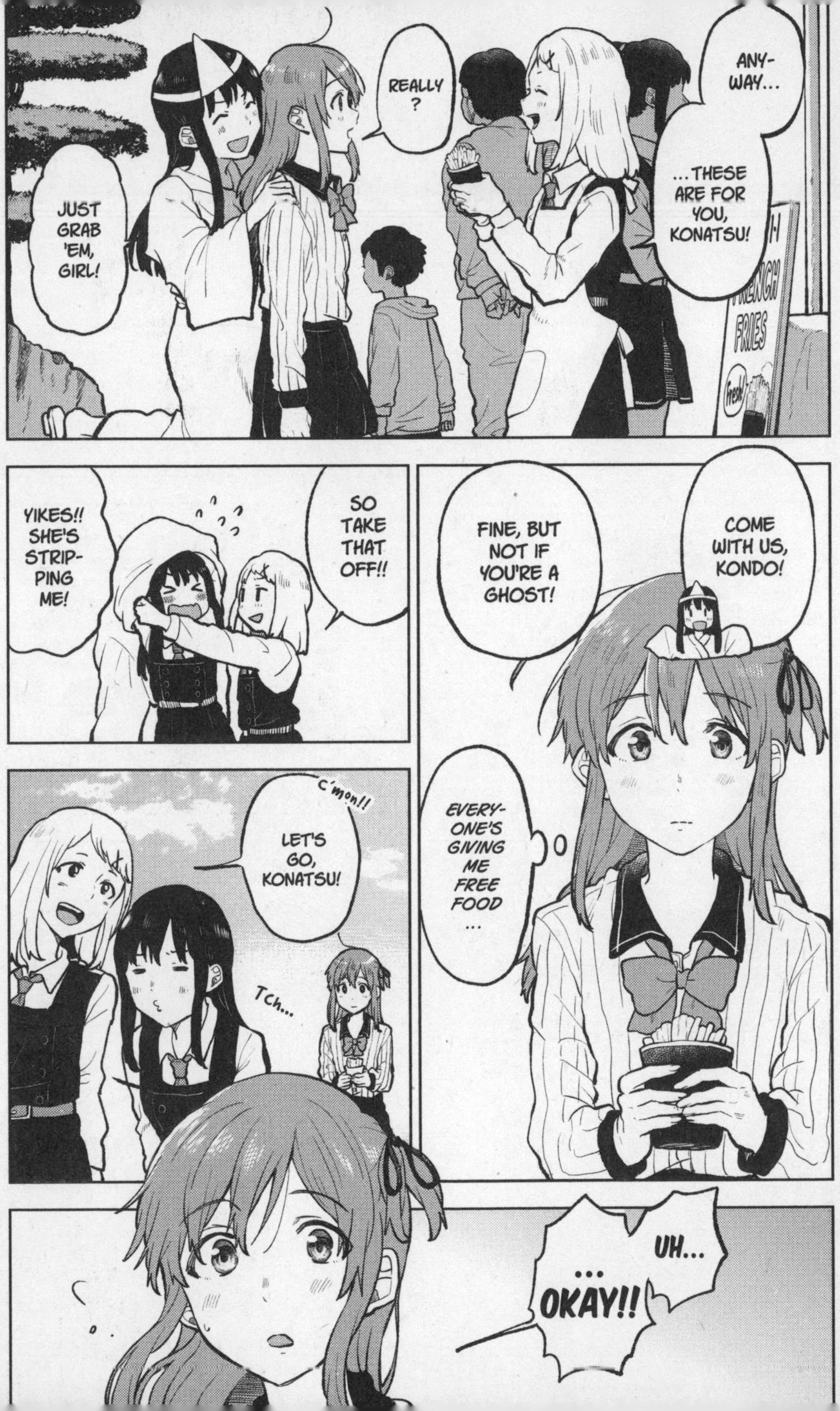
ANY-WAY...
...THESE ARE FOR YOU, KONATSU!
FRENCH FRIES
Fresh!
REALLY?
JUST GRAB 'EM, GIRL!
COME WITH US, KONDO!
FINE, BUT NOT IF YOU'RE A GHOST!
EVERY-ONE'S GIVING ME FREE FOOD...
SO TAKE THAT OFF!!
YIKES!! SHE'S STRIP-PING ME!
C'mon!!
LET'S GO, KONATSU!
Tch...
UH...
...OKAY!!

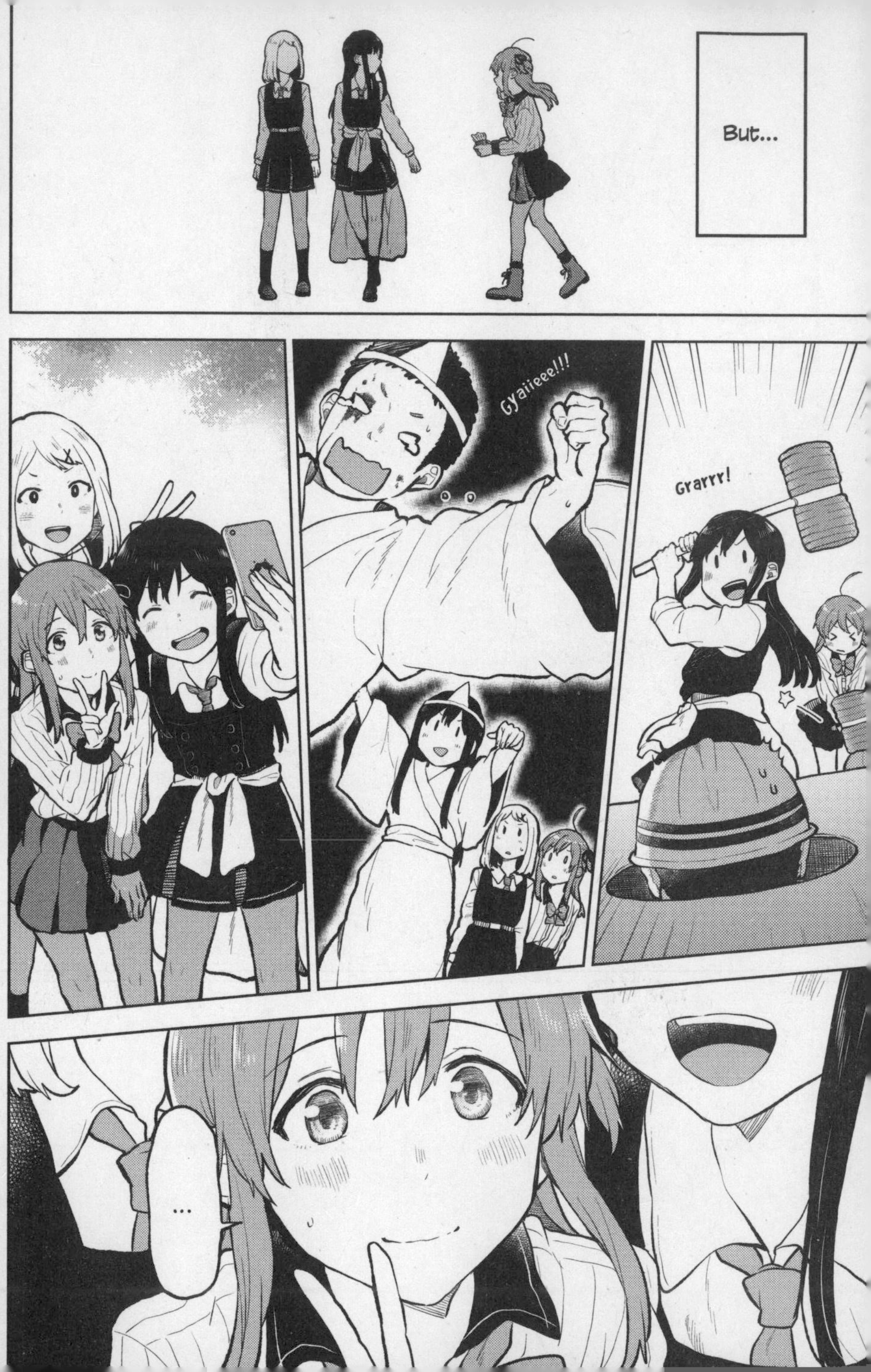
But...
Grarrr!
Gyaiieee!!!
...

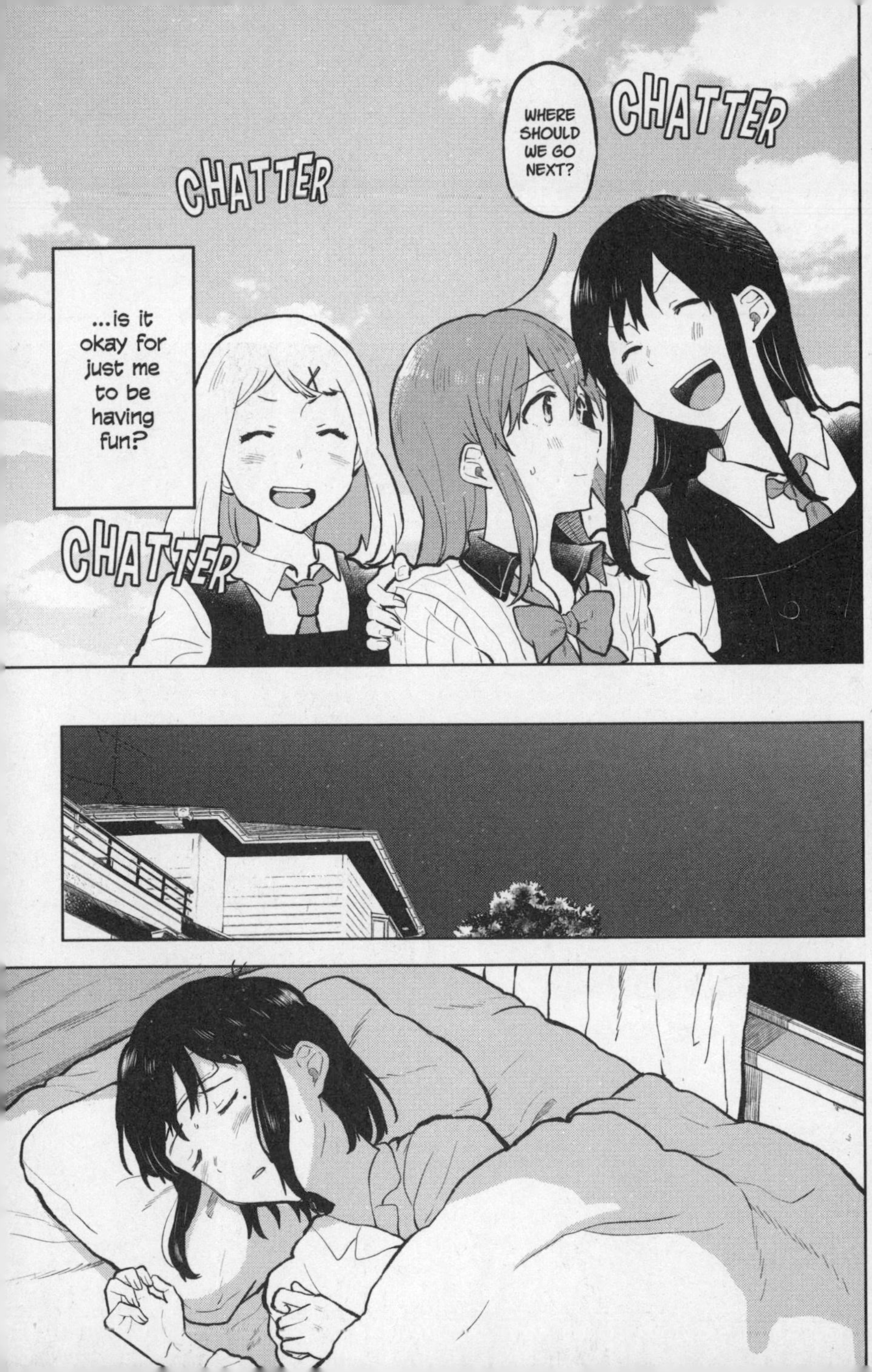
CHATTER
WHERE SHOULD WE GO NEXT?
CHATTER
...is it okay for just me to be having fun?
CHATTER

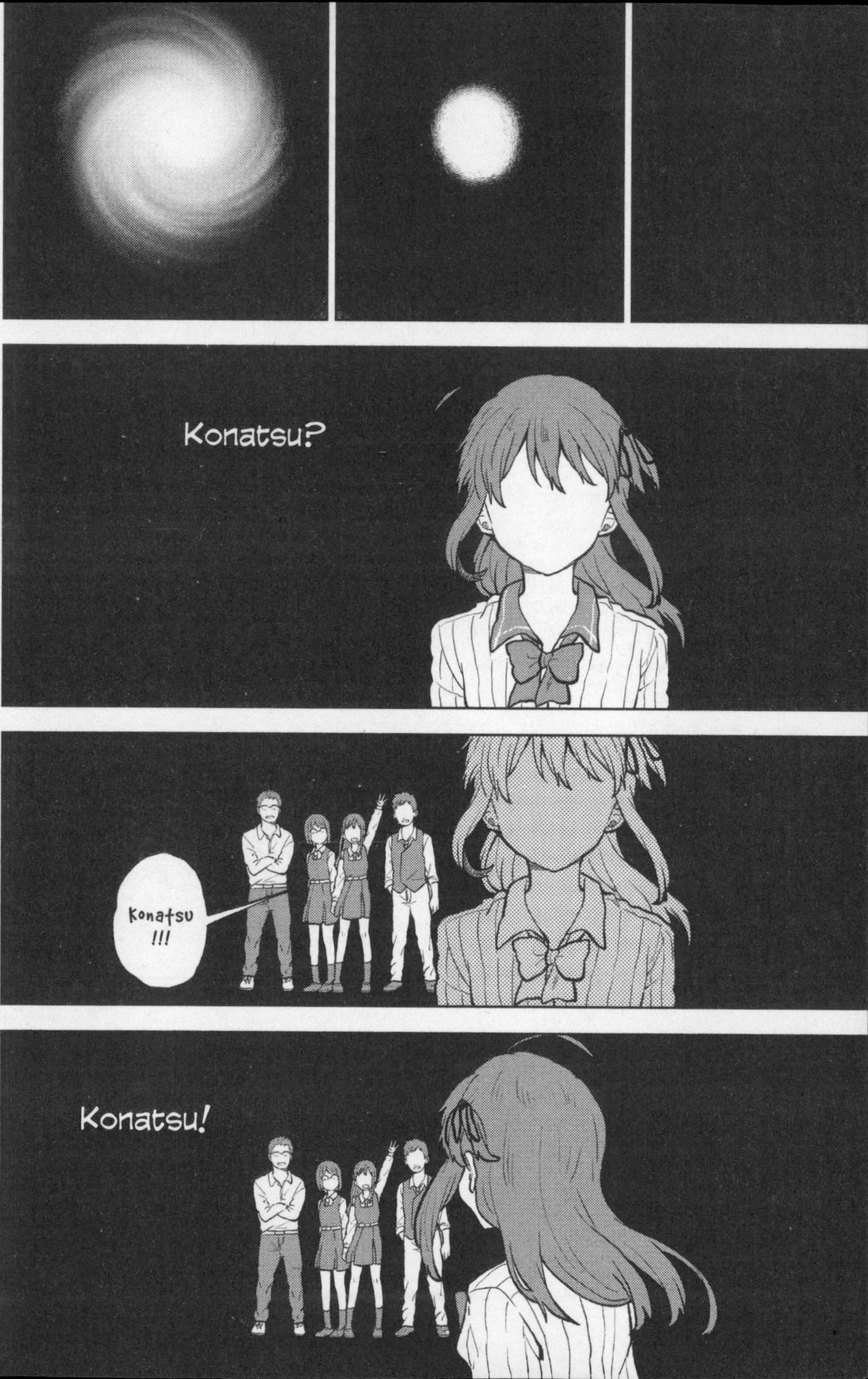
Konatsu?
Konatsu!!!
Konatsu!

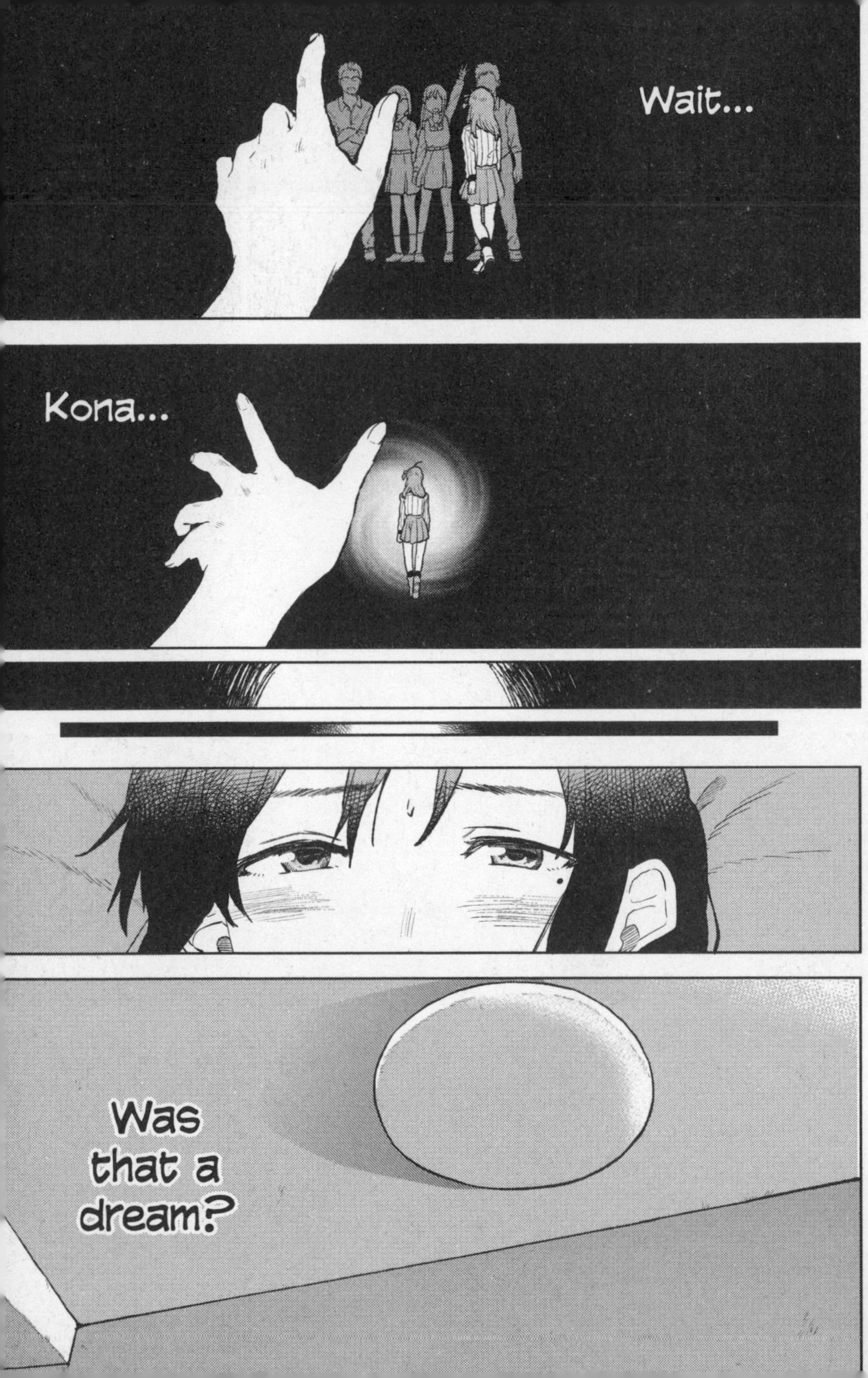
Wait...
Kona...
Was that a dream?

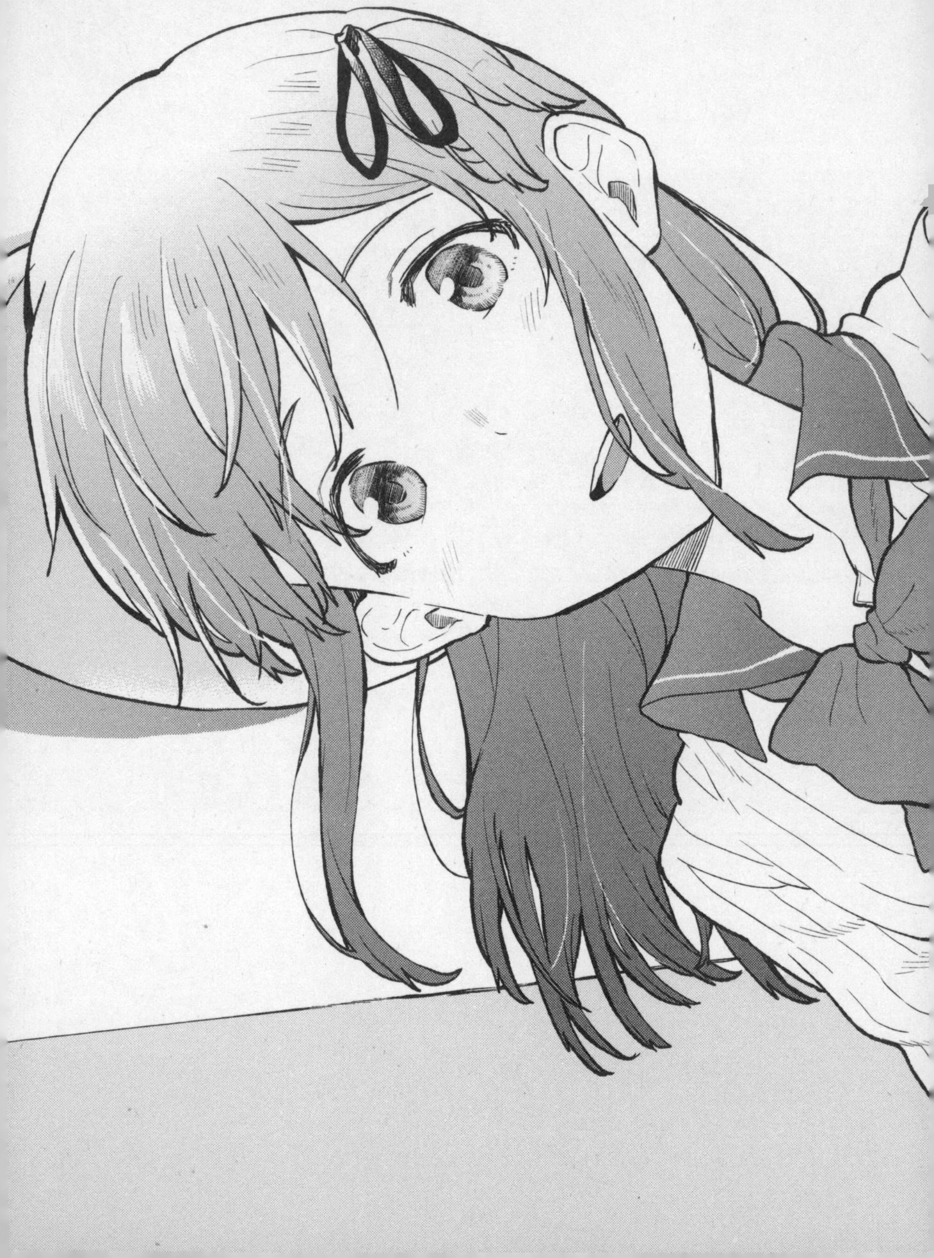

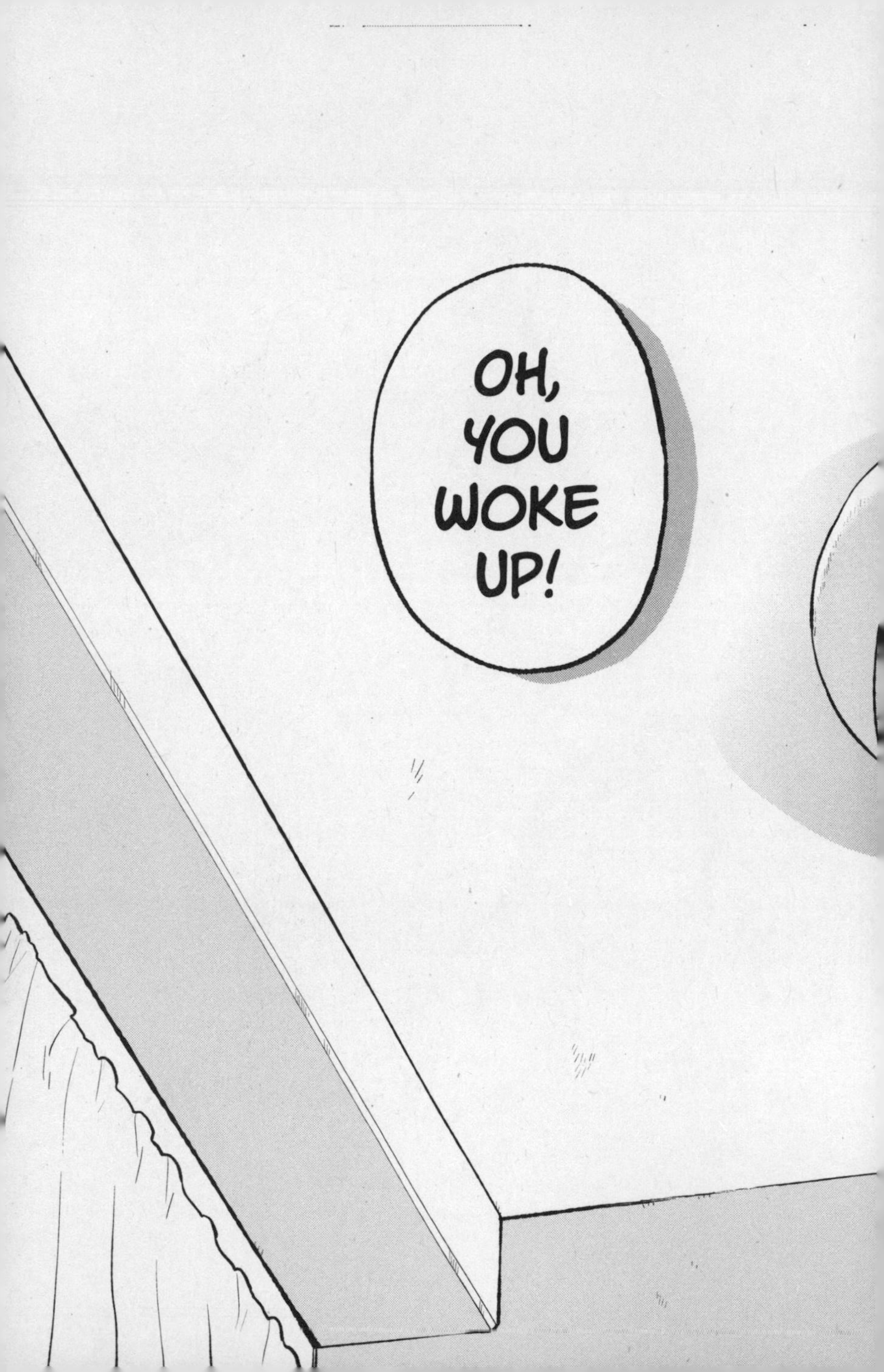
OH, YOU WOKE UP!

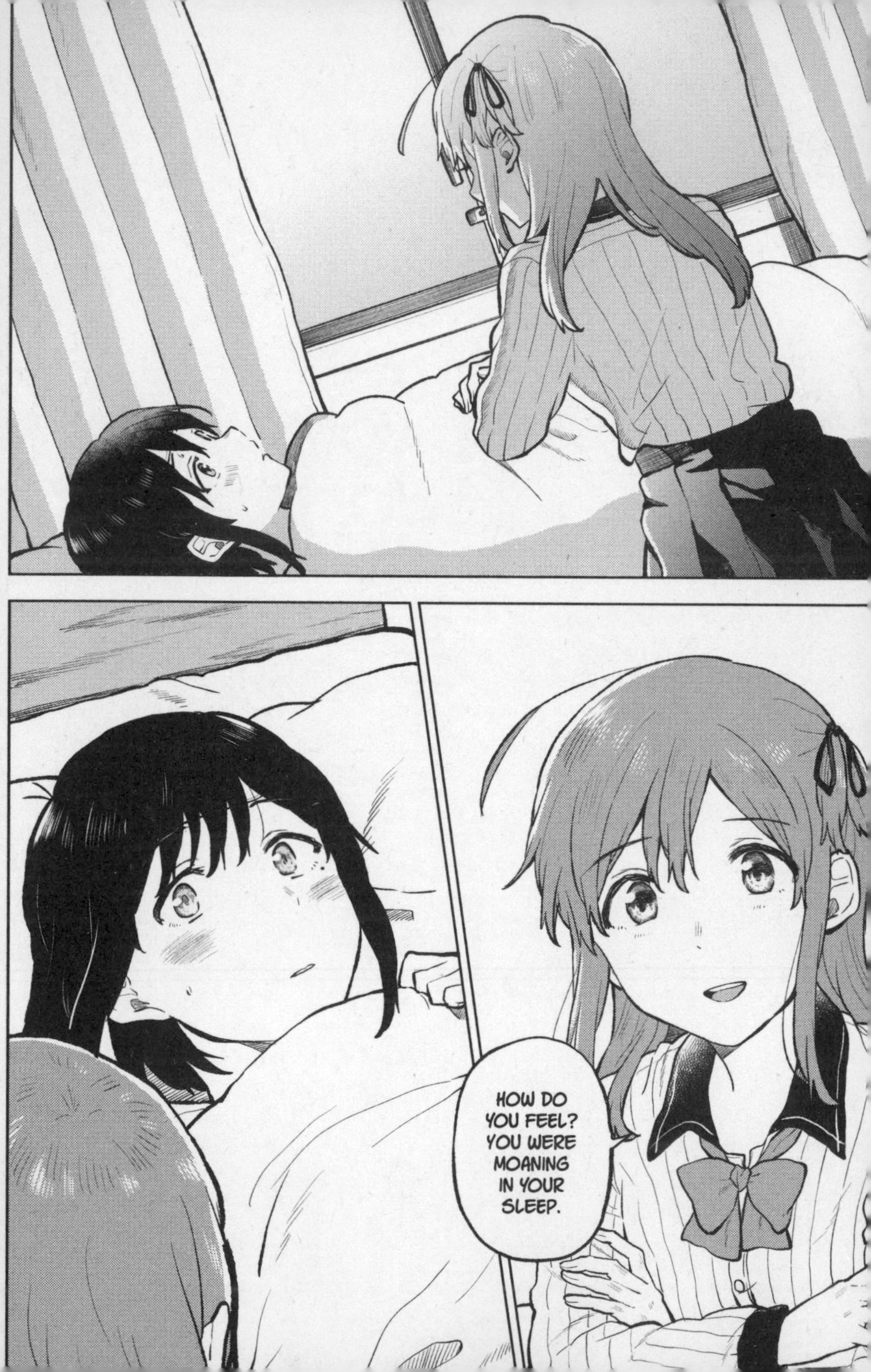
HOW DO YOU FEEL? YOU WERE MOANING IN YOUR SLEEP.

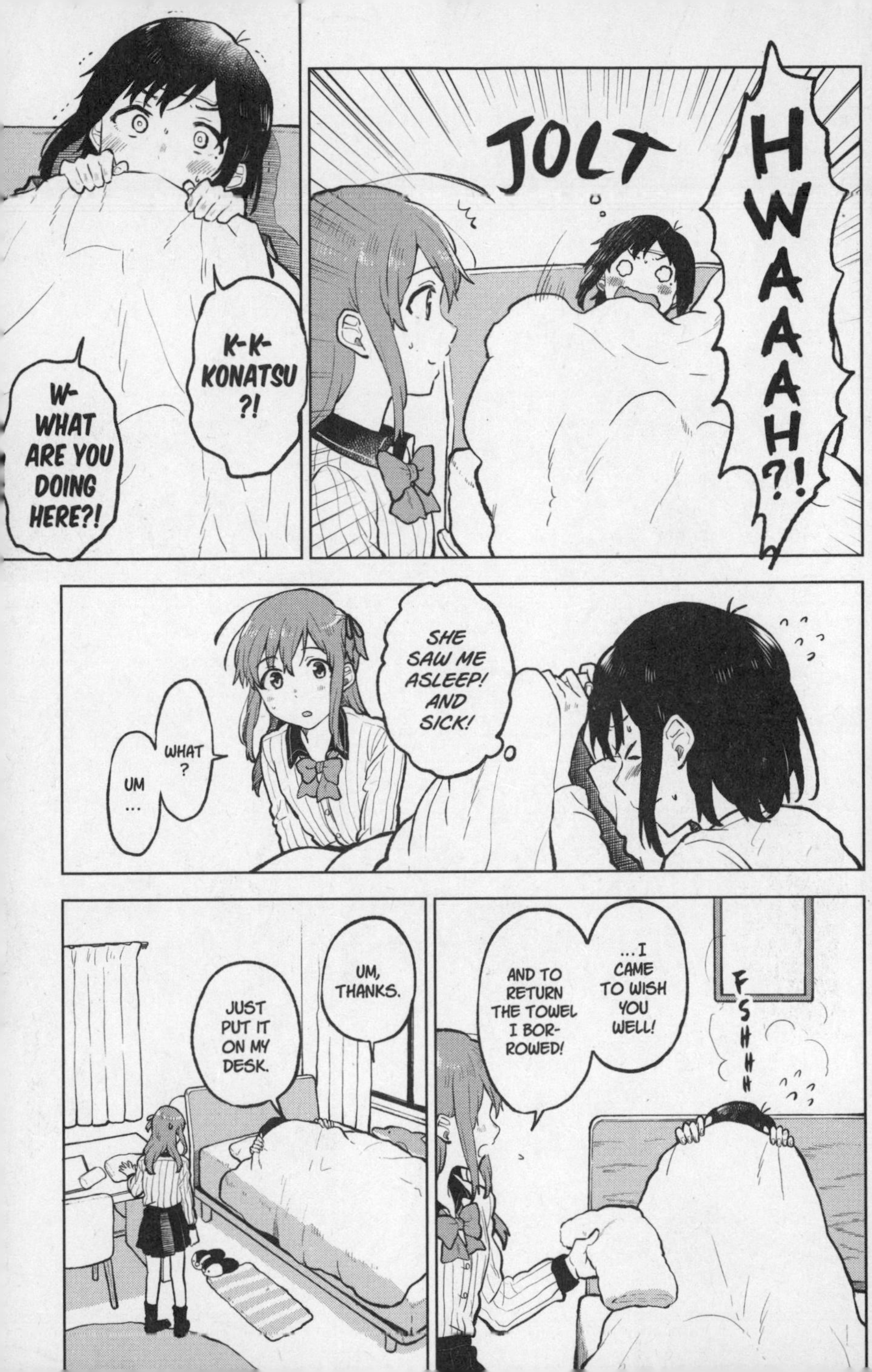
HWAAAH?!
JOLT
K-K-KONATSU?!
W-WHAT ARE YOU DOING HERE?!
SHE SAW ME ASLEEP! AND SICK!
WHAT?
UM...
...I CAME TO WISH YOU WELL!
AND TO RETURN THE TOWEL I BOR-ROWED!
FSHHH
UM, THANKS.
JUST PUT IT ON MY DESK.

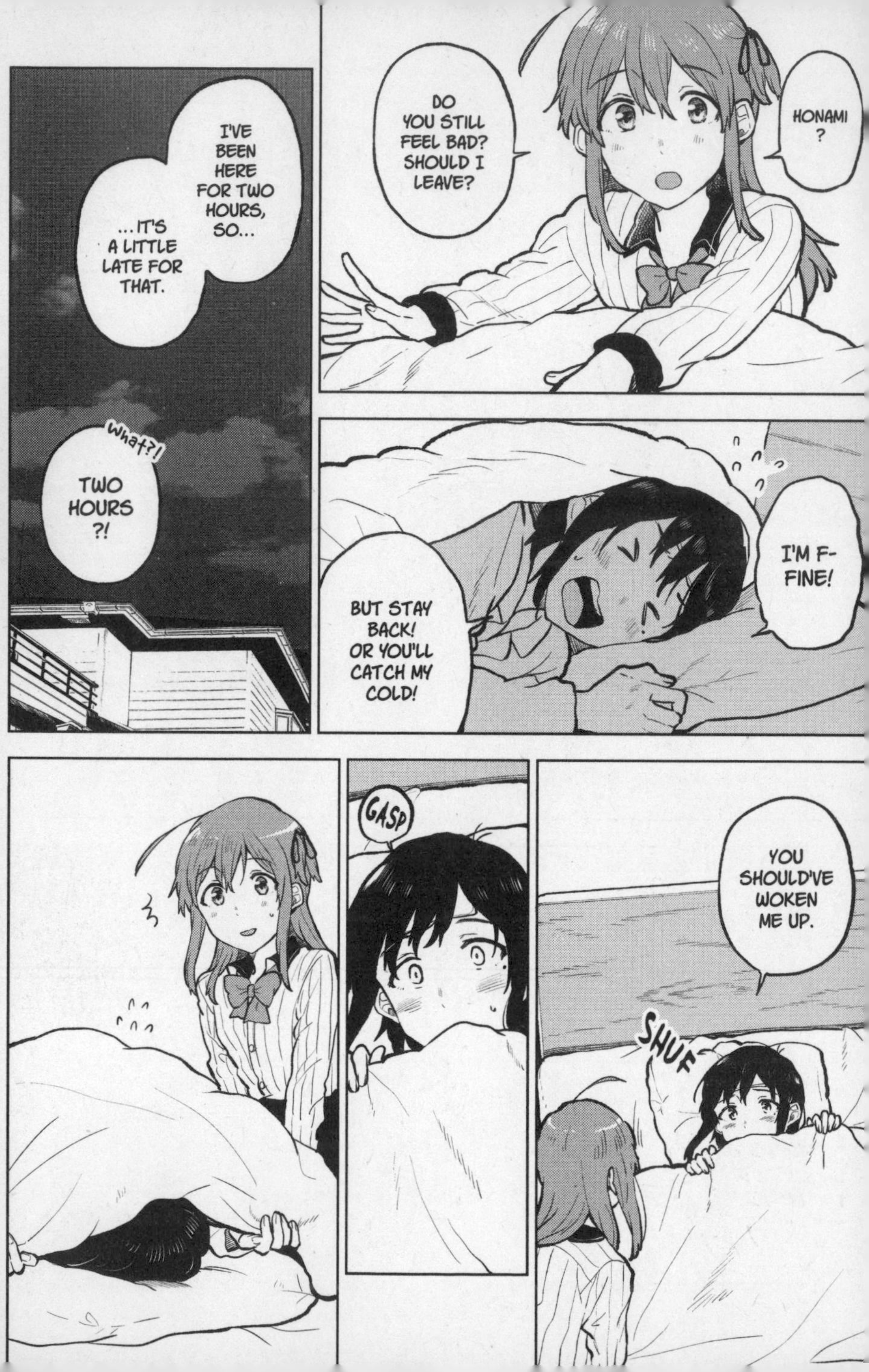
HONAMI ?
DO YOU STILL FEEL BAD? SHOULD I LEAVE?
I'M F-FINE!
BUT STAY BACK! OR YOU'LL CATCH MY COLD!
I'VE BEEN HERE FOR TWO HOURS, SO...
...IT'S A LITTLE LATE FOR THAT.
What?!
TWO HOURS ?!
YOU SHOULD'VE WOKEN ME UP.
SHUF
GASP

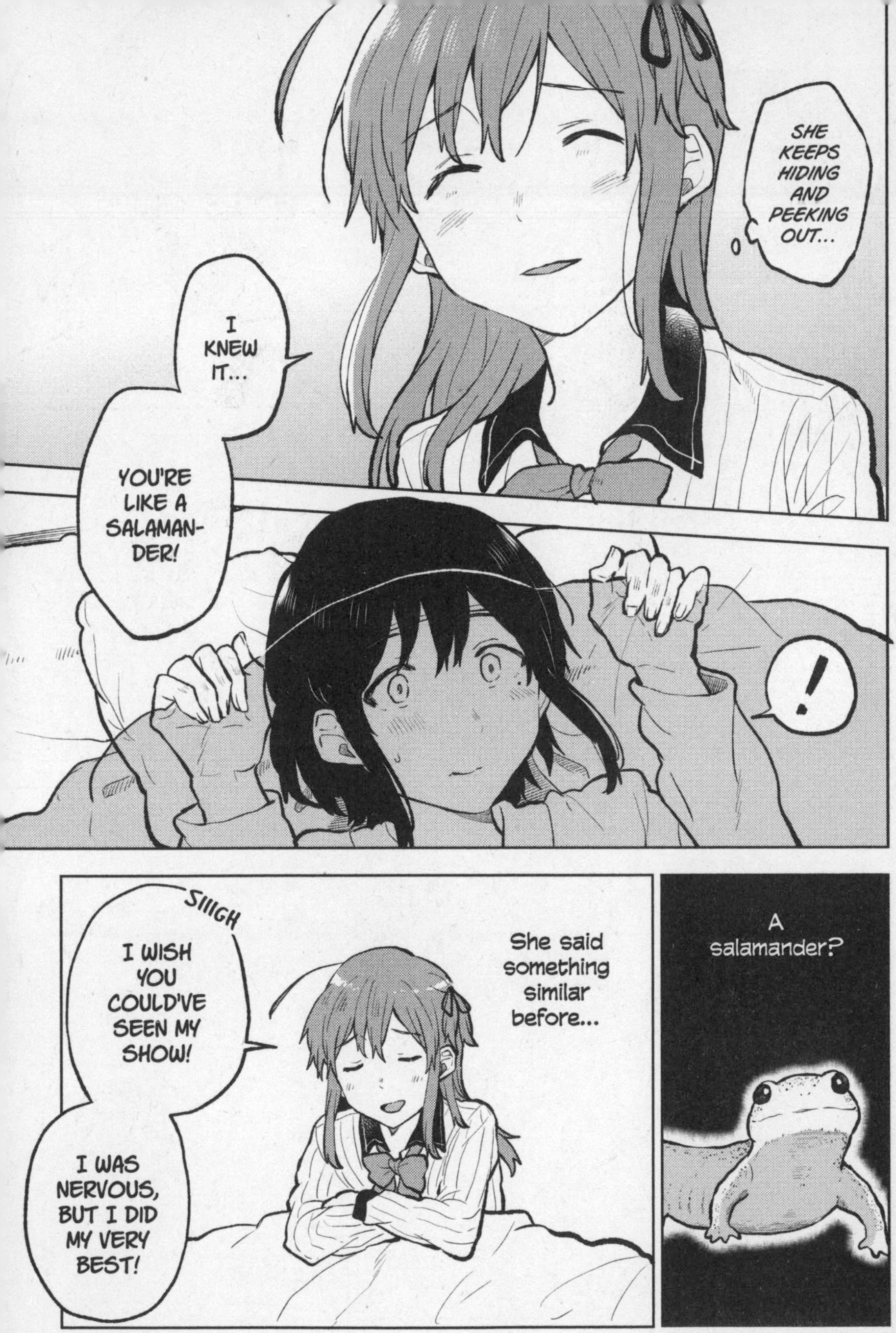
SHE KEEPS HIDING AND PEEKING OUT...
I KNEW IT...
YOU'RE LIKE A SALAMAN-DER!
!
A salamander?
She said something similar before...
SIIIGH
I WISH YOU COULD'VE SEEN MY SHOW!
I WAS NERVOUS, BUT I DID MY VERY BEST!

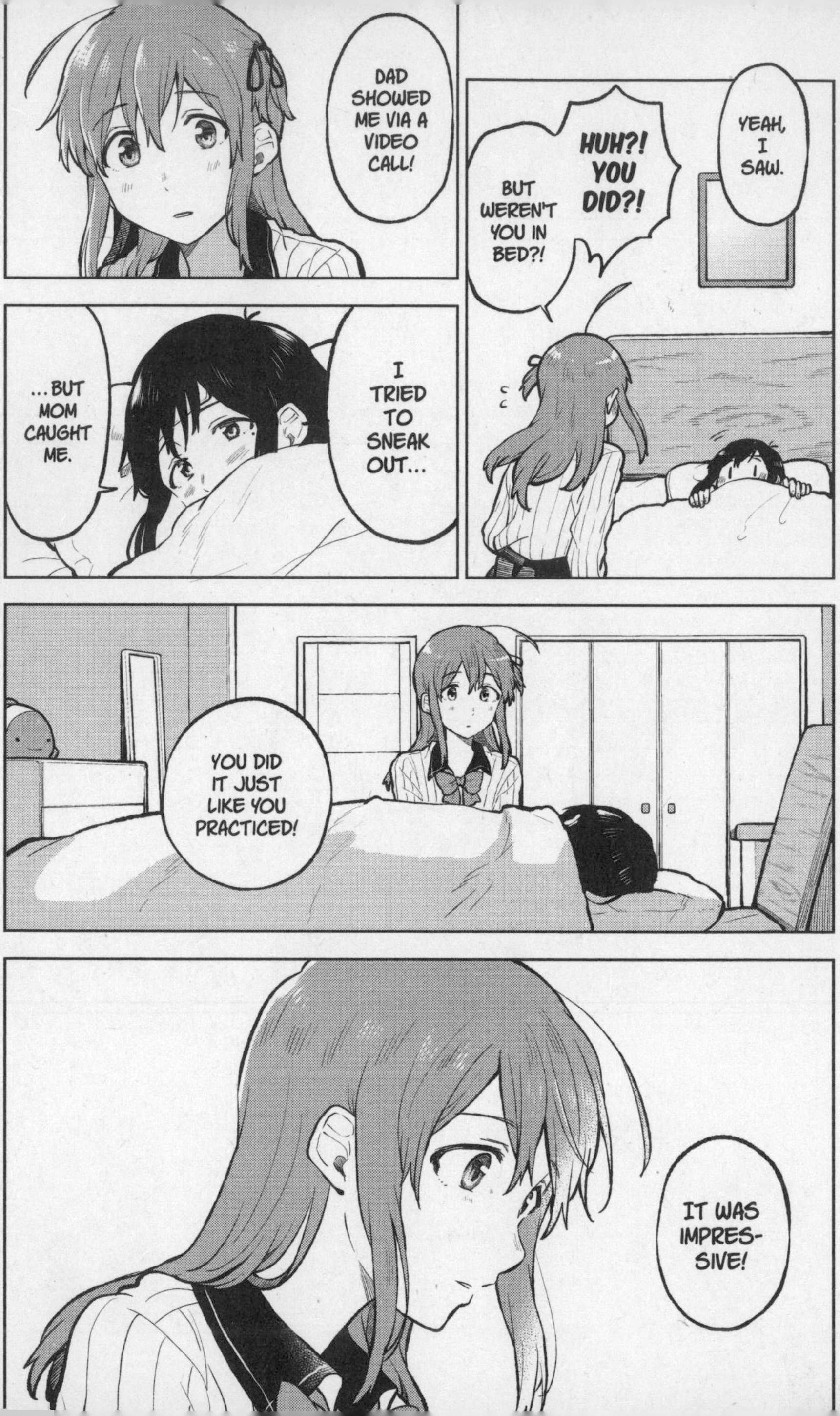
YEAH, I SAW.
HUH?! YOU DID?!
BUT WEREN'T YOU IN BED?!
DAD SHOWED ME VIA A VIDEO CALL!
I TRIED TO SNEAK OUT...
...BUT MOM CAUGHT ME.
YOU DID IT JUST LIKE YOU PRACTICED!
IT WAS IMPRES-SIVE!

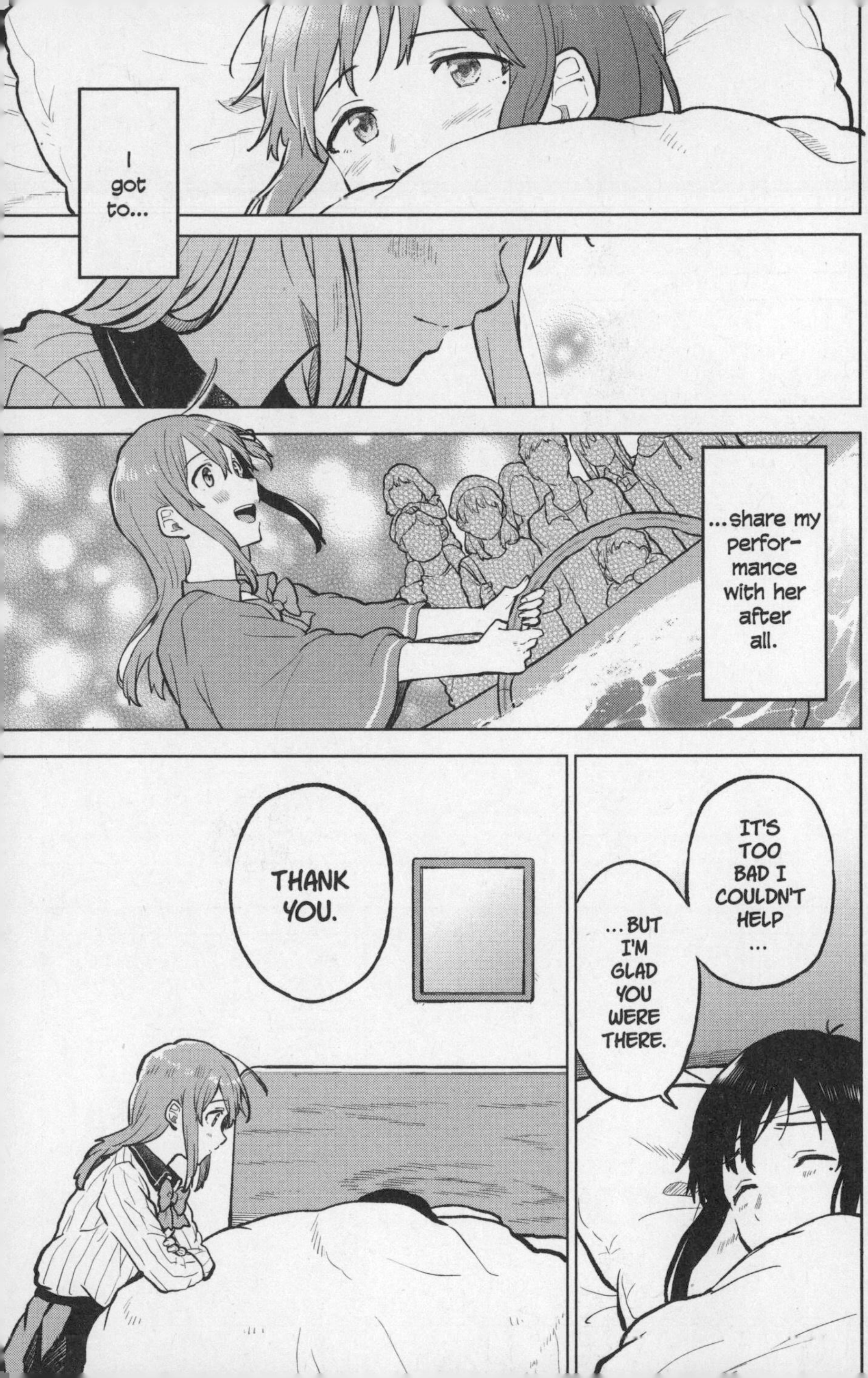
I got to...
...share my performance with her after all.
IT'S TOO BAD I COULDN'T HELP...
...BUT I'M GLAD YOU WERE THERE.
THANK YOU.

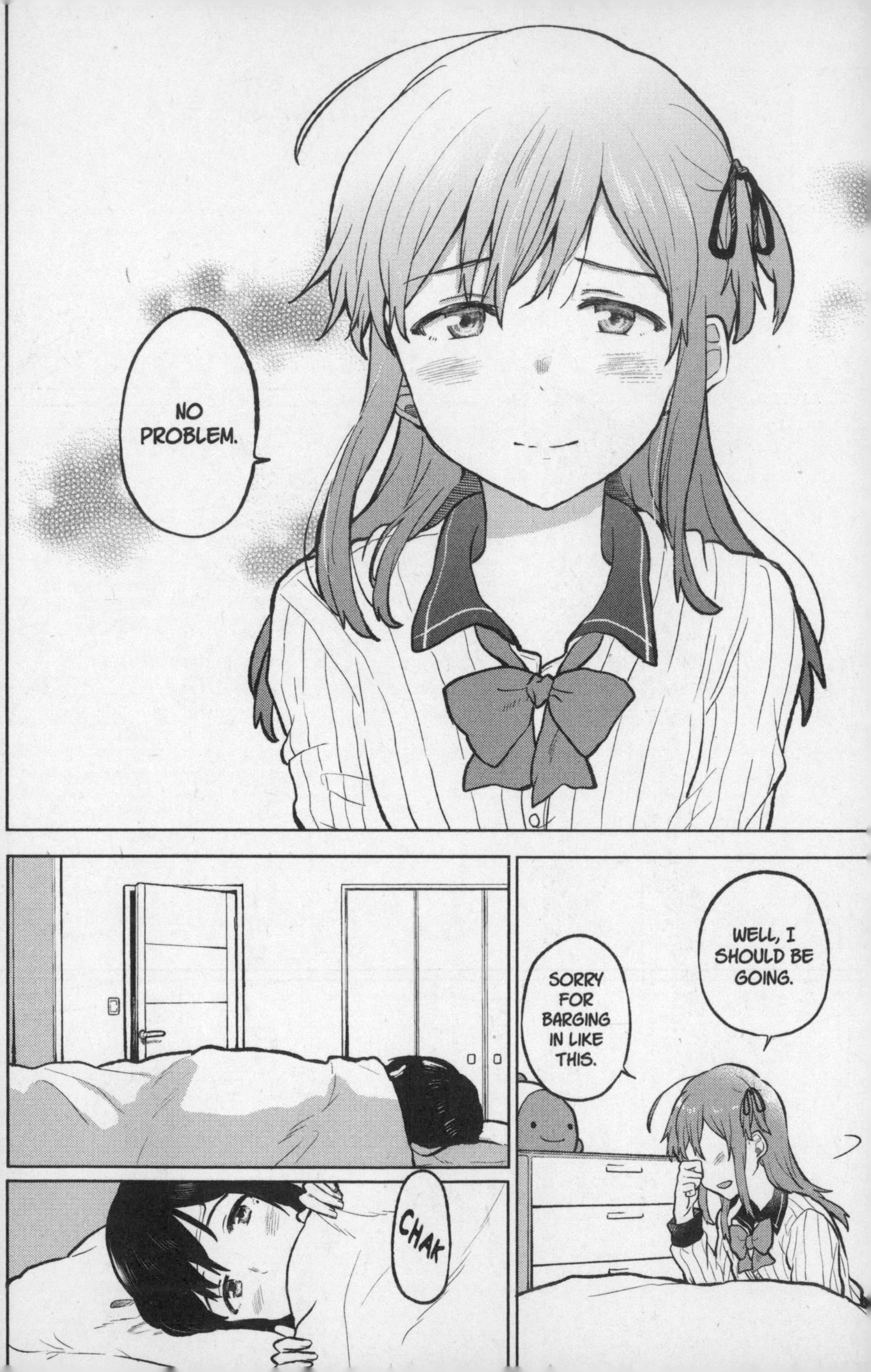
NO PROBLEM.
WELL, I SHOULD BE GOING.
SORRY FOR BARGING IN LIKE THIS.
CHAK

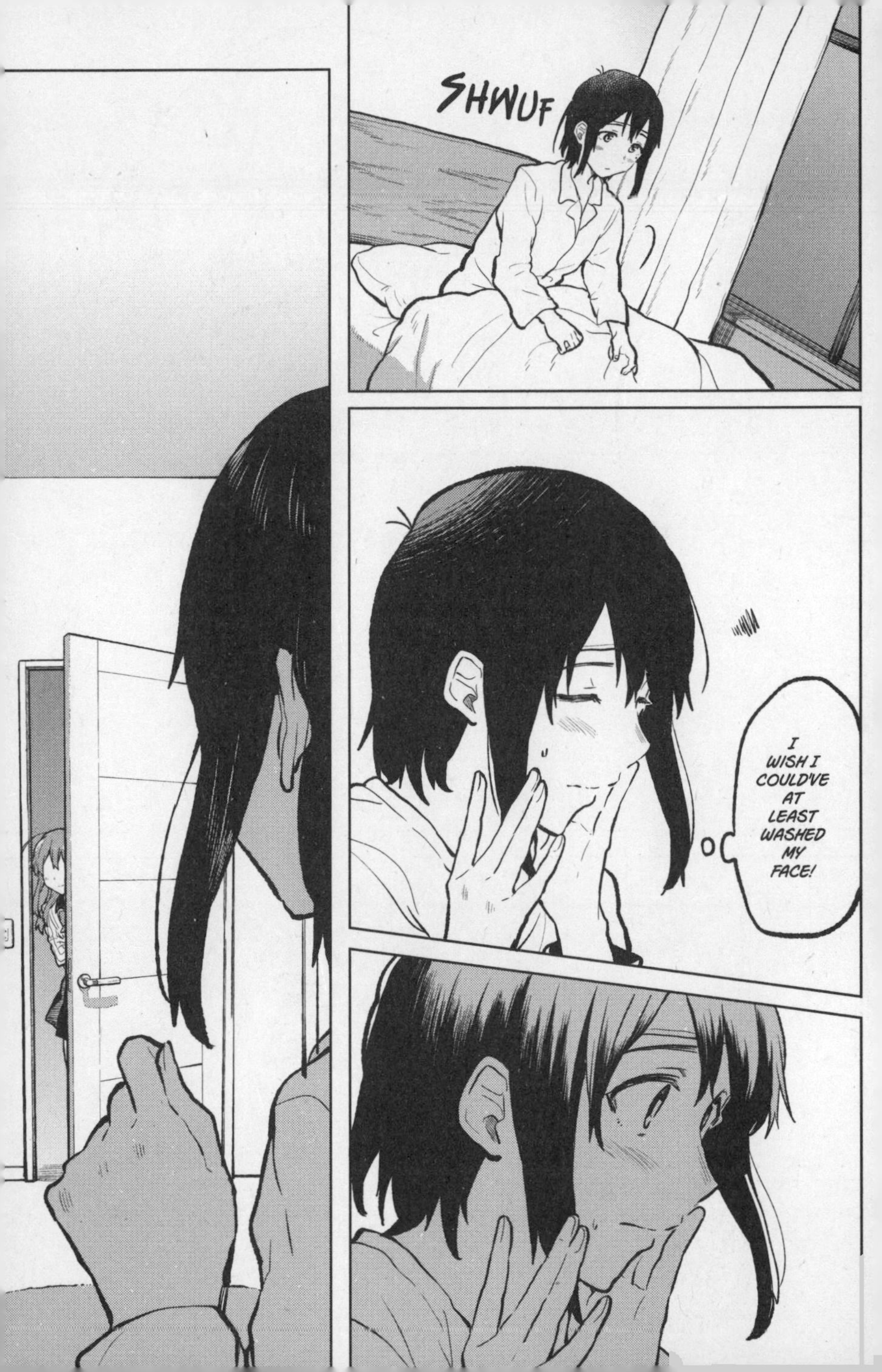
SHWUF
I WISH I COULD'VE AT LEAST WASHED MY FACE!

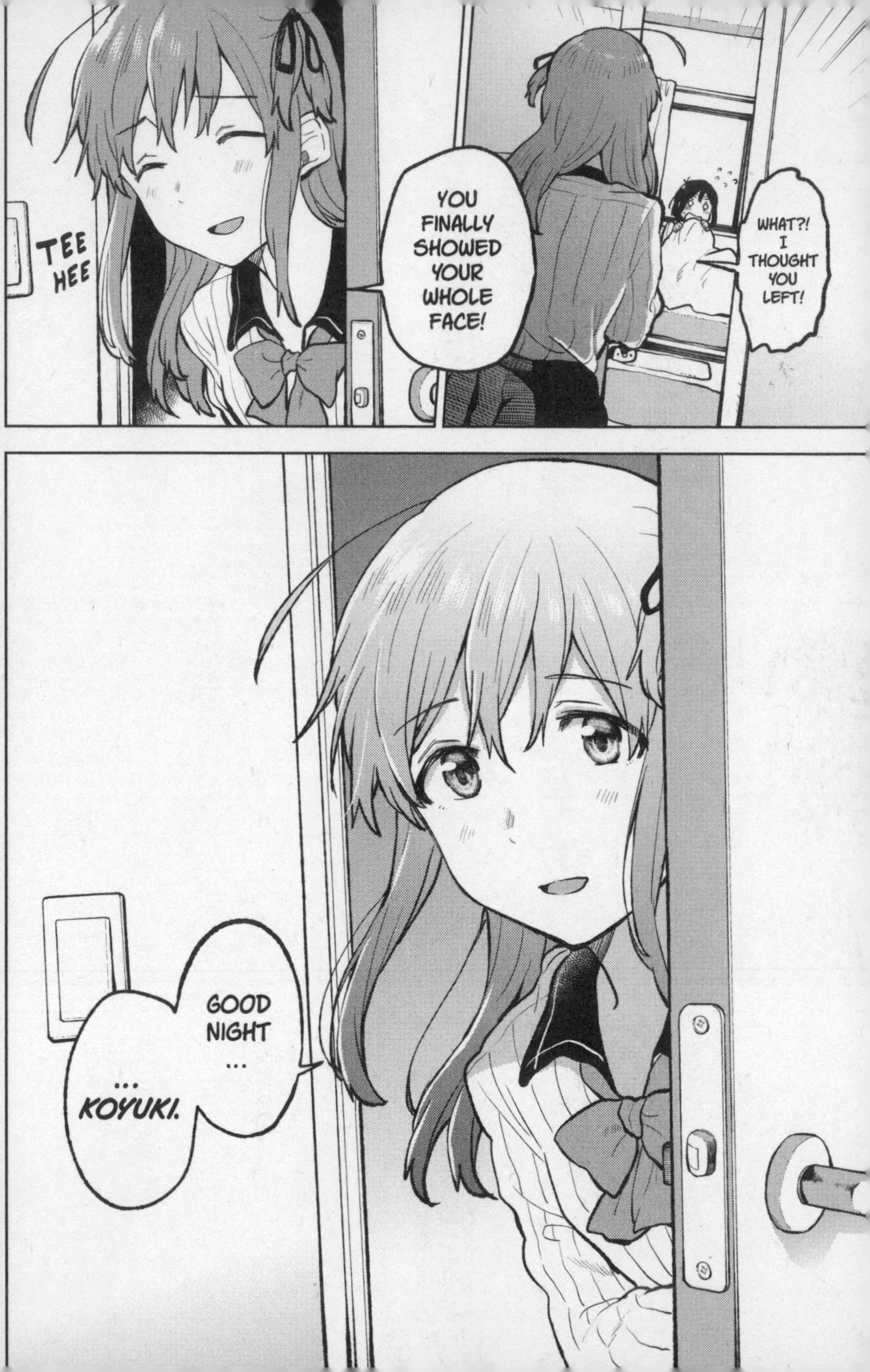
WHAT?! I THOUGHT YOU LEFT!
YOU FINALLY SHOWED YOUR WHOLE FACE!
TEE HEE
GOOD NIGHT ... ... KOYUKI.

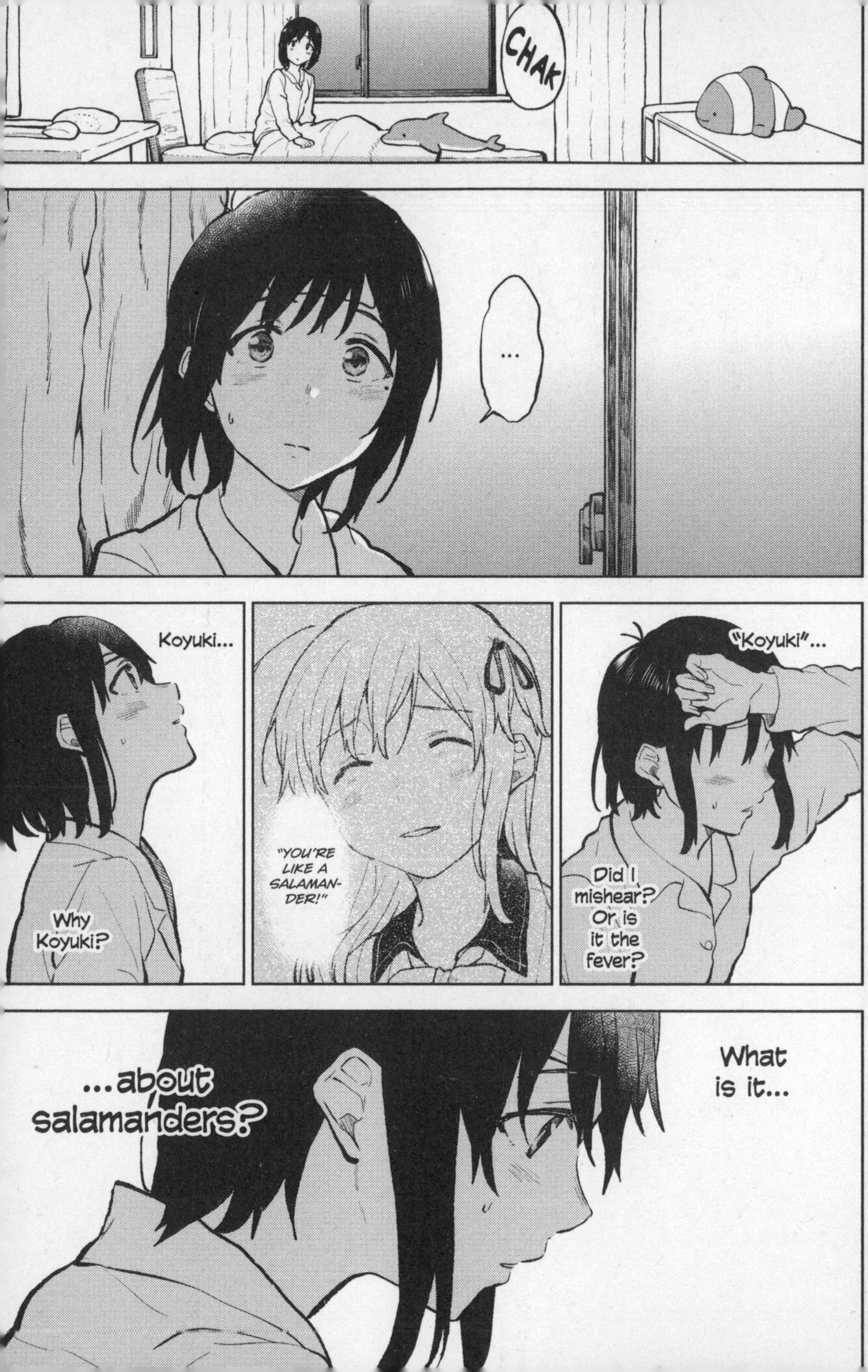
CHAK
...
"Koyuki"...
Did I mishear? Or is it the fever?
"YOU'RE LIKE A SALAMANDER!"
Koyuki...
Why Koyuki?
What is it...
...about salamanders?

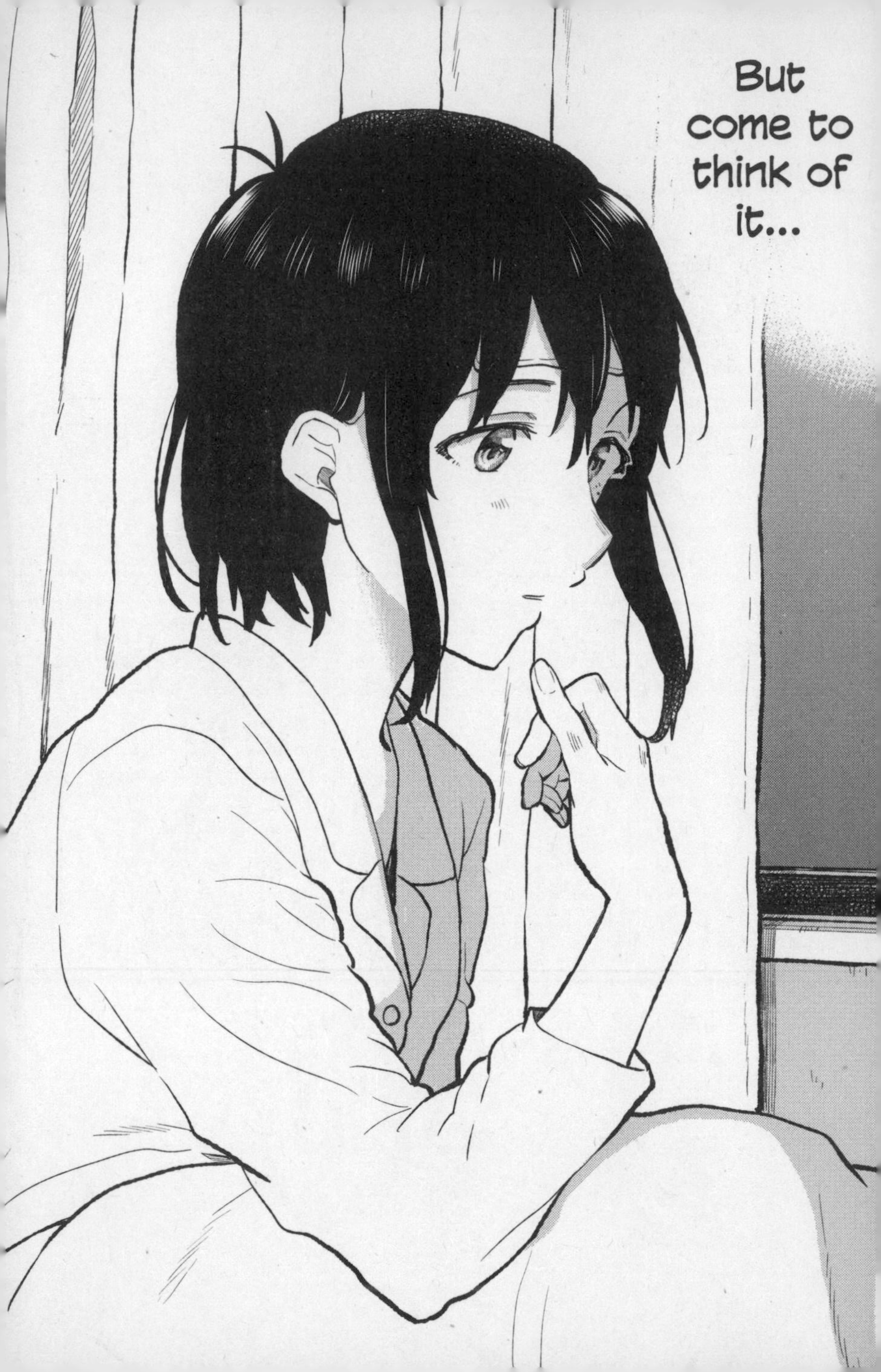
But come to think of it...

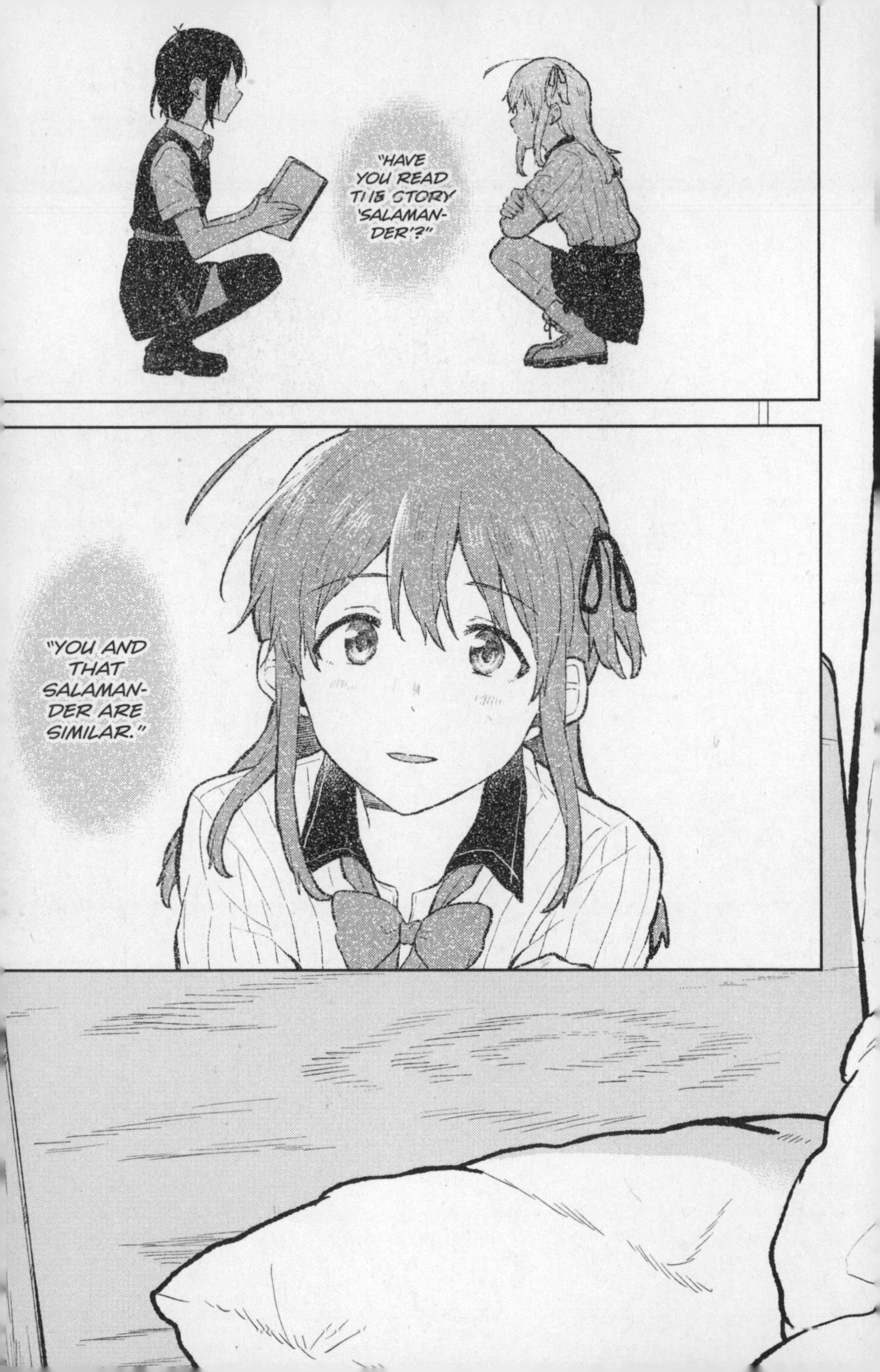
"HAVE YOU READ THE STORY 'SALAMANDER'?"
"YOU AND THAT SALAMANDER ARE SIMILAR."

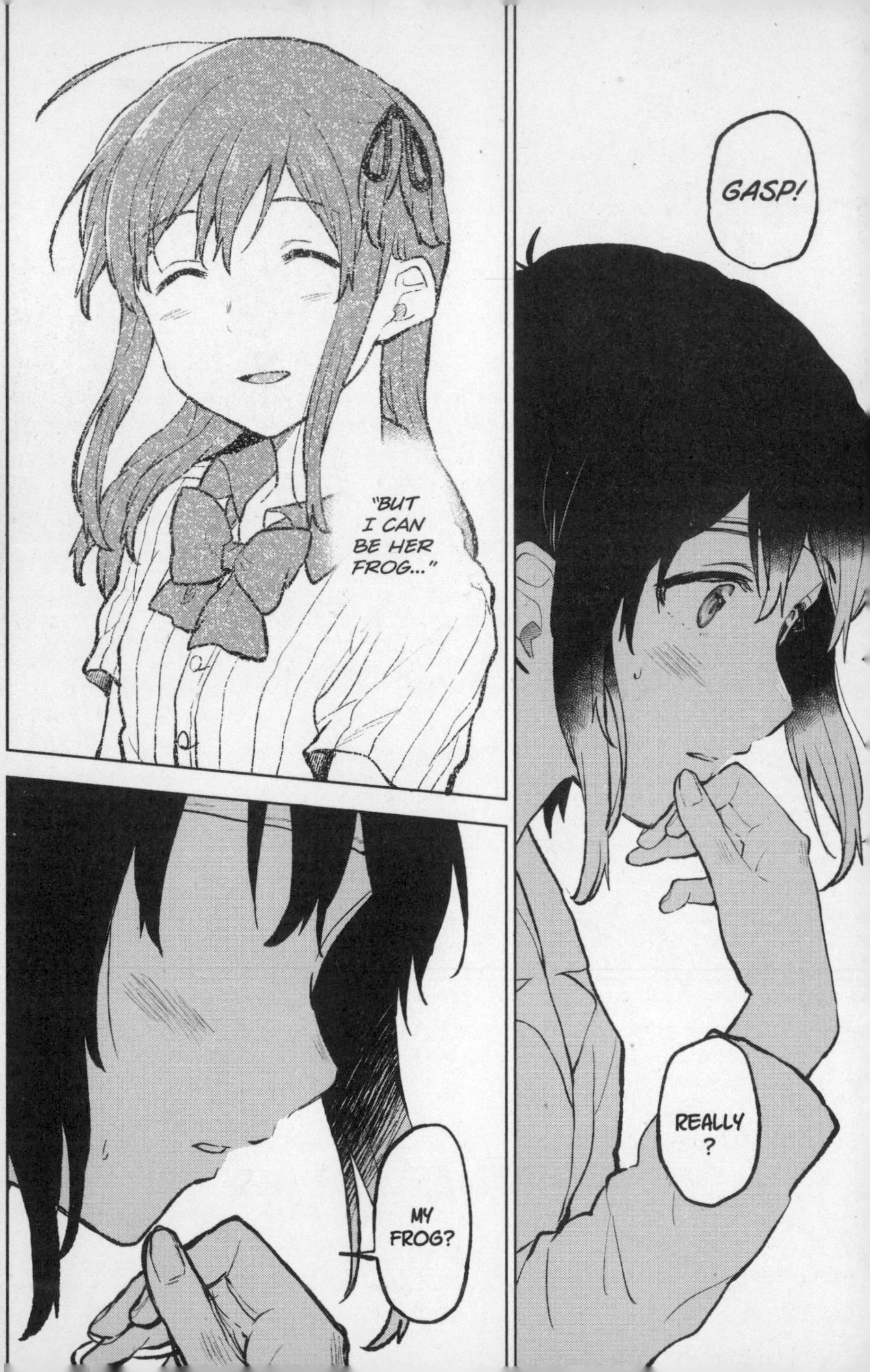
GASP!
REALLY?
"BUT I CAN BE HER FROG..."
MY FROG?

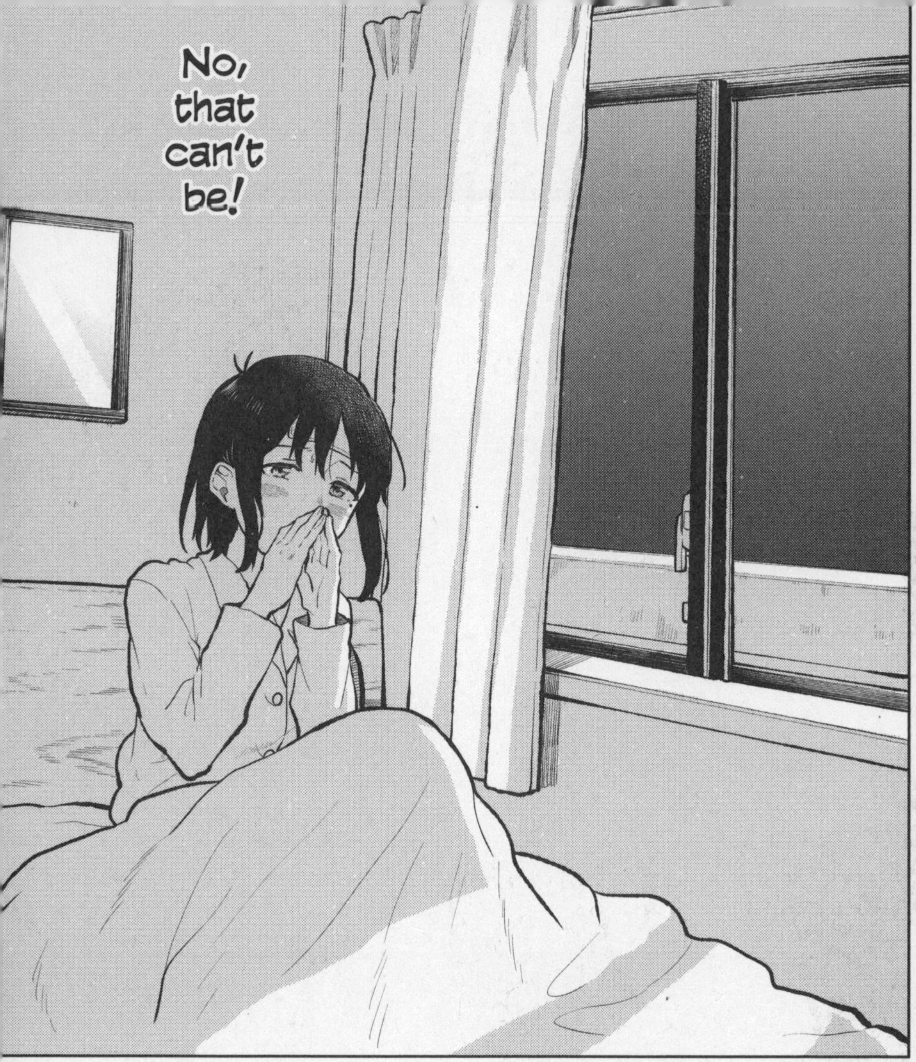
No, that can't be!

Tank 13:
Koyuki Honami Can't Sleep

A Tropical Fish
Years for Snow

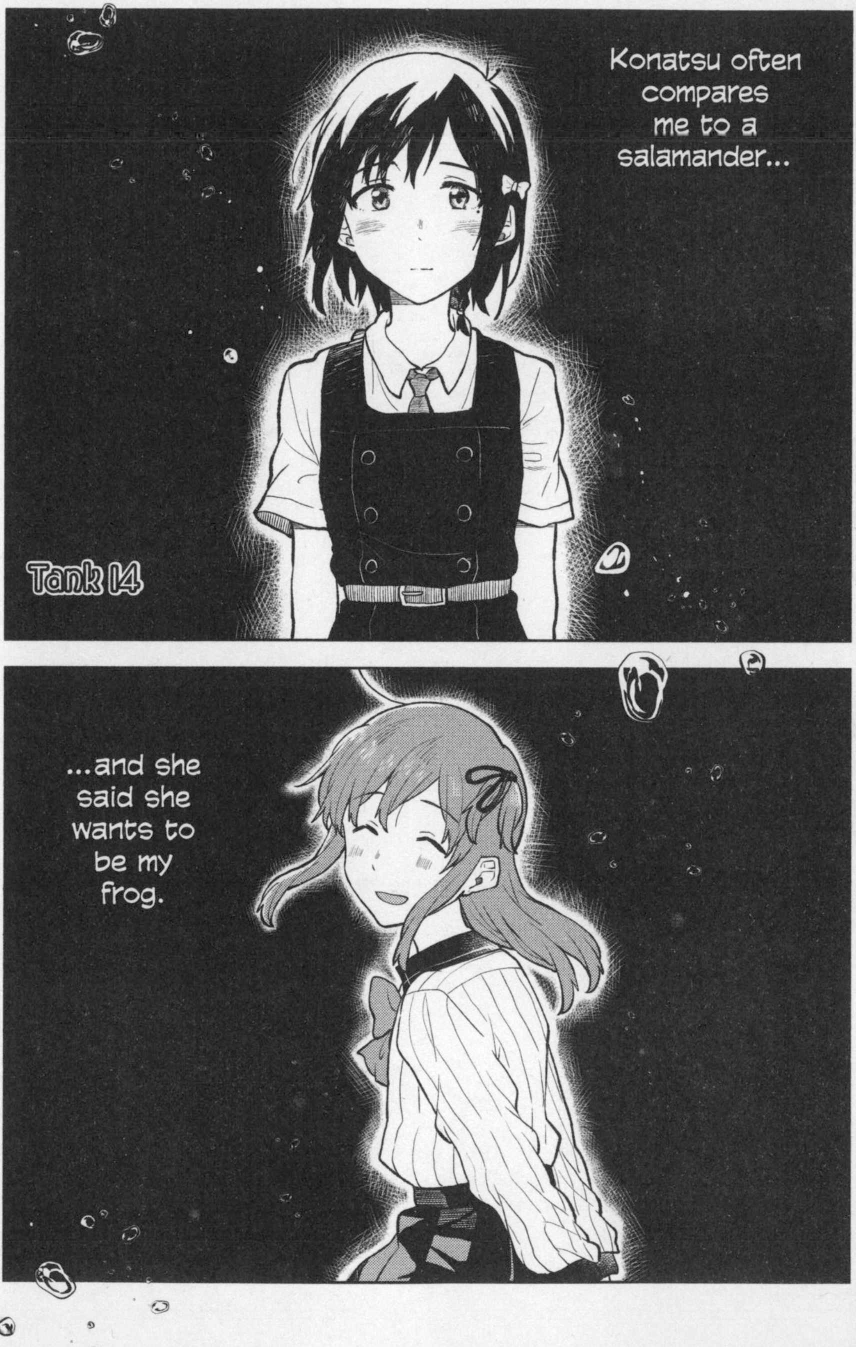
Konatsu often compares me to a salamander...
Tank 14
...and she said she wants to be my frog.

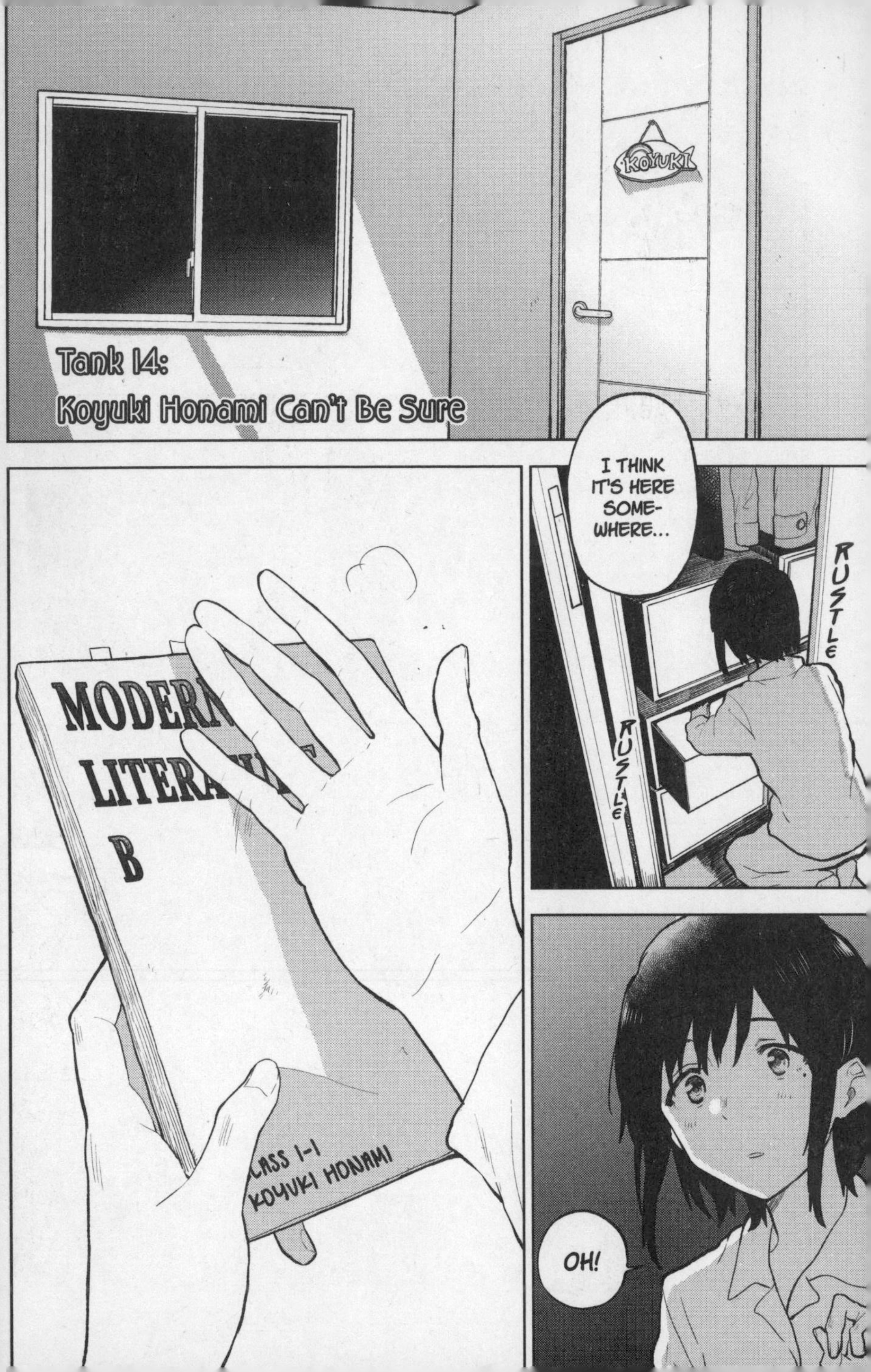
KOYUKI
Tank 14:
Koyuki Honami Can't Be Sure
I THINK IT'S HERE SOME-WHERE...
RUSTLE
RUSTLE
OH!
MODER
LITERA
B
CLASS 1-1
KOYUKI HONAMI

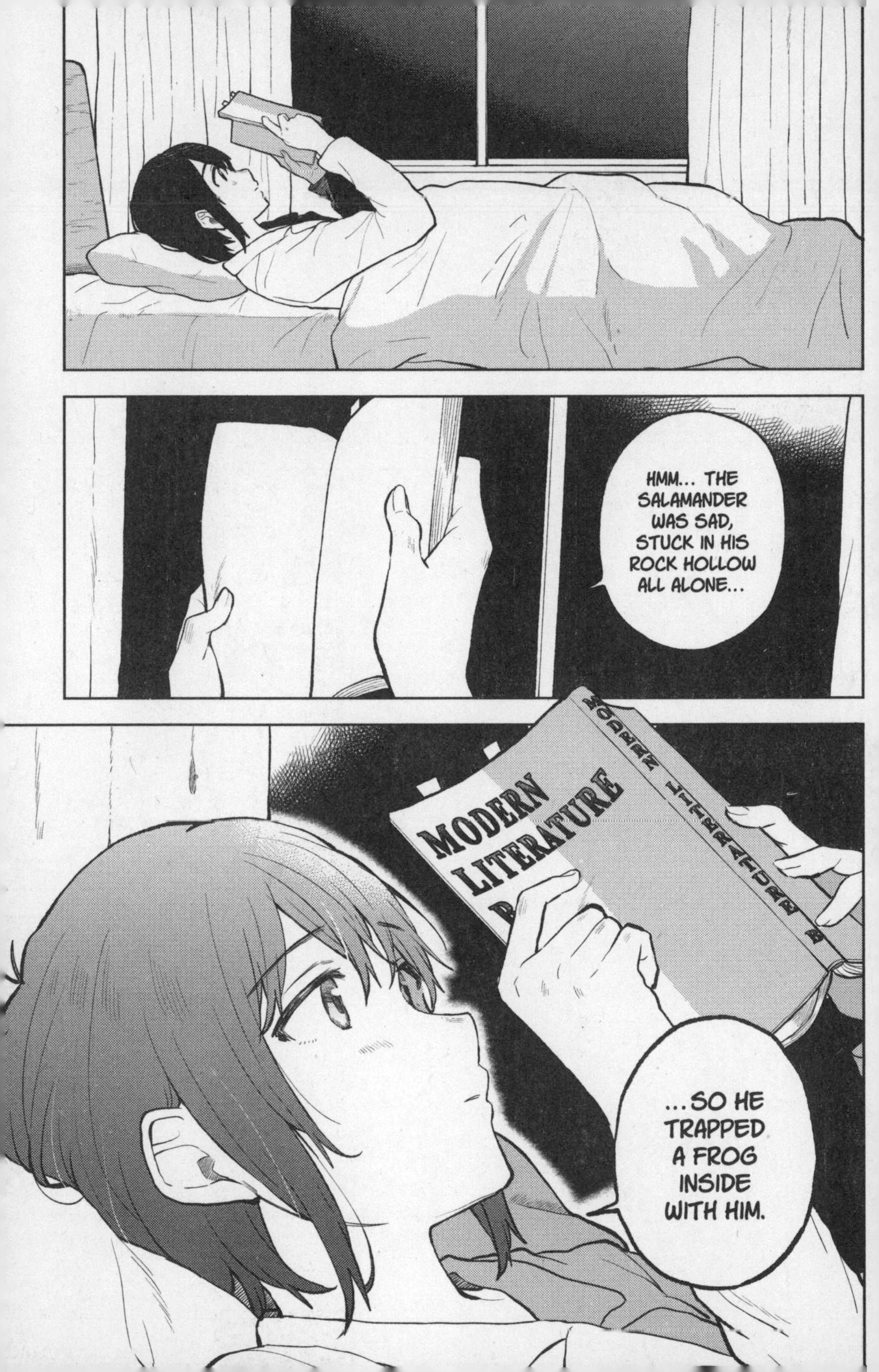
HMM... THE SALAMANDER WAS SAD, STUCK IN HIS ROCK HOLLOW ALL ALONE...
MODERN LITERATURE
...SO HE TRAPPED A FROG INSIDE WITH HIM.

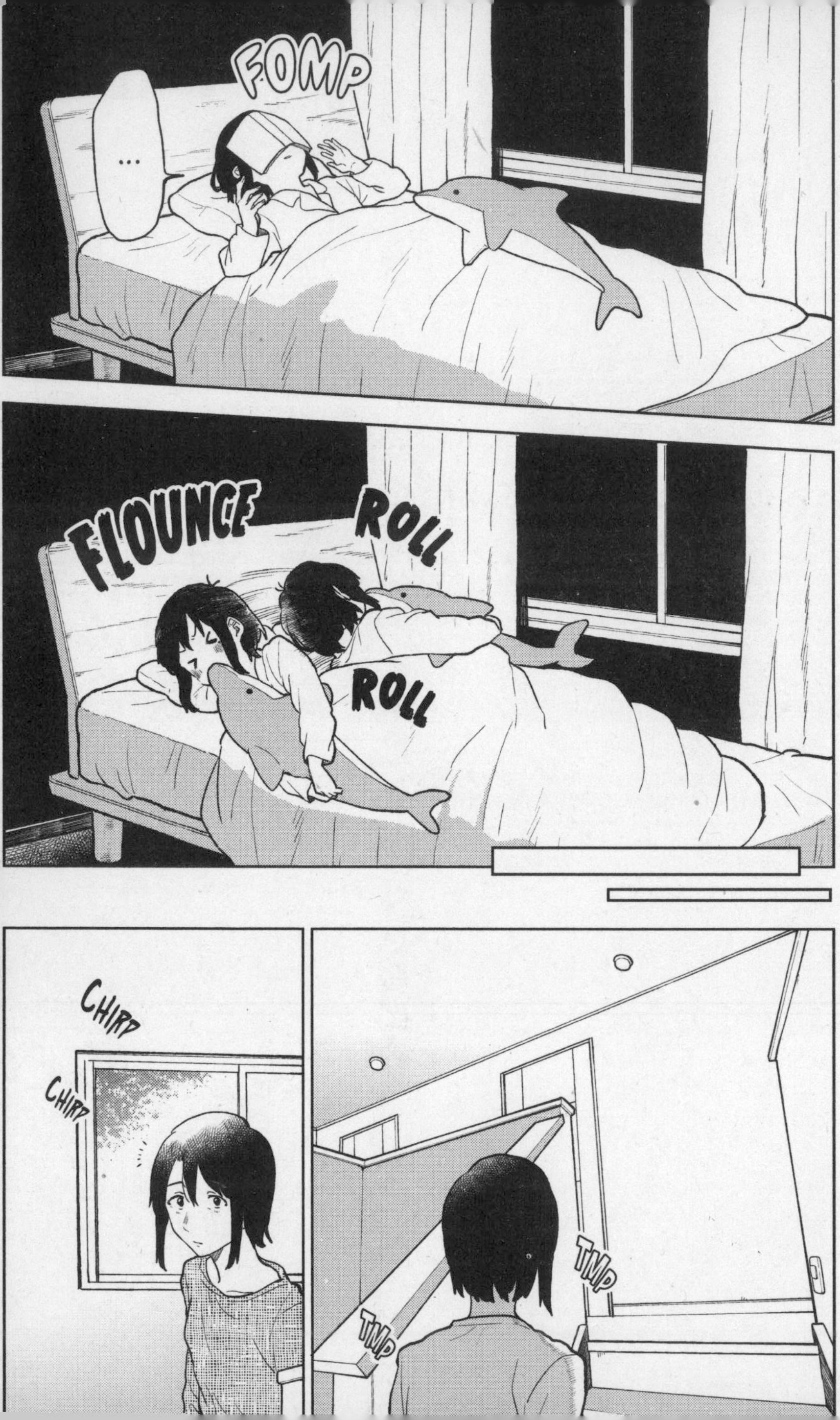
FOMP
...
FLOUNCE
ROLL
ROLL
TMP
TMP
CHIRP
CHIRP

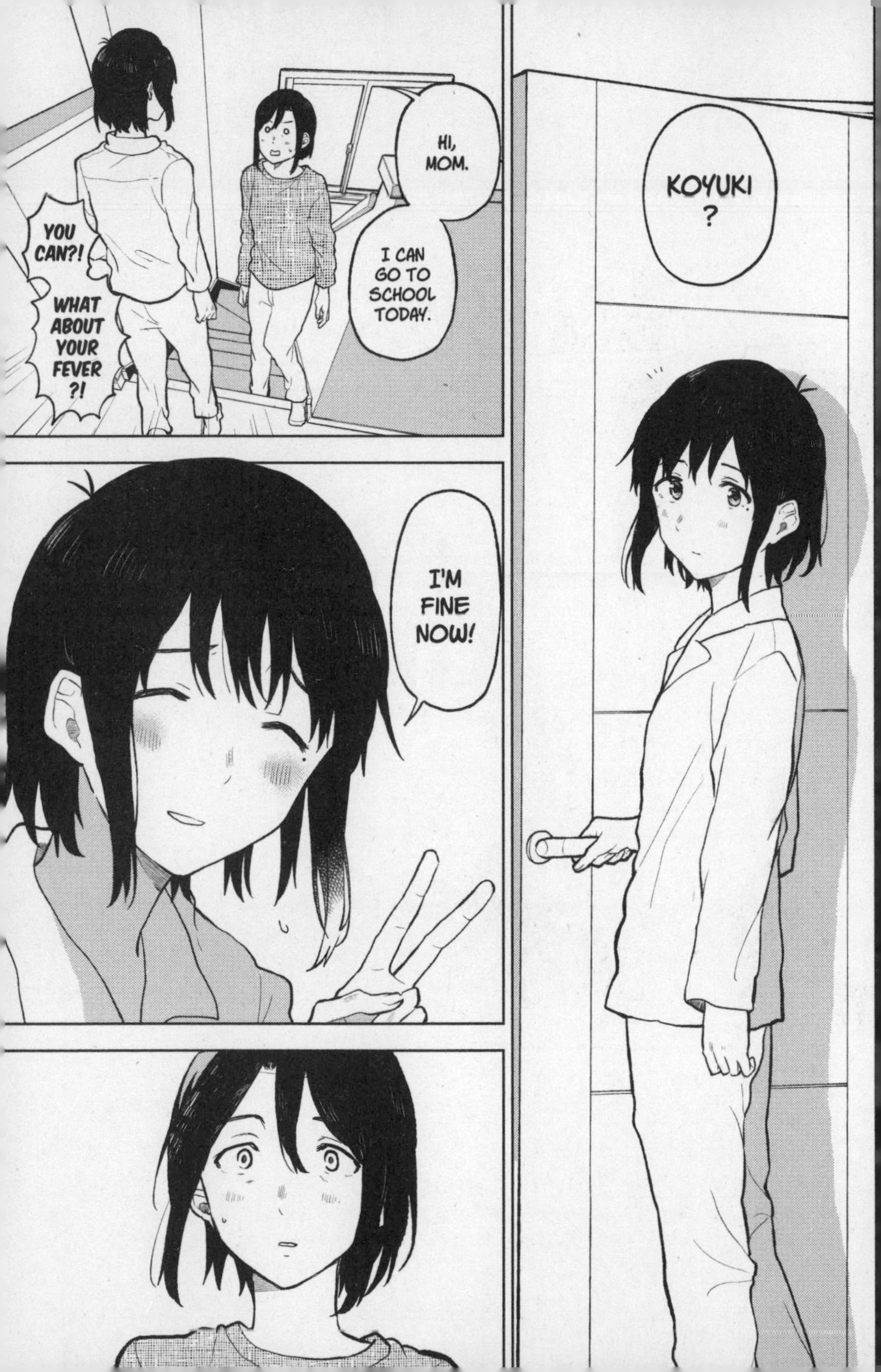
KOYUKI ?
HI, MOM.
I CAN GO TO SCHOOL TODAY.
YOU CAN?!
WHAT ABOUT YOUR FEVER ?!
I'M FINE NOW!

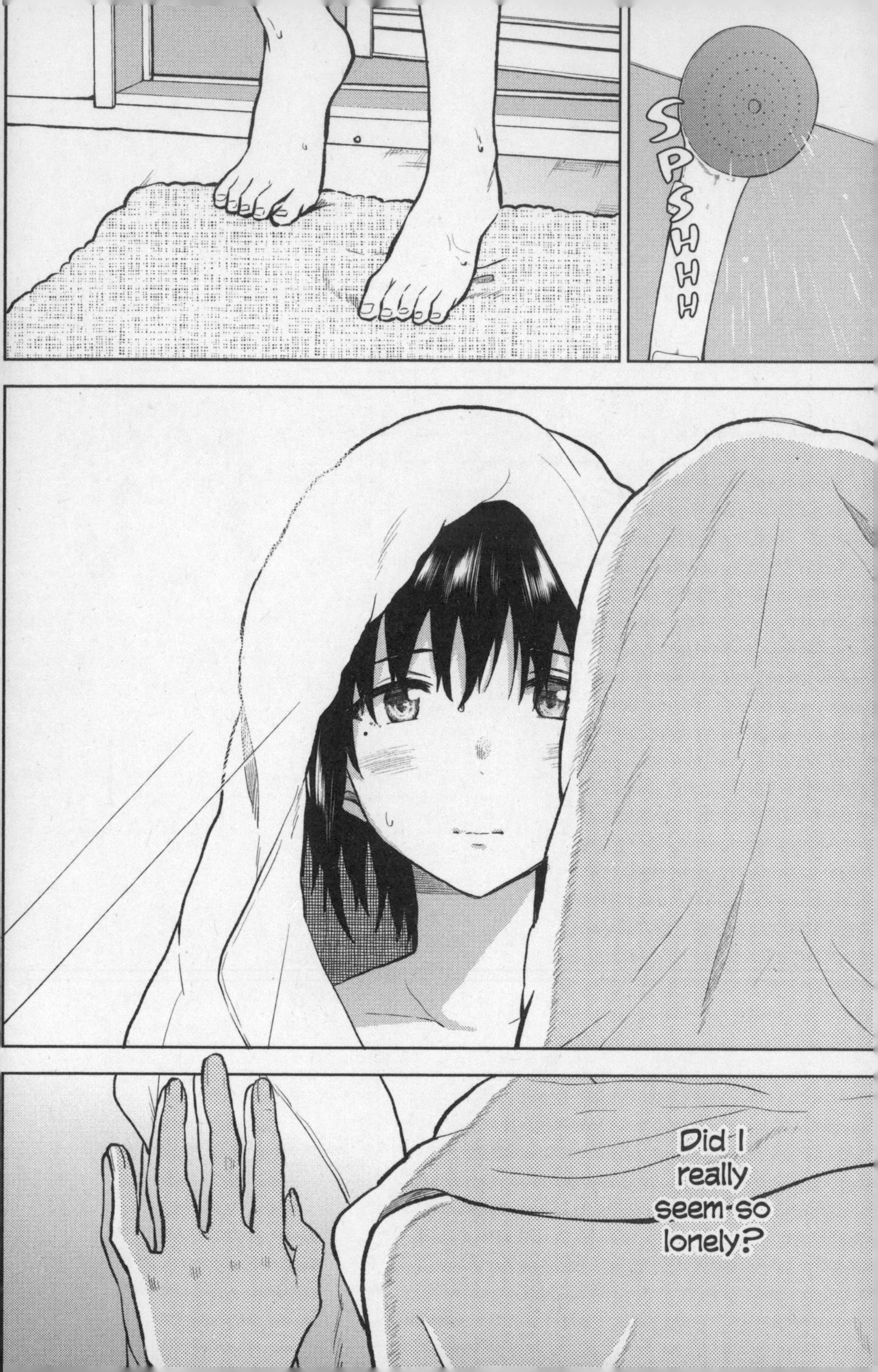
SPSHHH
Did I really seem so lonely?

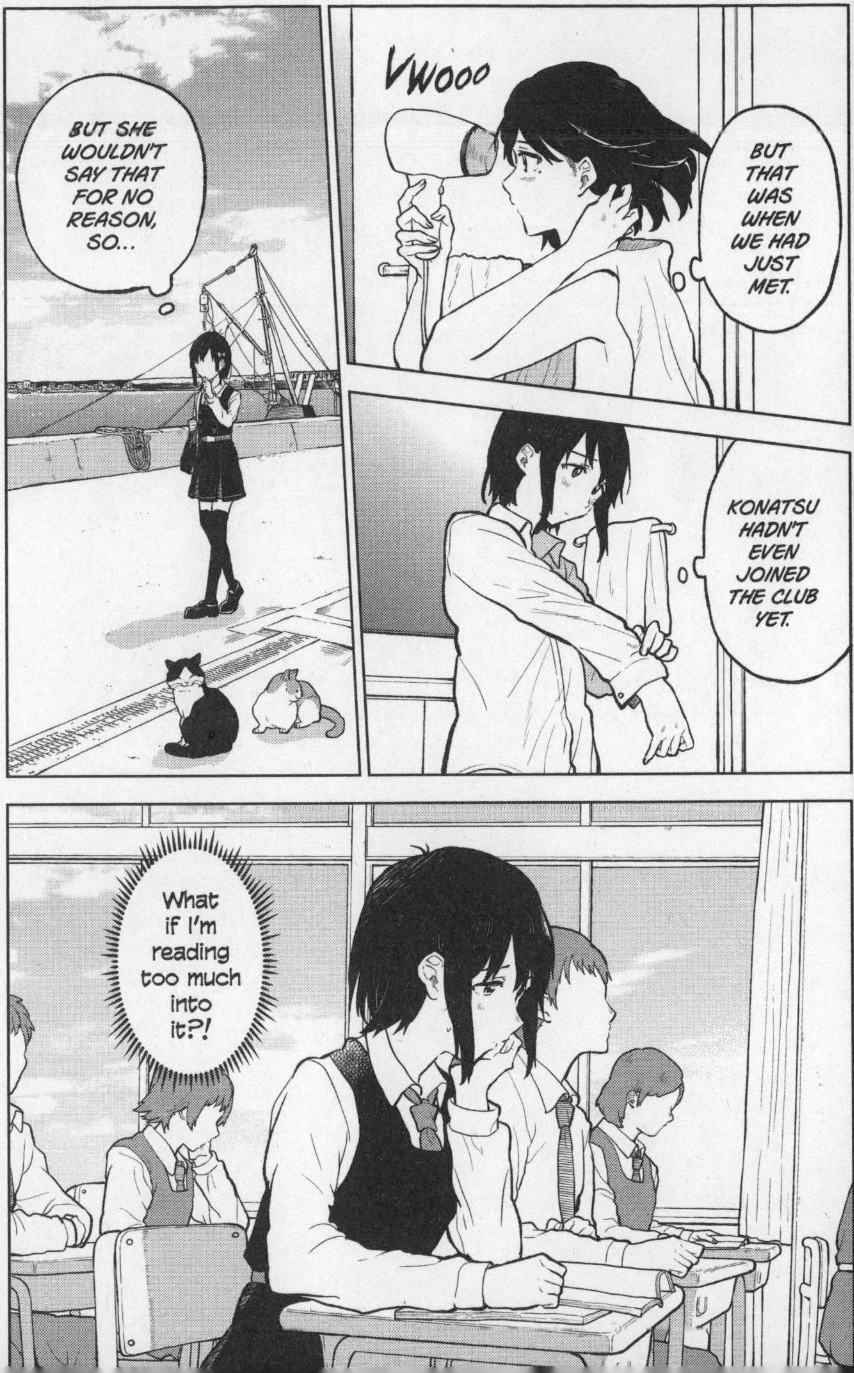
VWOOO
BUT THAT WAS WHEN WE HAD JUST MET.
KONATSU HADN'T EVEN JOINED THE CLUB YET.
BUT SHE WOULDN'T SAY THAT FOR NO REASON, SO...
What if I'm reading too much into it?!

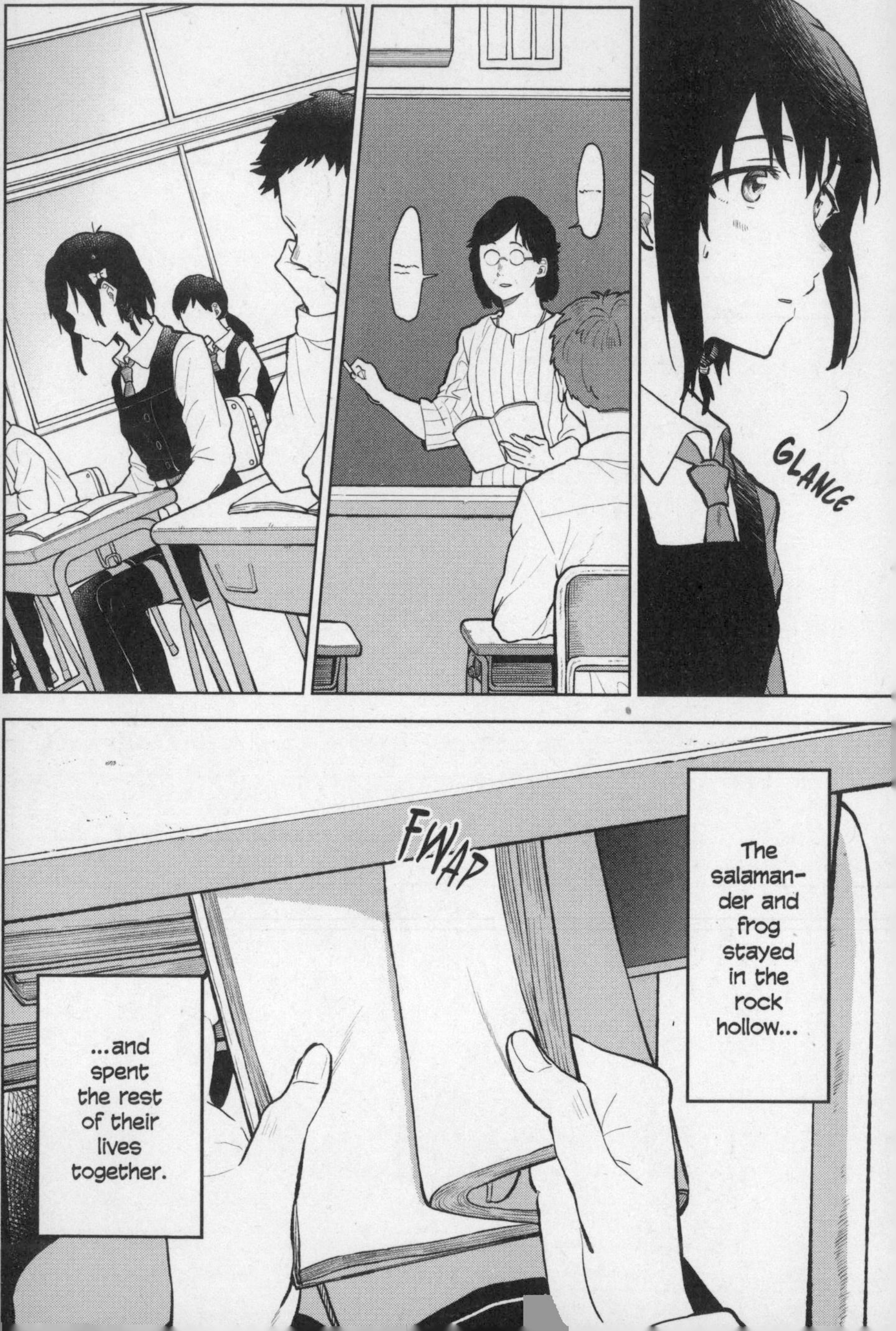
GLANCE
FWAP
The salamander and frog stayed in the rock hollow...
...and spent the rest of their lives together.

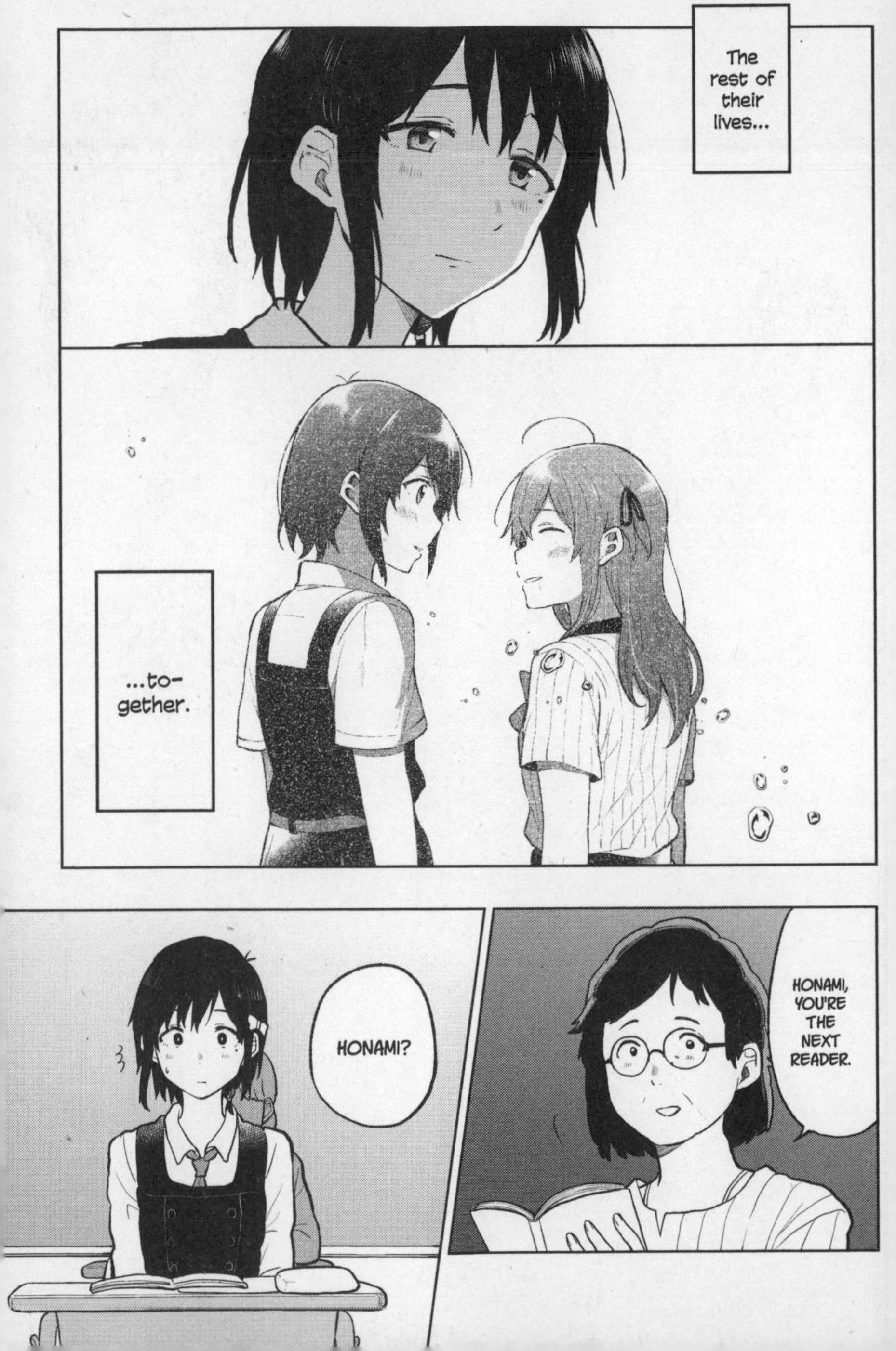
The rest of their lives...
...to-gether.
HONAMI, YOU'RE THE NEXT READER.
HONAMI?

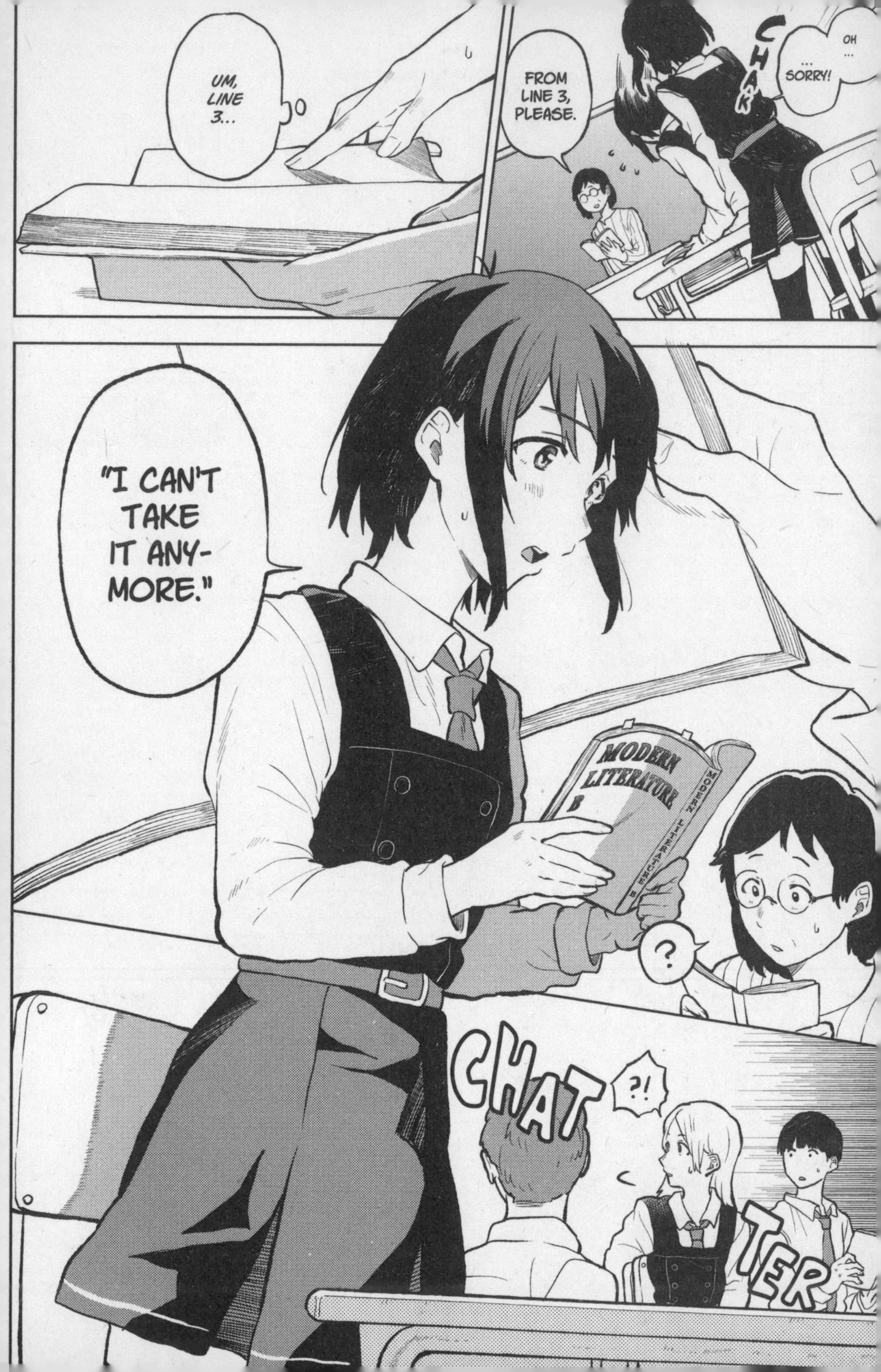
OH ... SORRY!
CHAK
FROM LINE 3, PLEASE.
UM, LINE 3...
"I CAN'T TAKE IT ANY-MORE."
MODERN LITERATURE B
?
CHAT
?!
TER

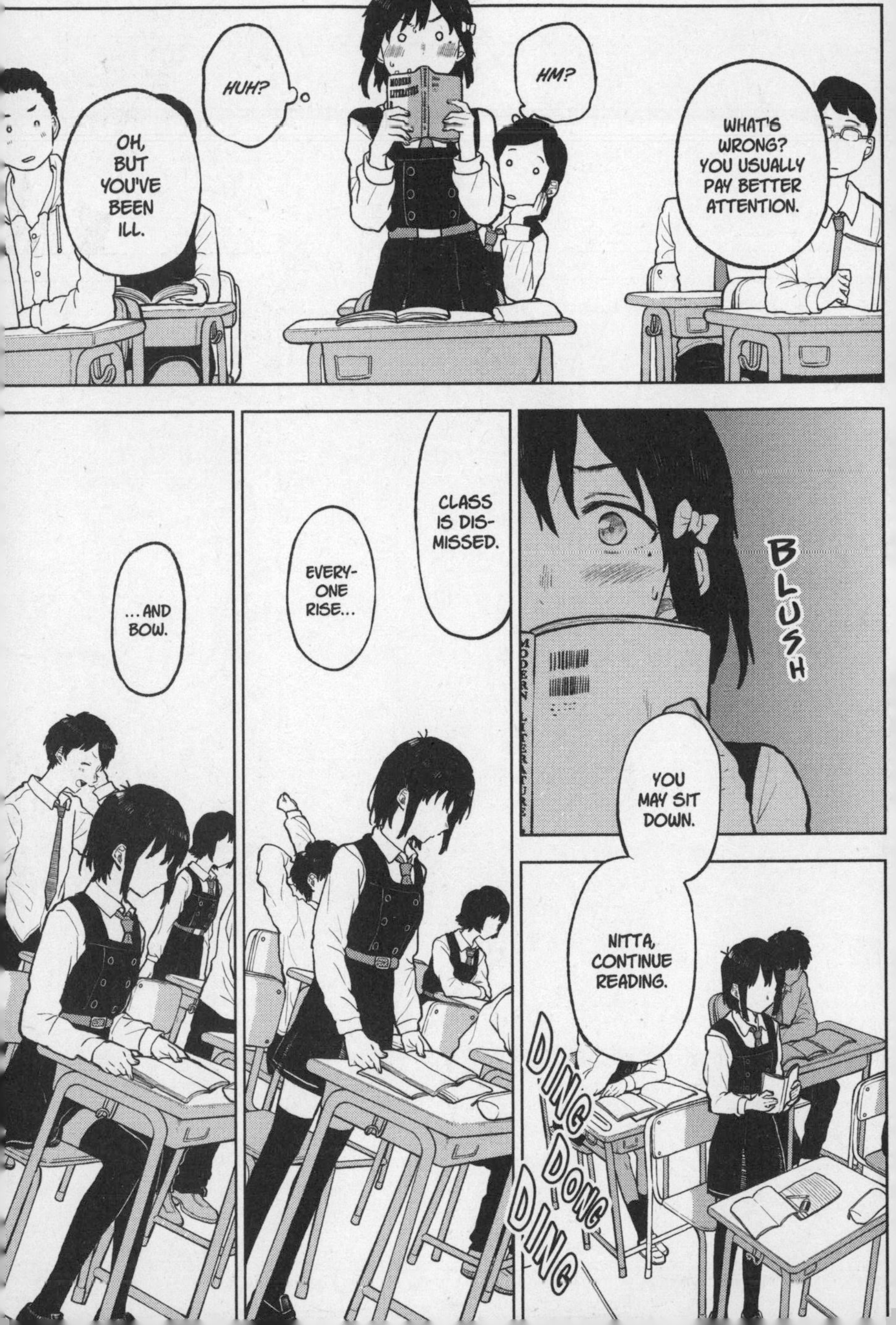
WHAT'S WRONG? YOU USUALLY PAY BETTER ATTENTION.
HM?
HUH?
OH, BUT YOU'VE BEEN ILL.
MODERN LITERATURE
BLUSH
YOU MAY SIT DOWN.
NITTA, CONTINUE READING.
DING DONG DING
CLASS IS DIS-MISSED.
EVERY-ONE RISE...
...AND BOW.

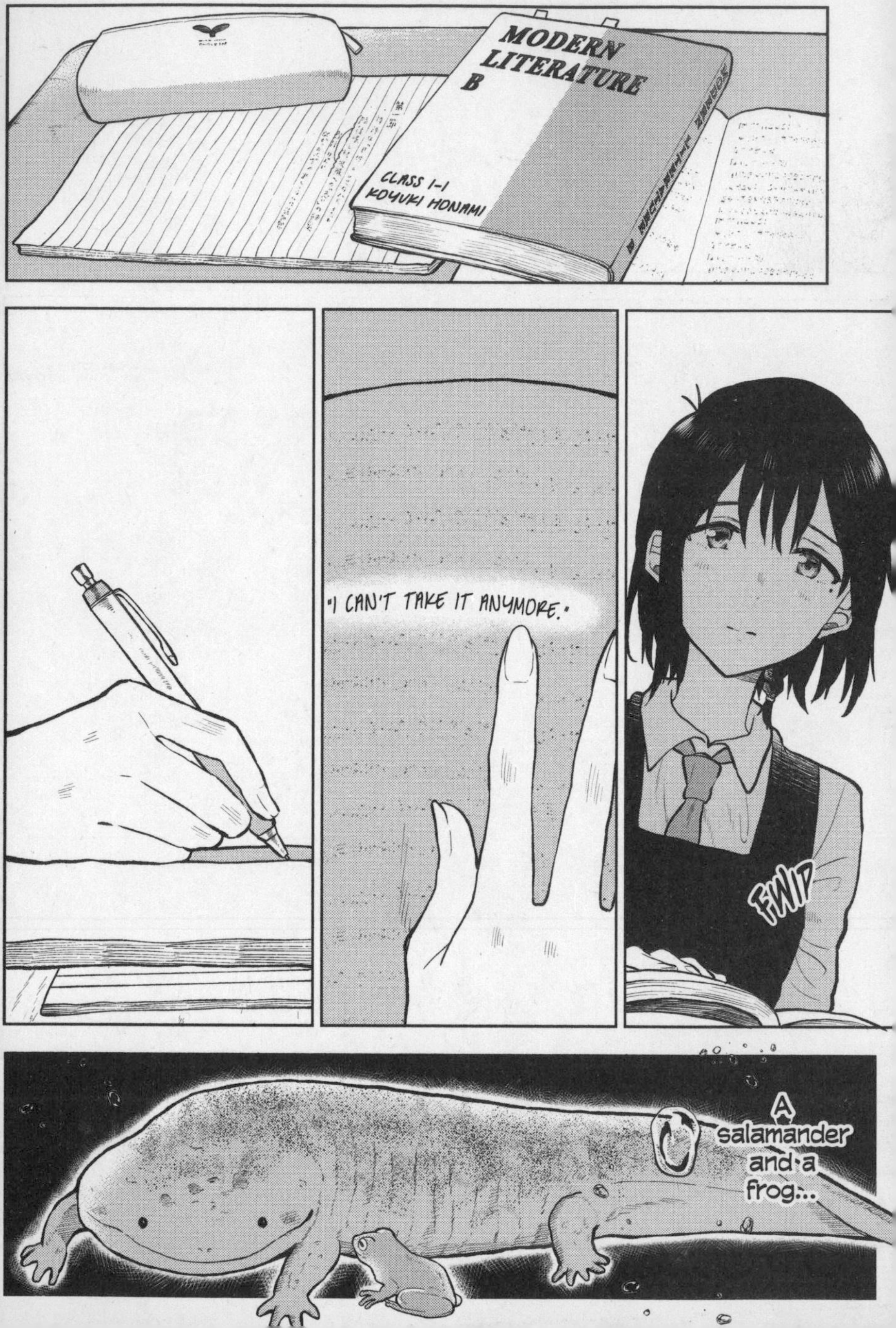
MODERN LITERATURE B
CLASS 1-1
KOYUKI HONAMI
FWIP
"I CAN'T TAKE IT ANYMORE."
A salamander and a frog...

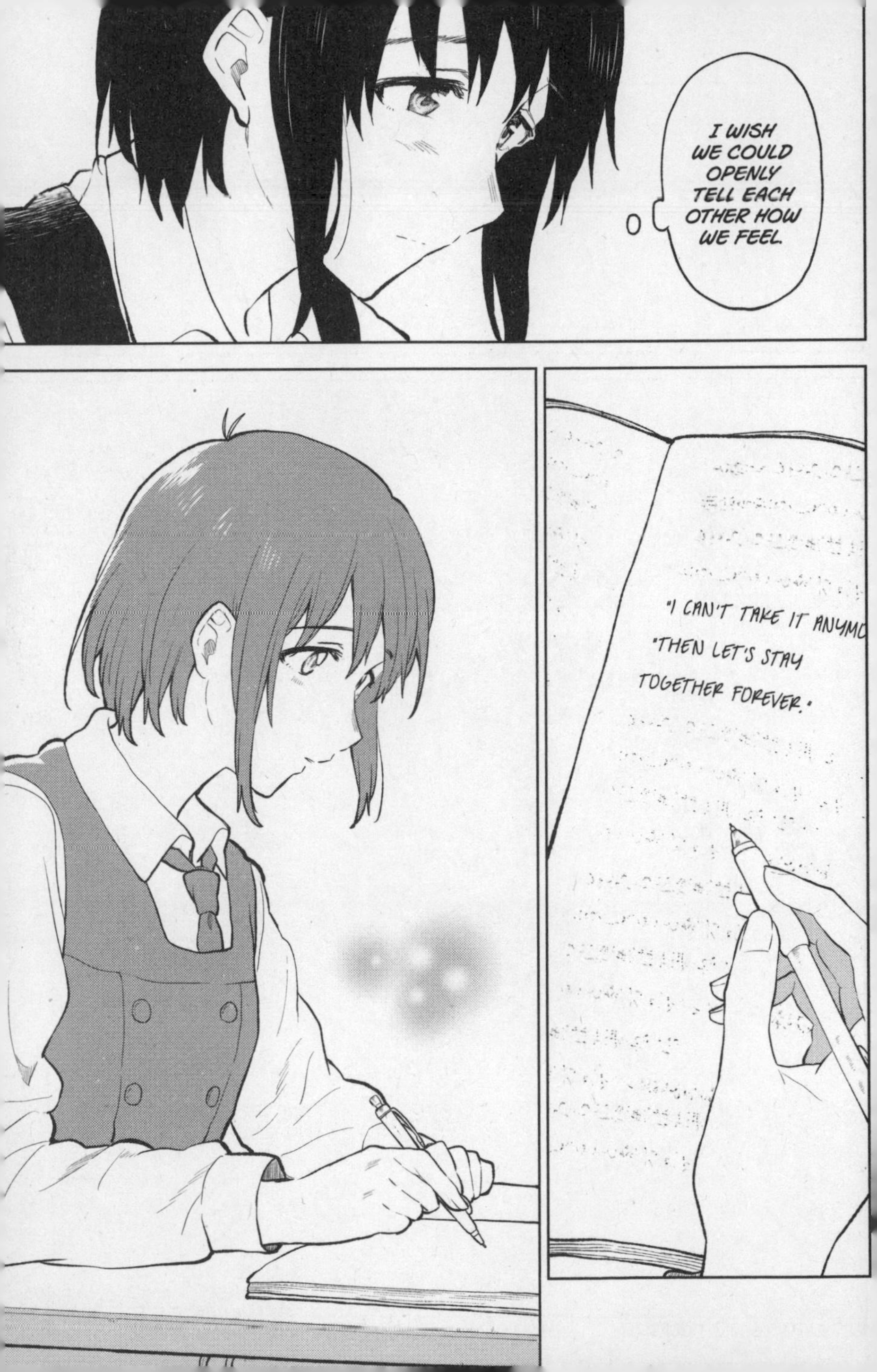
I WISH WE COULD OPENLY TELL EACH OTHER HOW WE FEEL.
"I CAN'T TAKE IT ANYMO
"THEN LET'S STAY TOGETHER FOREVER."

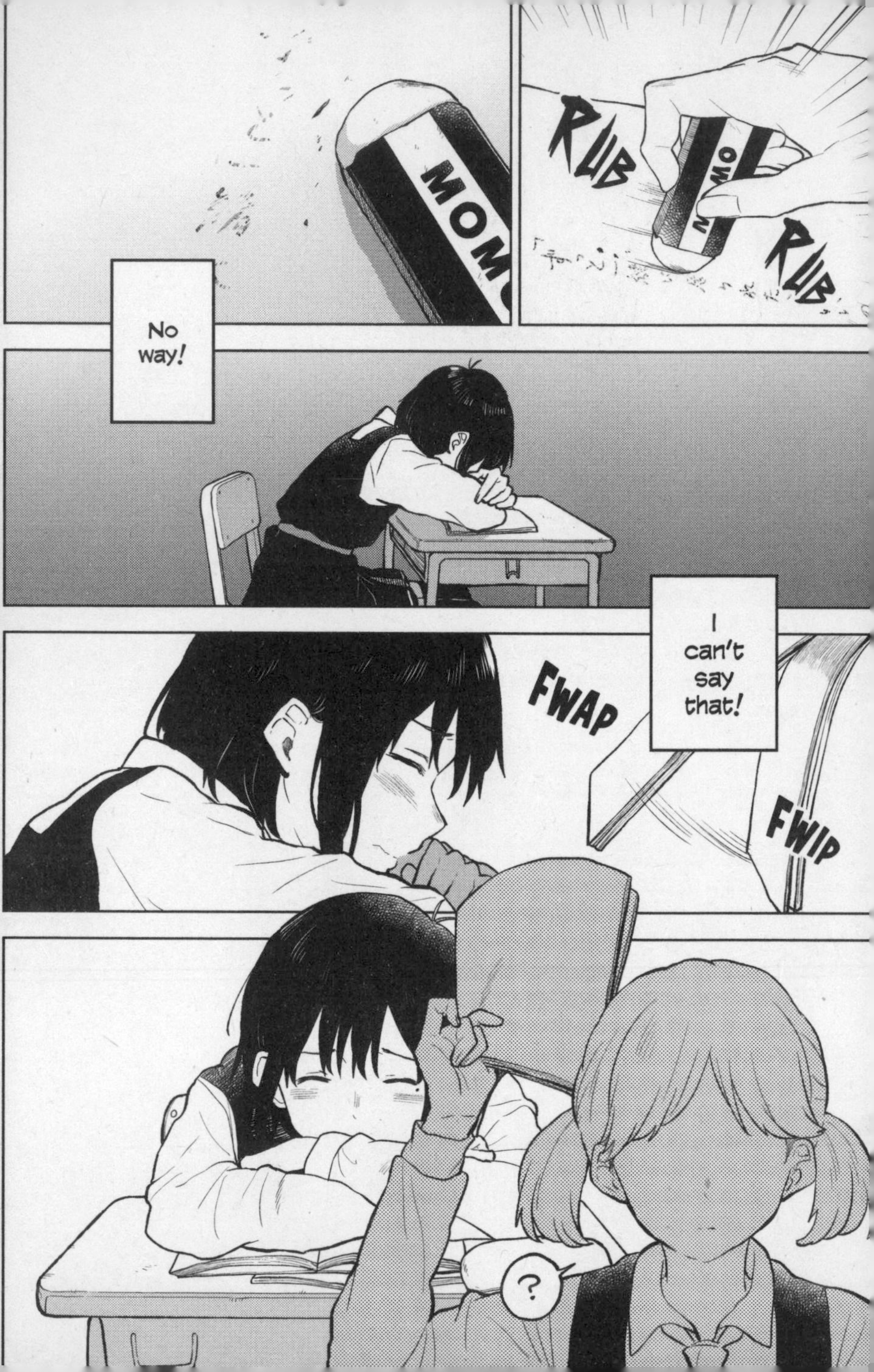
RUB
RUB
MOMO
No way!
I can't say that!
FWAP
FWIP
?

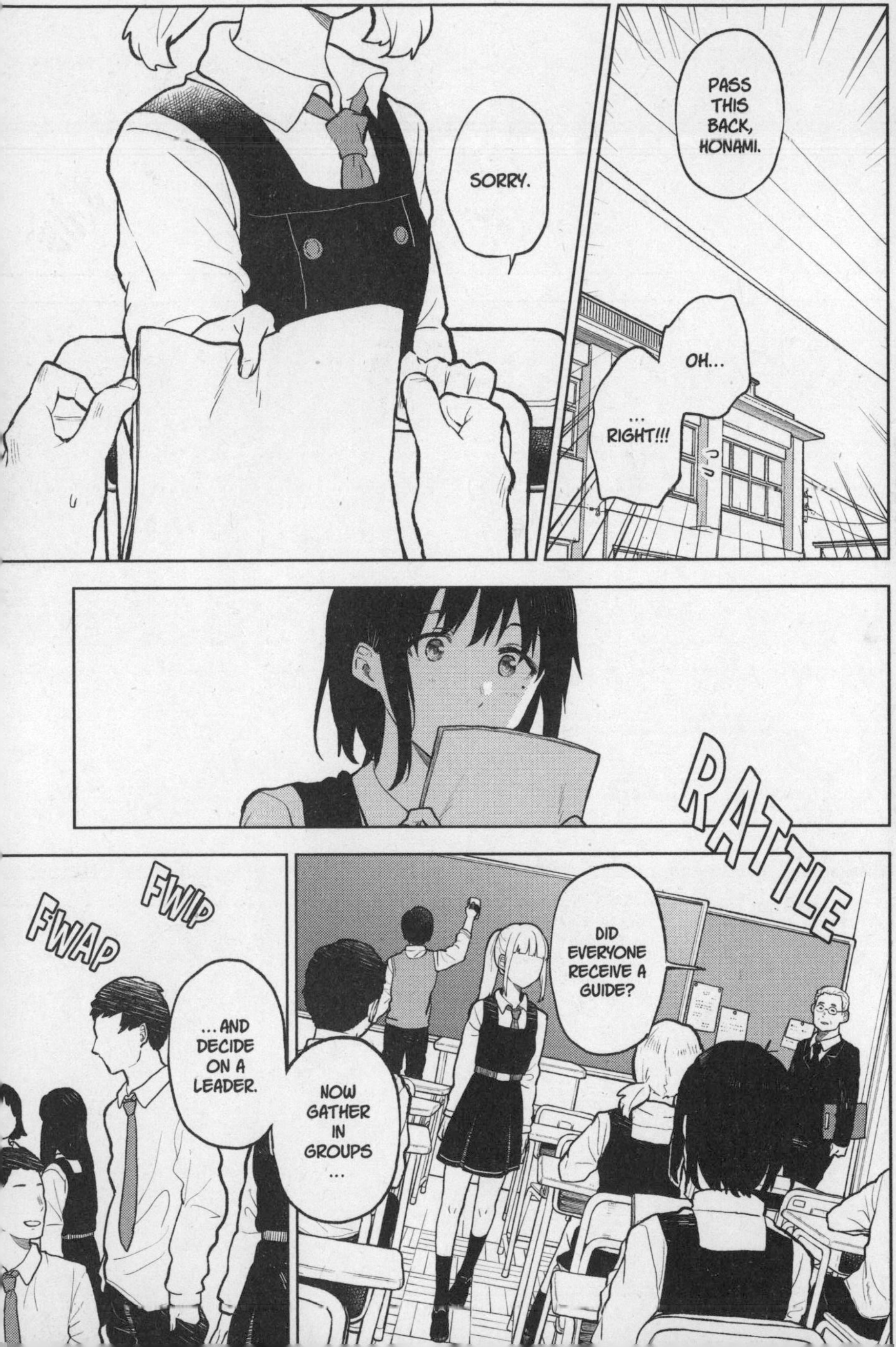
PASS THIS BACK, HONAMI.
OH...
...RIGHT!!!
SORRY.
RATTLE
DID EVERYONE RECEIVE A GUIDE?
FWIP
FWAP
NOW GATHER IN GROUPS...
...AND DECIDE ON A LEADER.

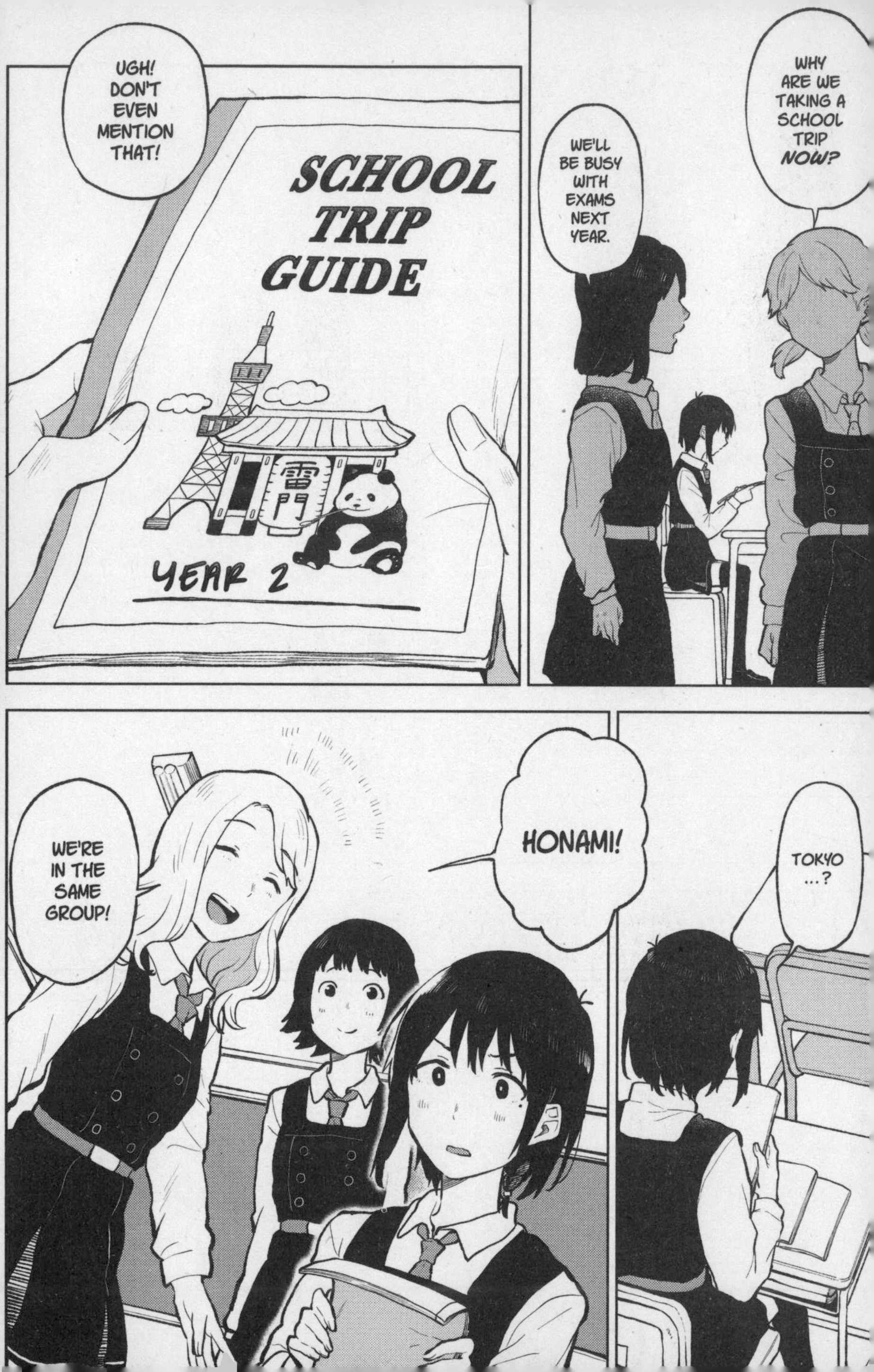
WHY ARE WE TAKING A SCHOOL TRIP NOW?
WE'LL BE BUSY WITH EXAMS NEXT YEAR.
UGH! DON'T EVEN MENTION THAT!
SCHOOL TRIP GUIDE
雷門
YEAR 2
TOKYO ...?
HONAMI!
WE'RE IN THE SAME GROUP!

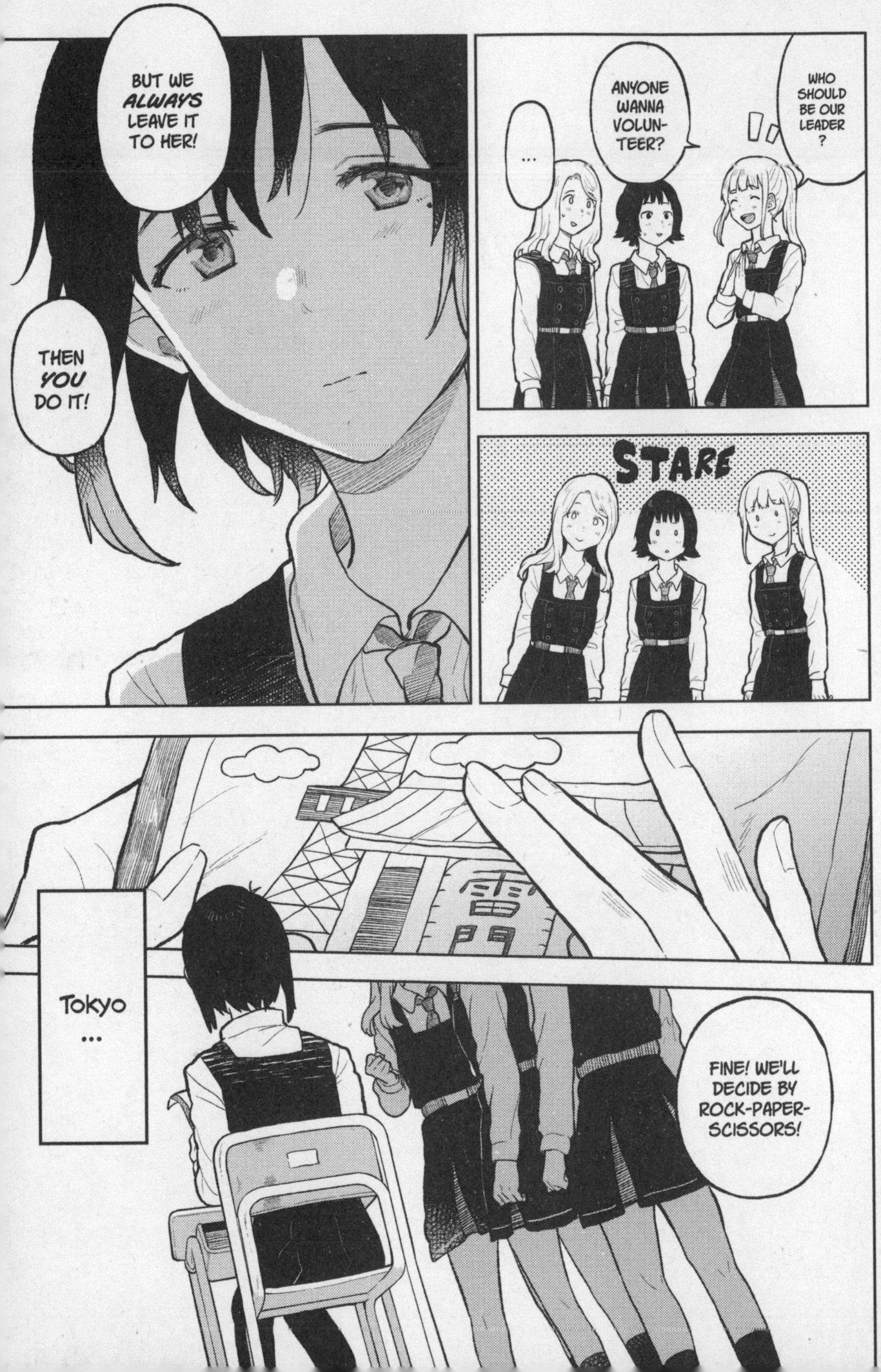
WHO SHOULD BE OUR LEADER?
ANYONE WANNA VOLUNTEER?
...
STARE
BUT WE *ALWAYS* LEAVE IT TO HER!
THEN *YOU* DO IT!
FINE! WE'LL DECIDE BY ROCK-PAPER-SCISSORS!
Tokyo ...

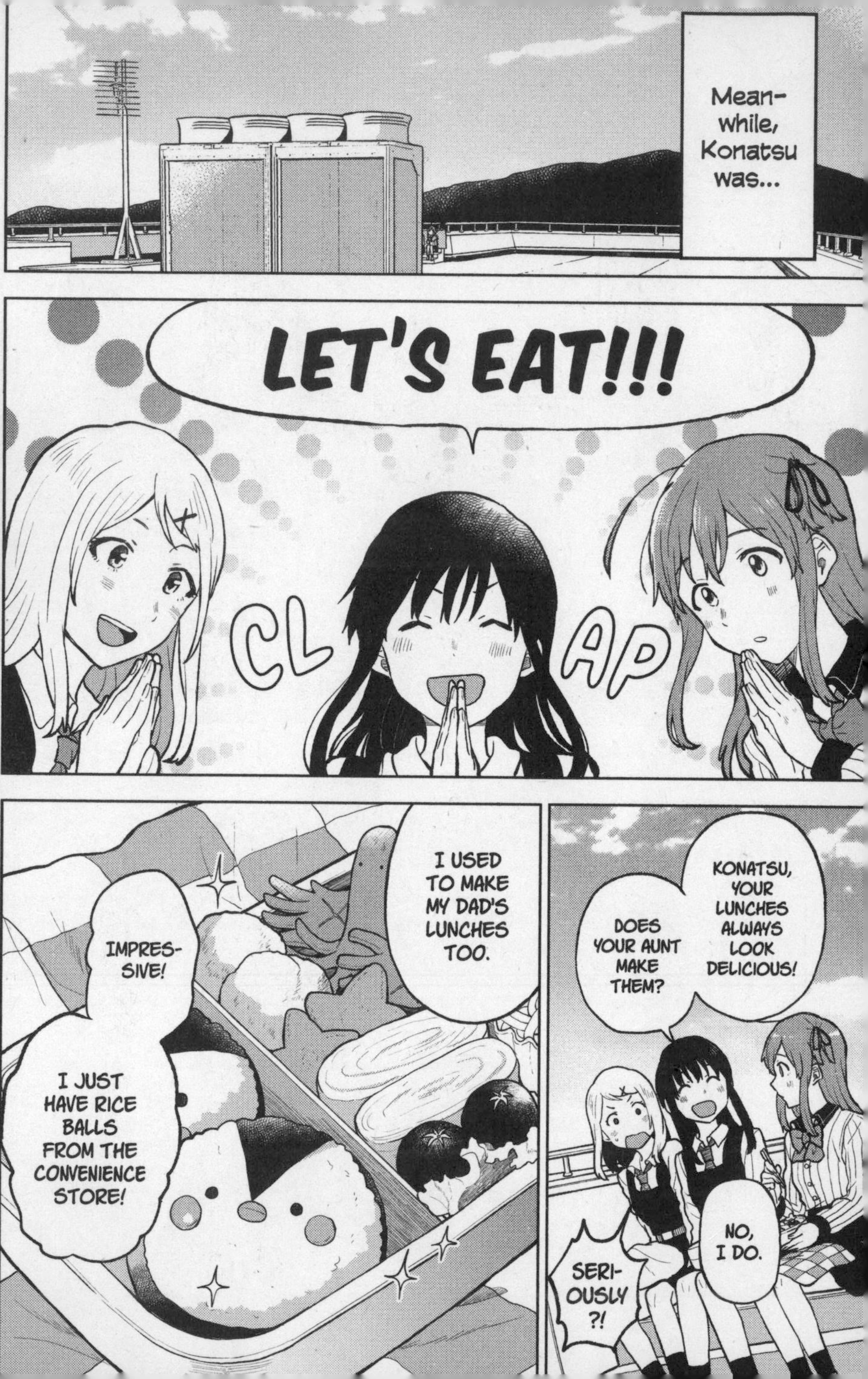

Mean-while, Konatsu was...
LET'S EAT!!!
CLAP
KONATSU, YOUR LUNCHES ALWAYS LOOK DELICIOUS!
DOES YOUR AUNT MAKE THEM?
NO, I DO.
SERI-OUSLY?!
I USED TO MAKE MY DAD'S LUNCHES TOO.
IMPRES-SIVE!
I JUST HAVE RICE BALLS FROM THE CONVENIENCE STORE!

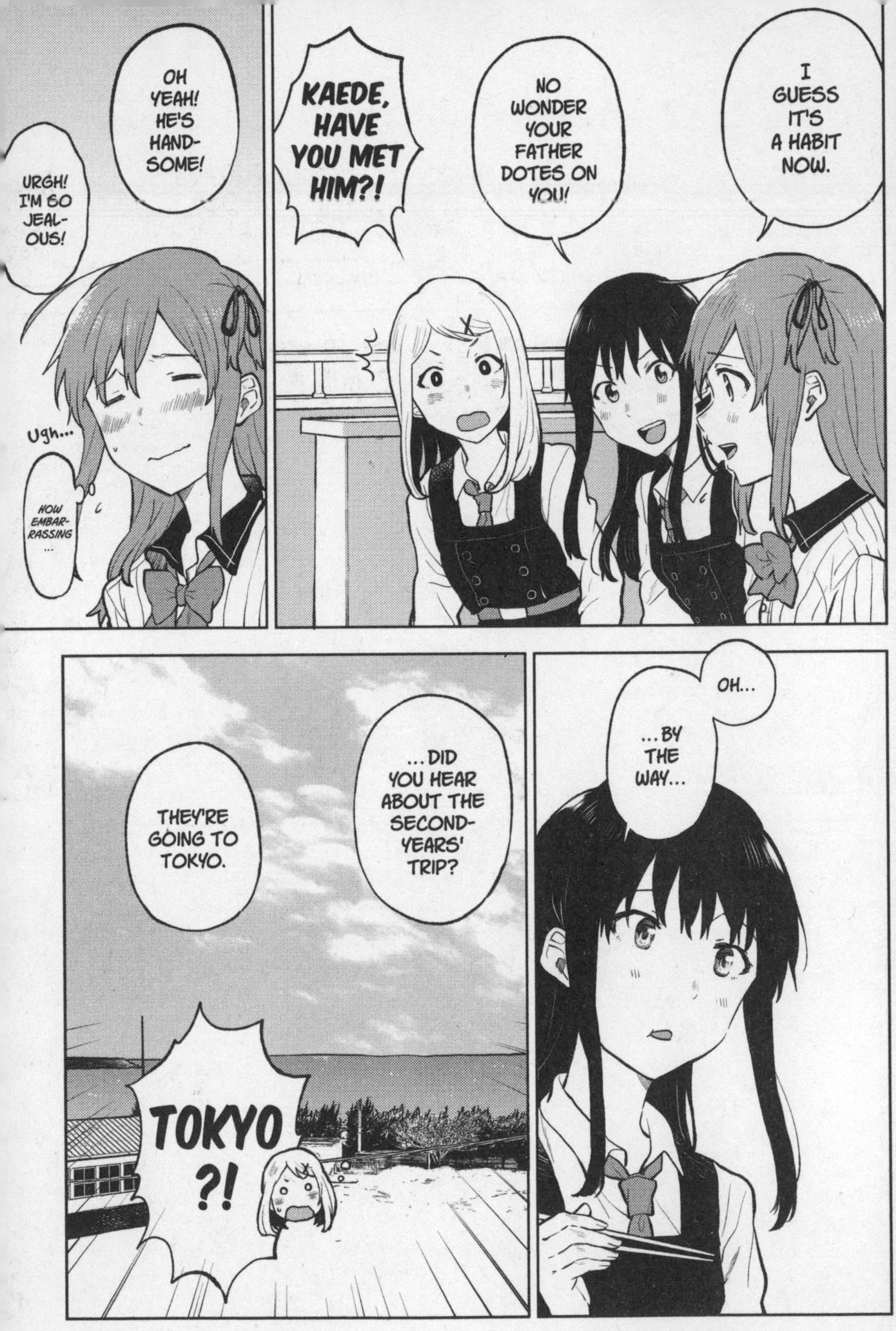
I GUESS IT'S A HABIT NOW.
NO WONDER YOUR FATHER DOTES ON YOU!
KAEDE, HAVE YOU MET HIM?!
OH YEAH! HE'S HAND-SOME!
URGH! I'M SO JEAL-OUS!
Ugh...
HOW EMBAR-RASSING...
OH...
...BY THE WAY...
...DID YOU HEAR ABOUT THE SECOND-YEARS' TRIP?
THEY'RE GOING TO TOKYO.
TOKYO?!

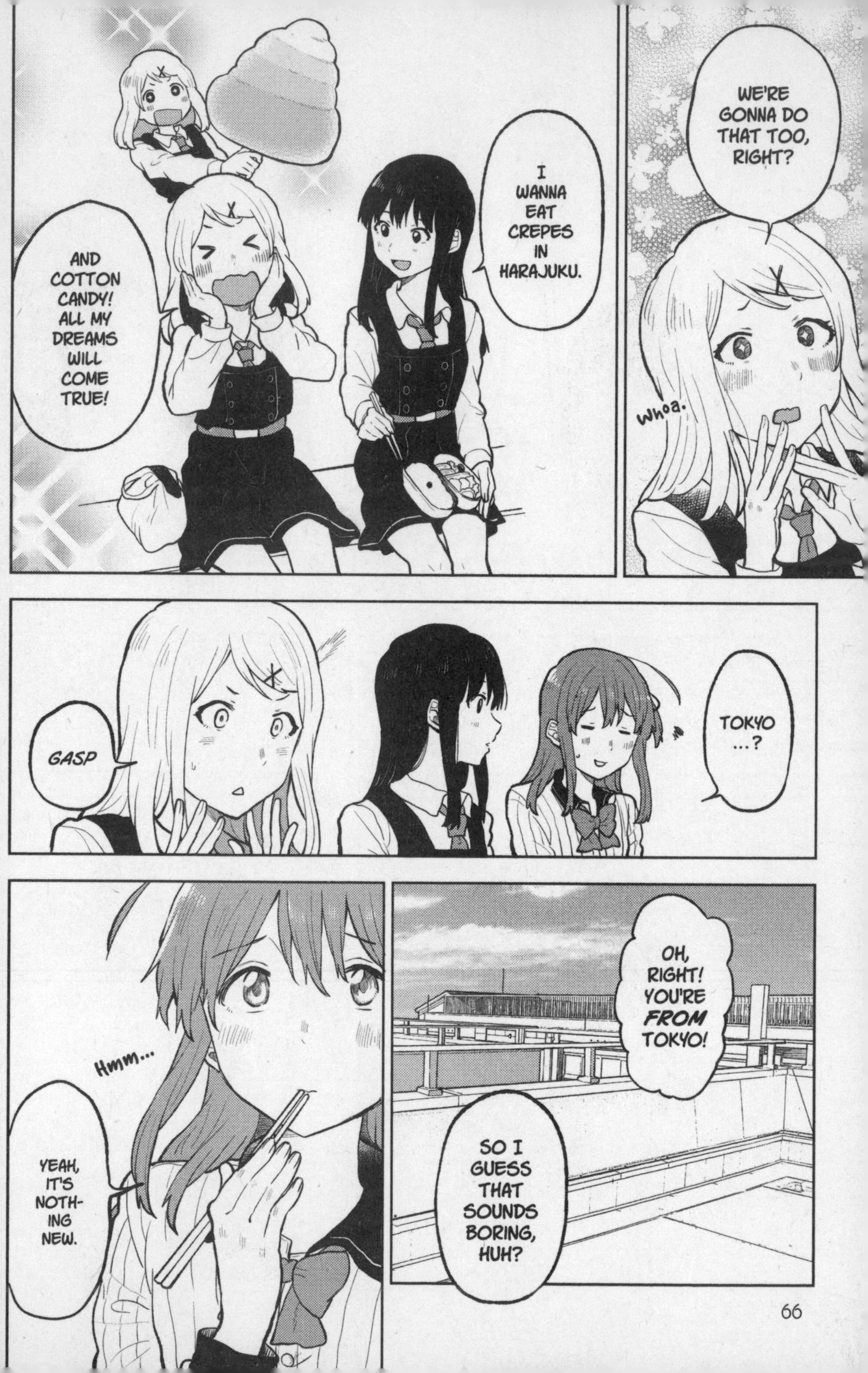
WE'RE GONNA DO THAT TOO, RIGHT?
Whoa.
I WANNA EAT CREPES IN HARAJUKU.
AND COTTON CANDY! ALL MY DREAMS WILL COME TRUE!
TOKYO ...?
GASP
OH, RIGHT! YOU'RE *FROM* TOKYO!
SO I GUESS THAT SOUNDS BORING, HUH?
Hmm...
YEAH, IT'S NOTH-ING NEW.

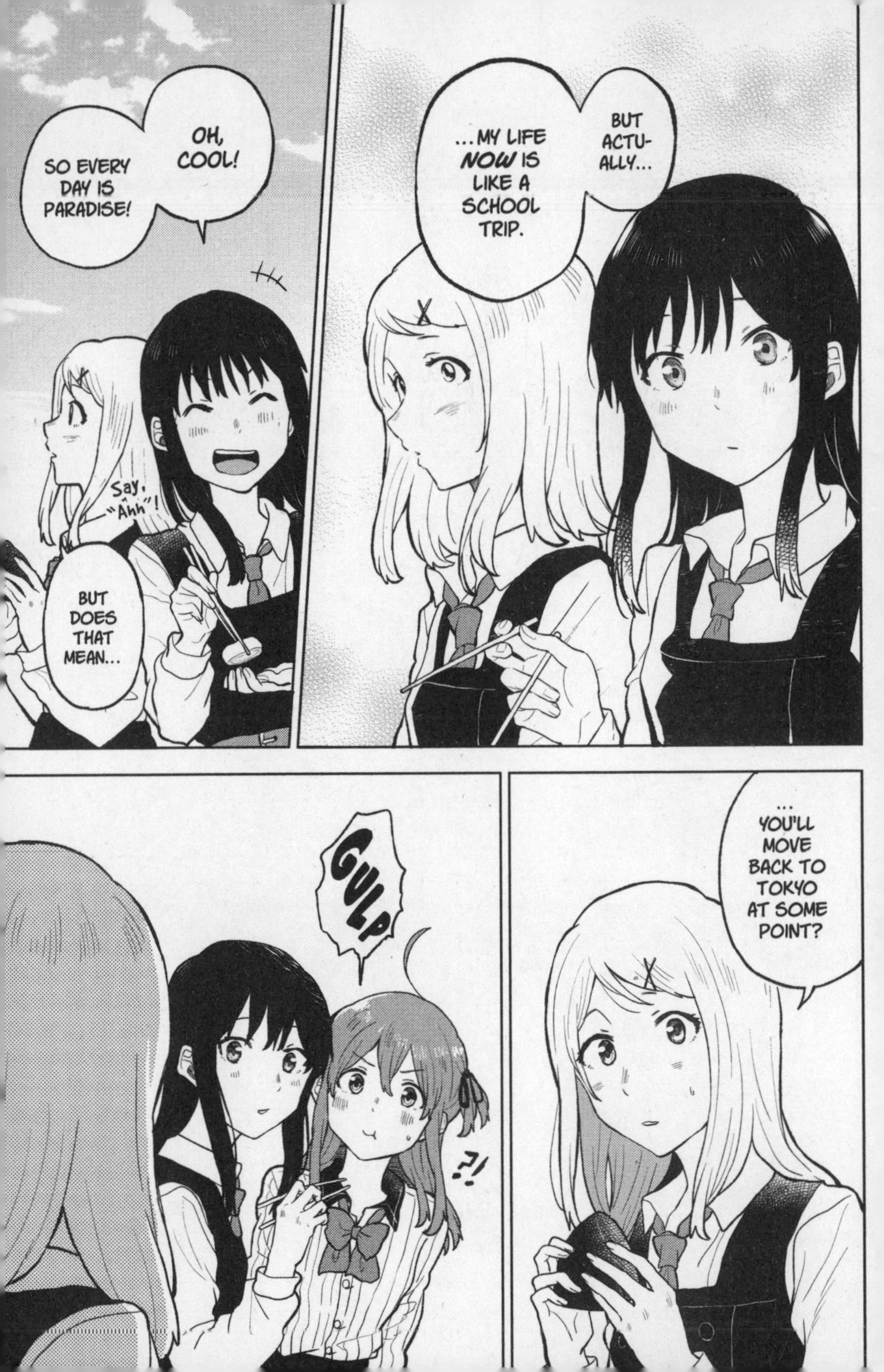
BUT ACTU-ALLY...
...MY LIFE NOW IS LIKE A SCHOOL TRIP.
OH, COOL!
SO EVERY DAY IS PARADISE!
Say, "Ahh"!
BUT DOES THAT MEAN...
... YOU'LL MOVE BACK TO TOKYO AT SOME POINT?
GULP
?!

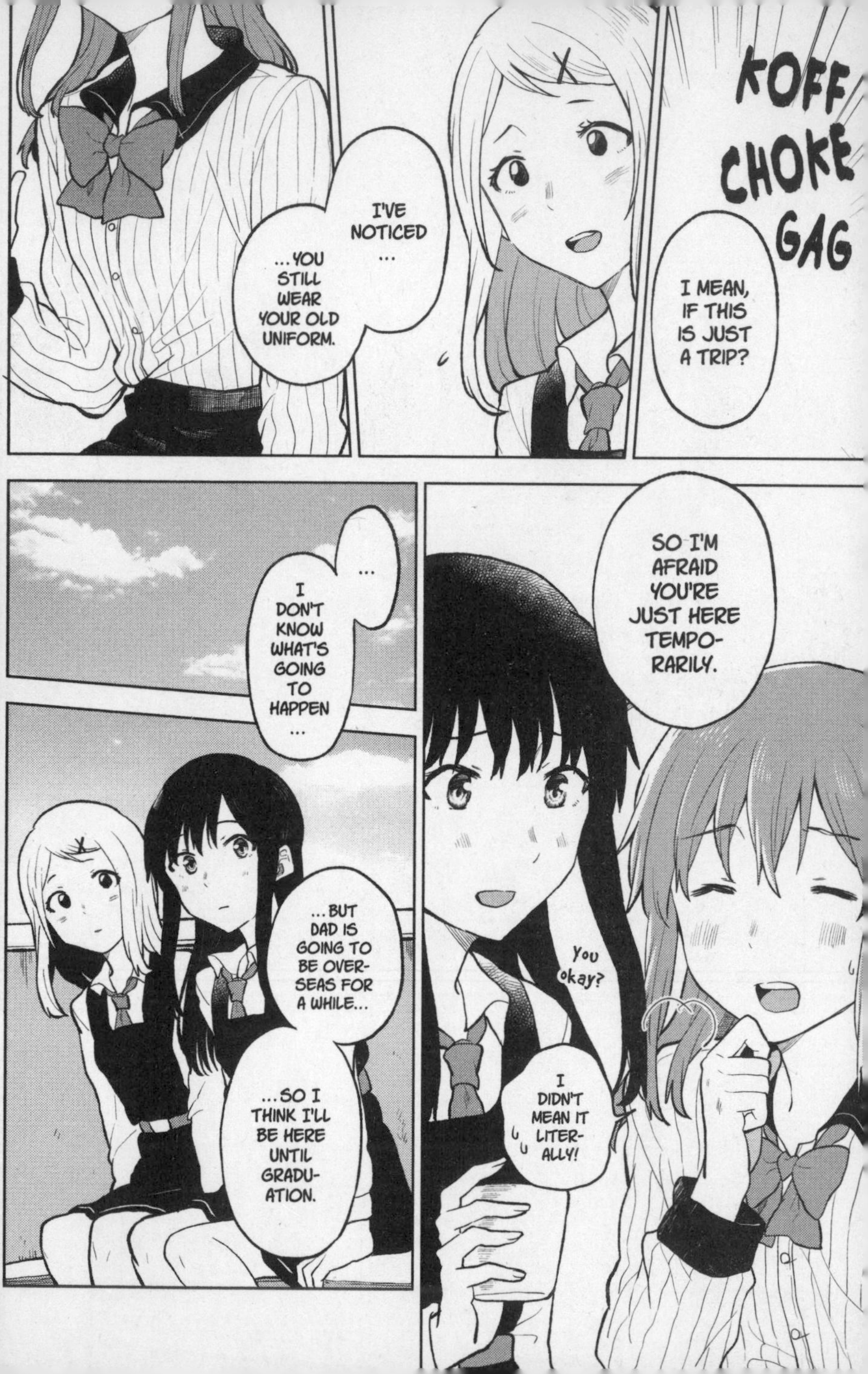
KOFF CHOKE GAG
I MEAN, IF THIS IS JUST A TRIP?
I'VE NOTICED ...
...YOU STILL WEAR YOUR OLD UNIFORM.
SO I'M AFRAID YOU'RE JUST HERE TEMPO-RARILY.
You okay?
I DIDN'T MEAN IT LITER-ALLY!
... I DON'T KNOW WHAT'S GOING TO HAPPEN ...
...BUT DAD IS GOING TO BE OVER-SEAS FOR A WHILE...
...SO I THINK I'LL BE HERE UNTIL GRADU-ATION.

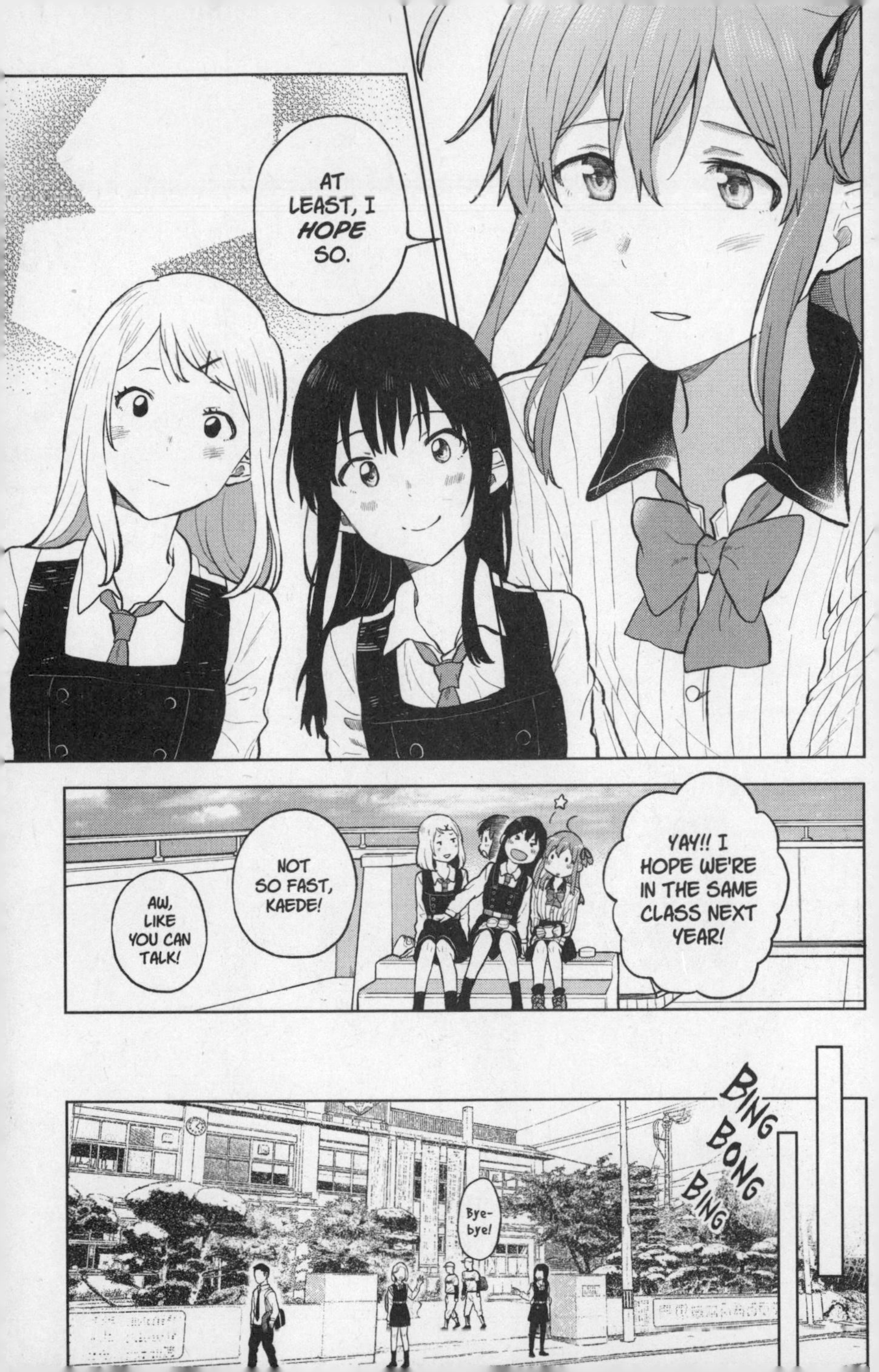
AT LEAST, I HOPE SO.
YAY!! I HOPE WE'RE IN THE SAME CLASS NEXT YEAR!
NOT SO FAST, KAEDE!
AW, LIKE YOU CAN TALK!
BING BONG BING
Bye-bye!

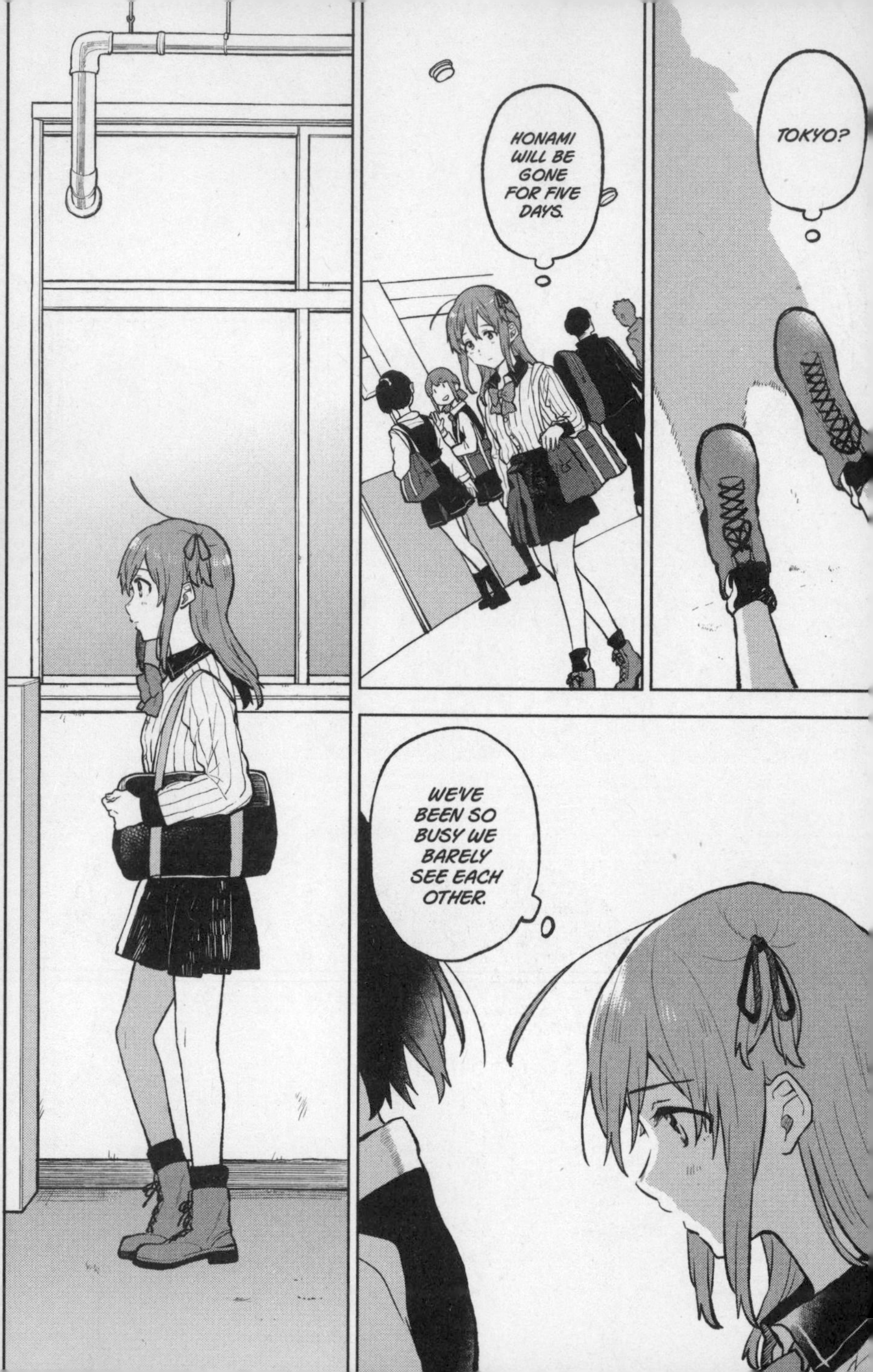
TOKYO?
HONAMI WILL BE GONE FOR FIVE DAYS.
WE'VE BEEN SO BUSY WE BARELY SEE EACH OTHER.

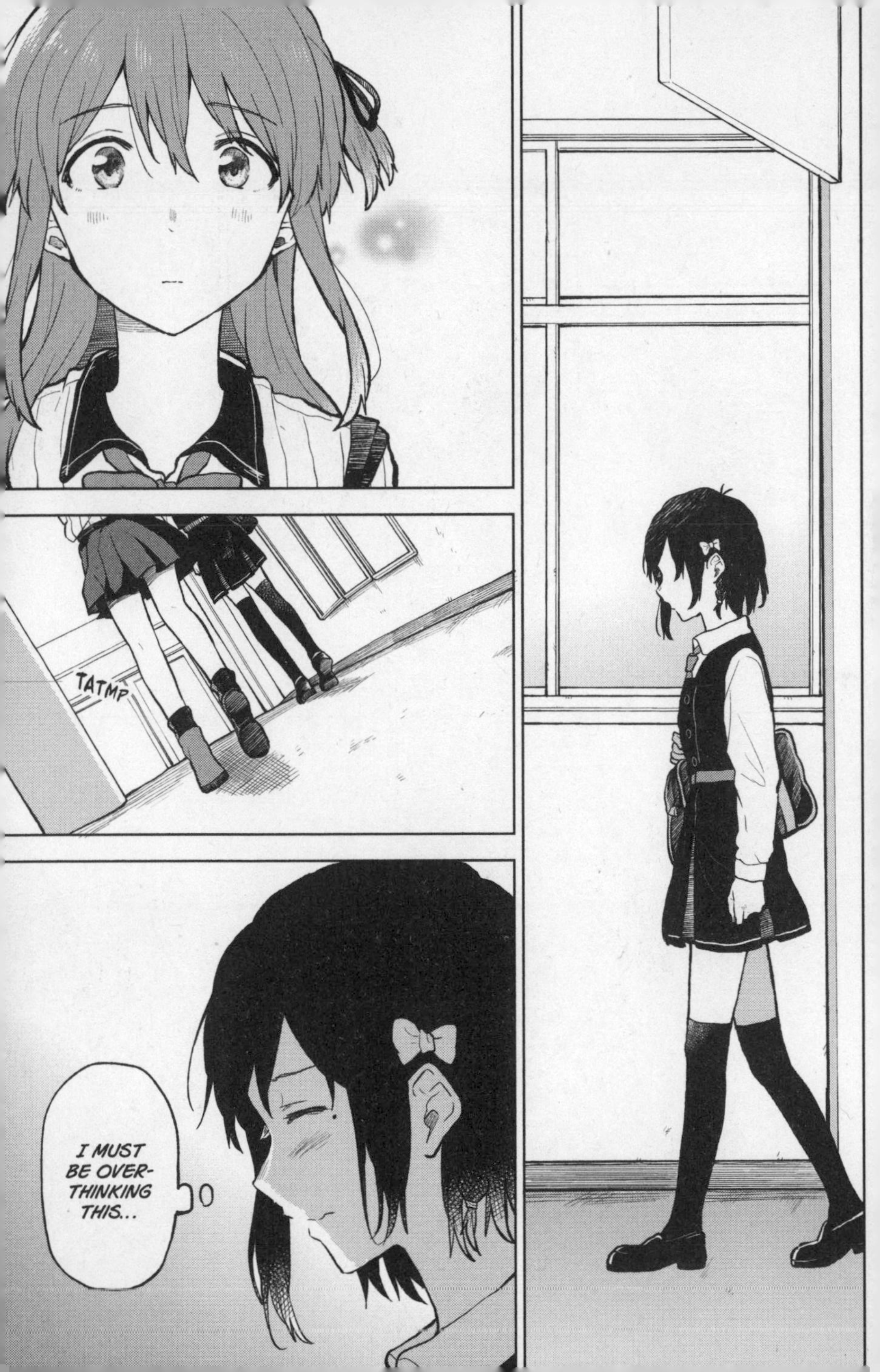
TATMP
I MUST BE OVER-THINKING THIS...

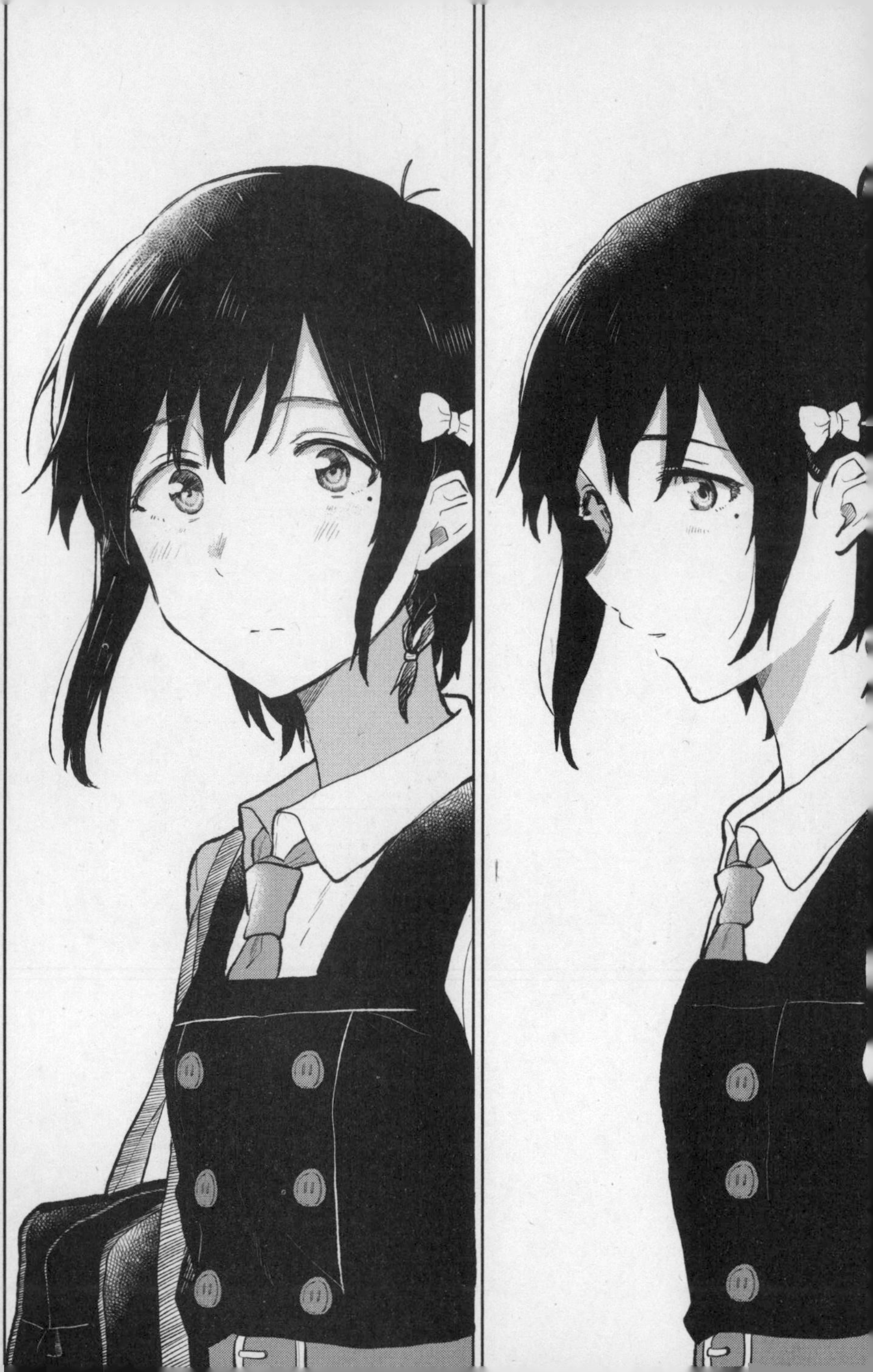

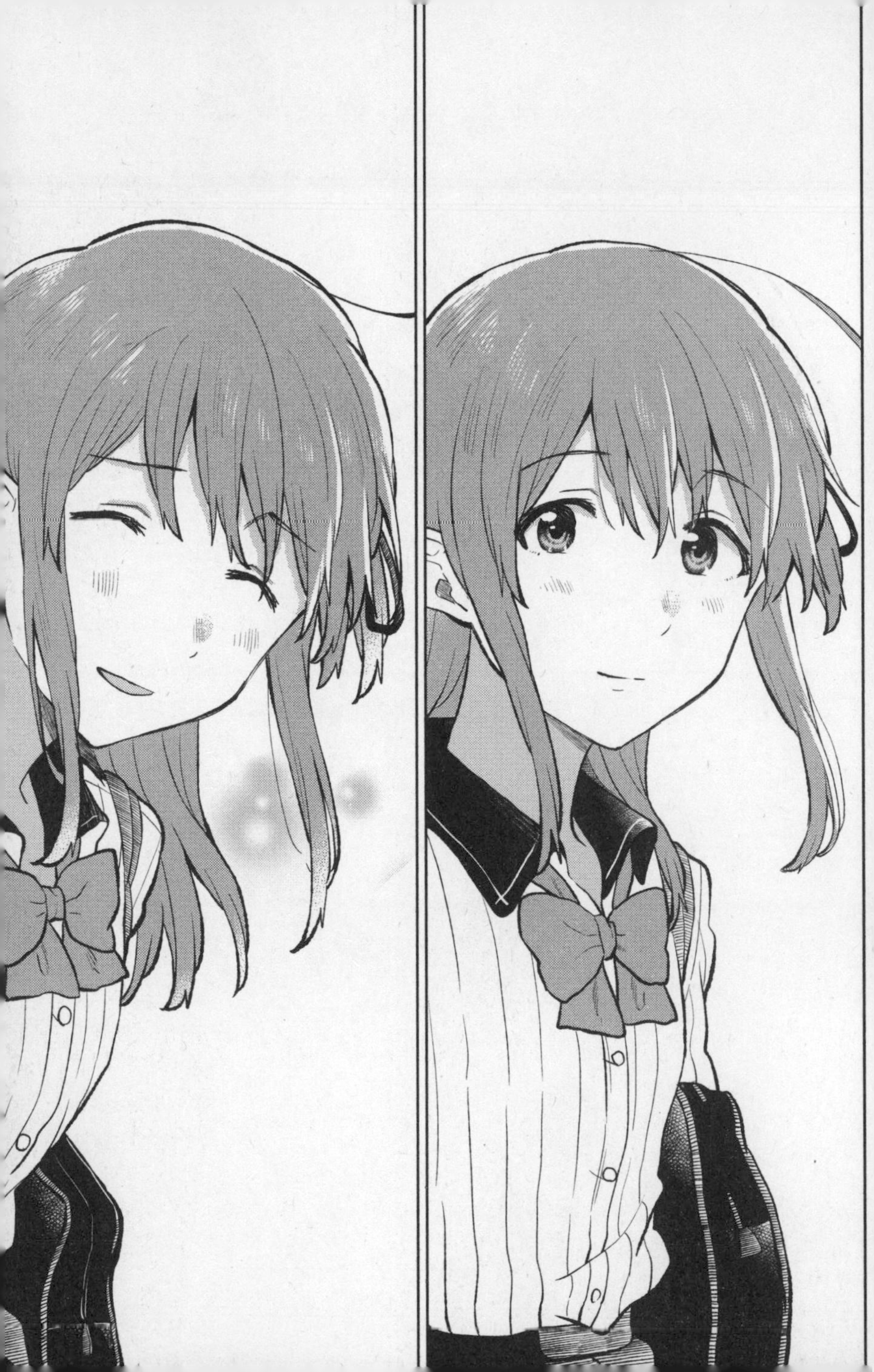

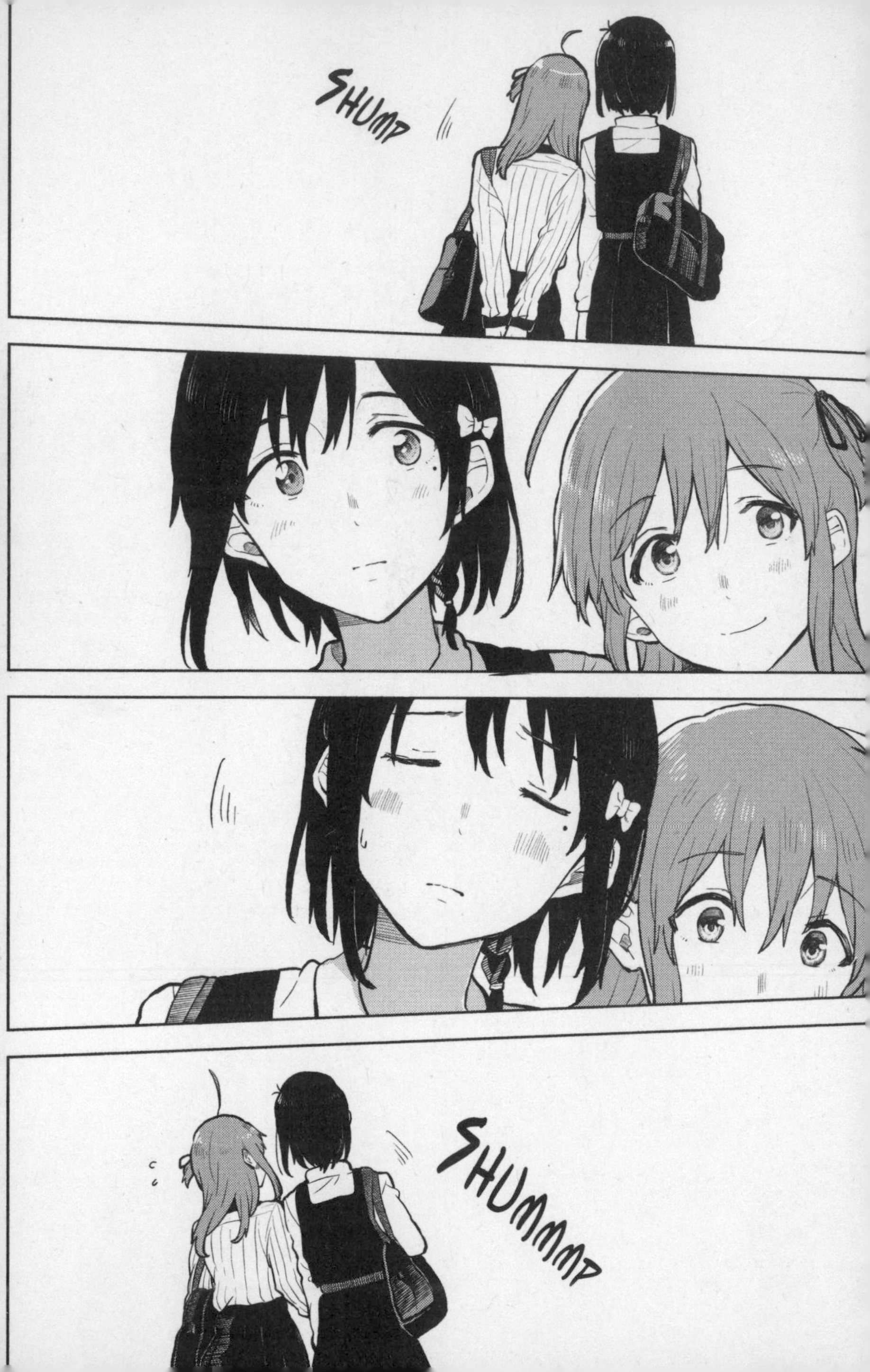
SHUMP
SHUMMMP

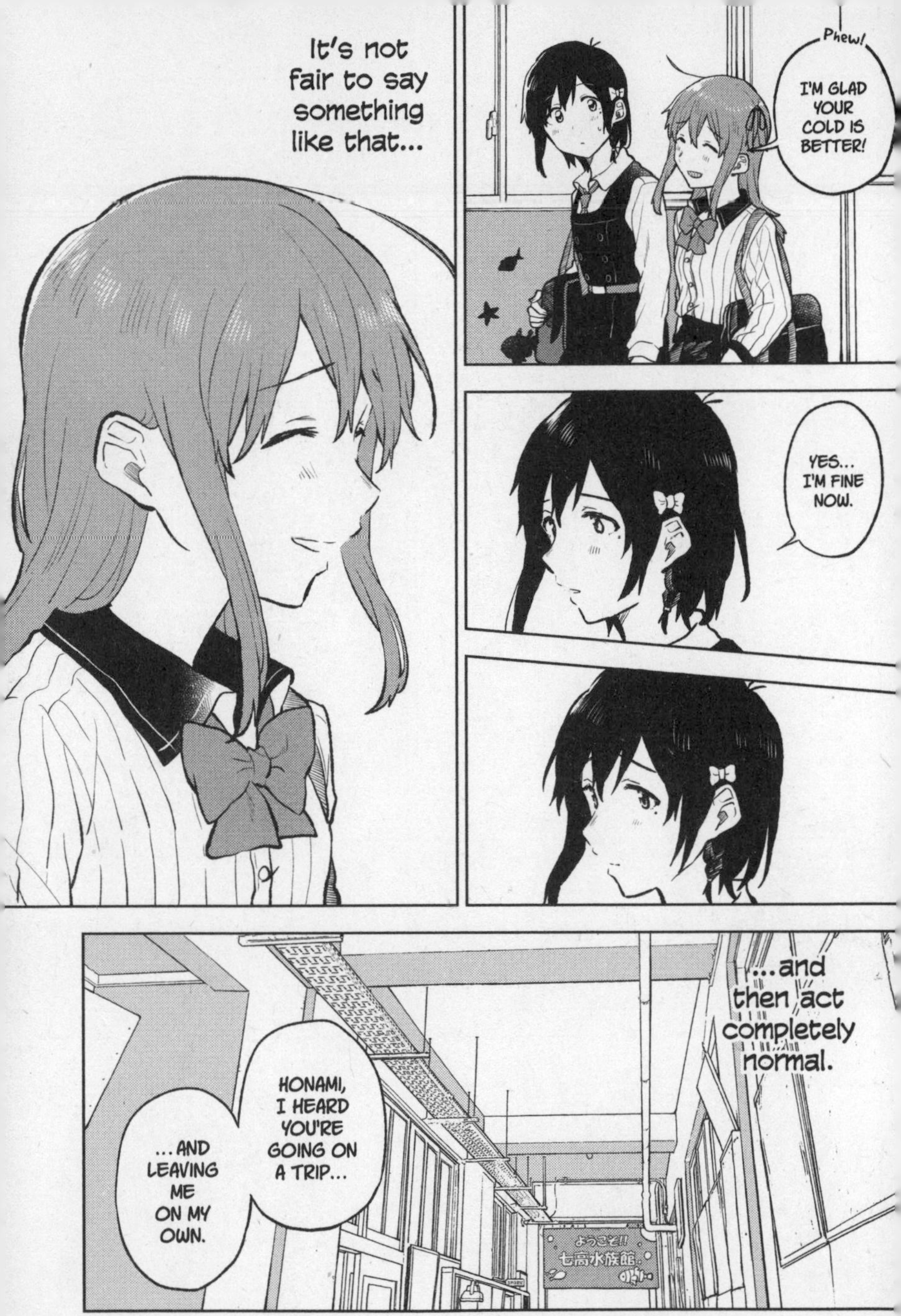
Phew!
I'M GLAD YOUR COLD IS BETTER!
YES... I'M FINE NOW.
It's not fair to say something like that...
...and then act completely normal.
HONAMI, I HEARD YOU'RE GOING ON A TRIP...
...AND LEAVING ME ON MY OWN.
ようこそ!! 七高水族館

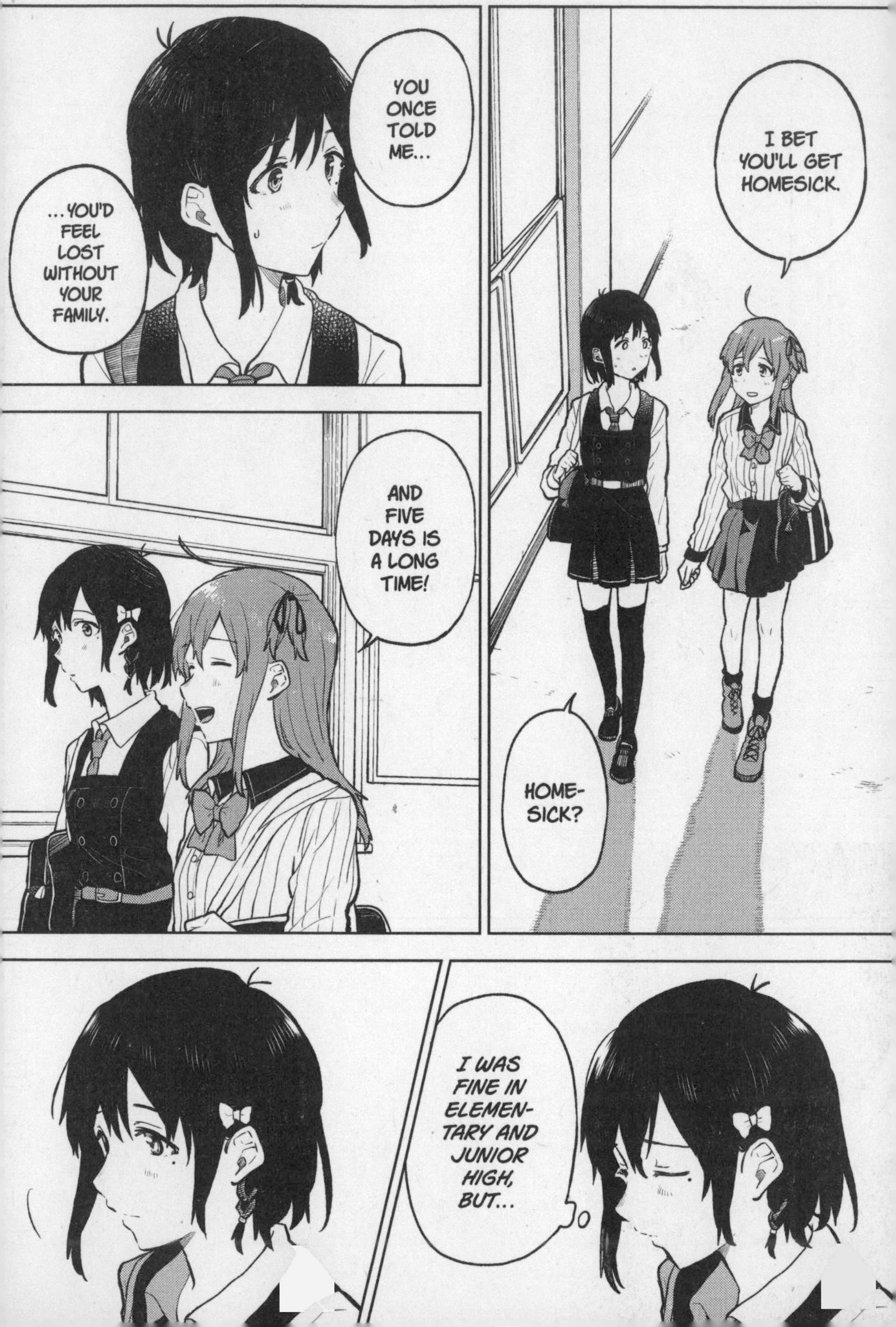
I BET YOU'LL GET HOMESICK.
HOME-SICK?
YOU ONCE TOLD ME...
...YOU'D FEEL LOST WITHOUT YOUR FAMILY.
AND FIVE DAYS IS A LONG TIME!
I WAS FINE IN ELEMENTARY AND JUNIOR HIGH, BUT...

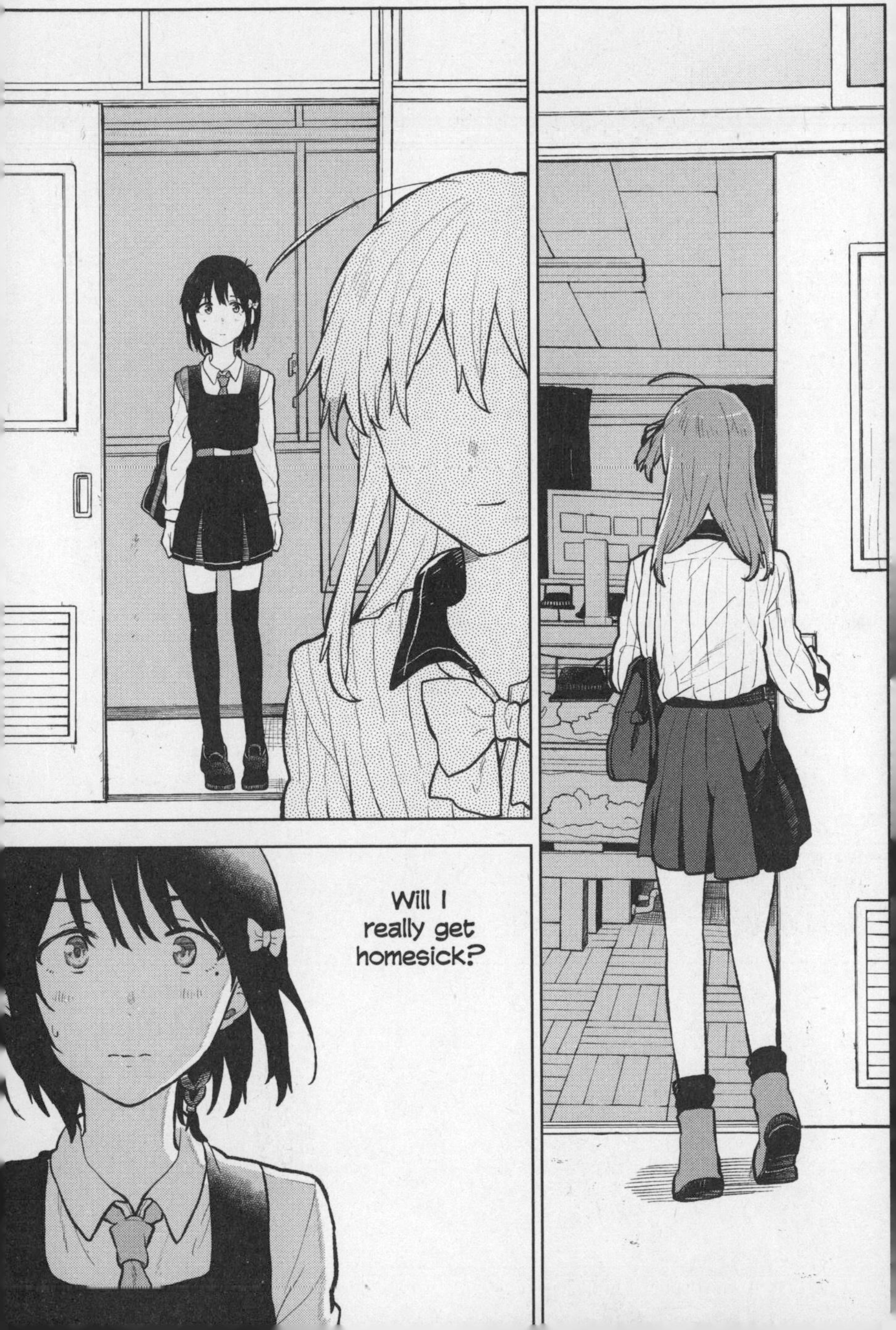
Will I
really get
homesick?

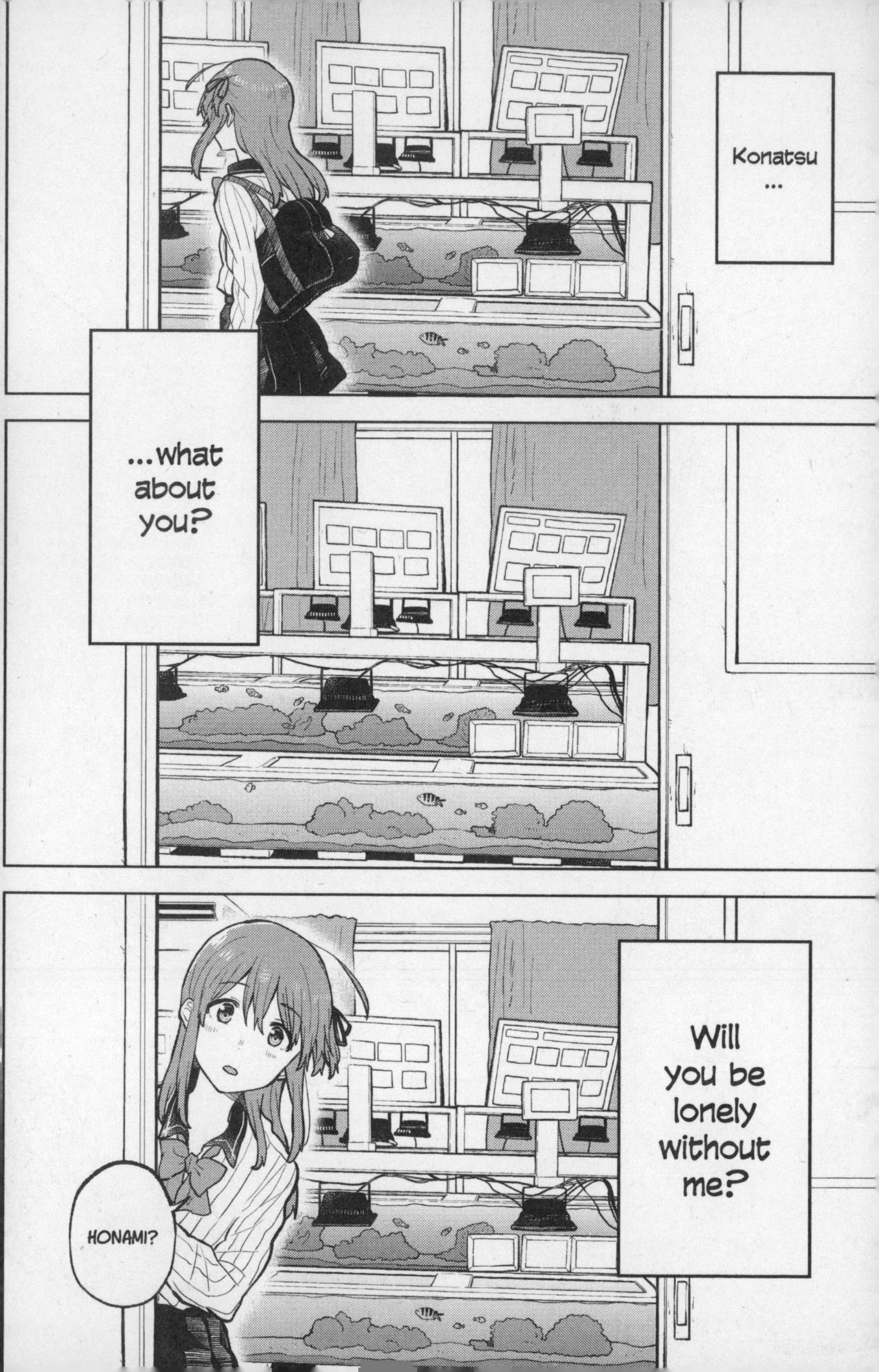
Konatsu ...
...what about you?
Will you be lonely without me?
HONAMI?

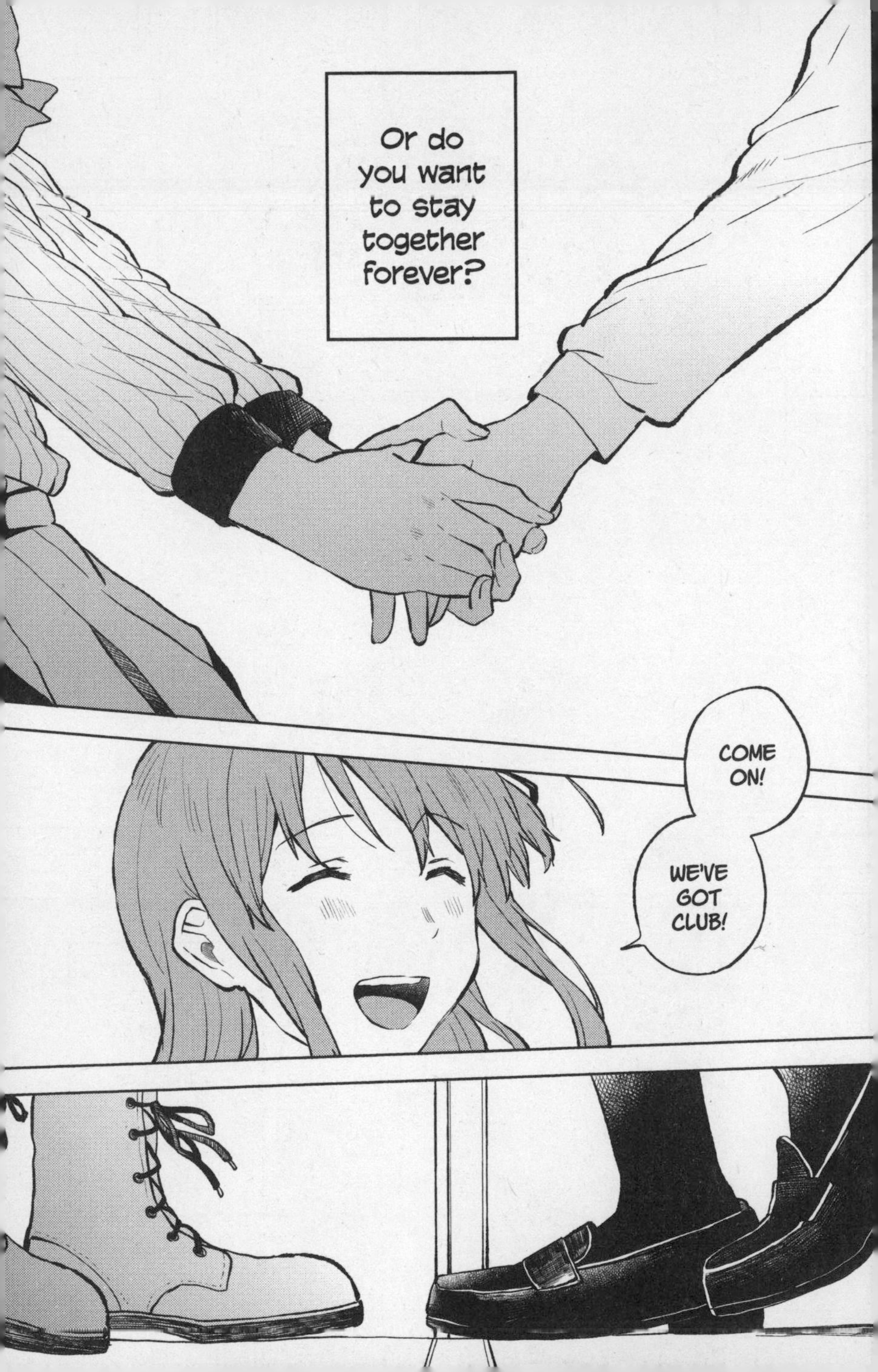
Or do you want to stay together forever?
COME ON!
WE'VE GOT CLUB!

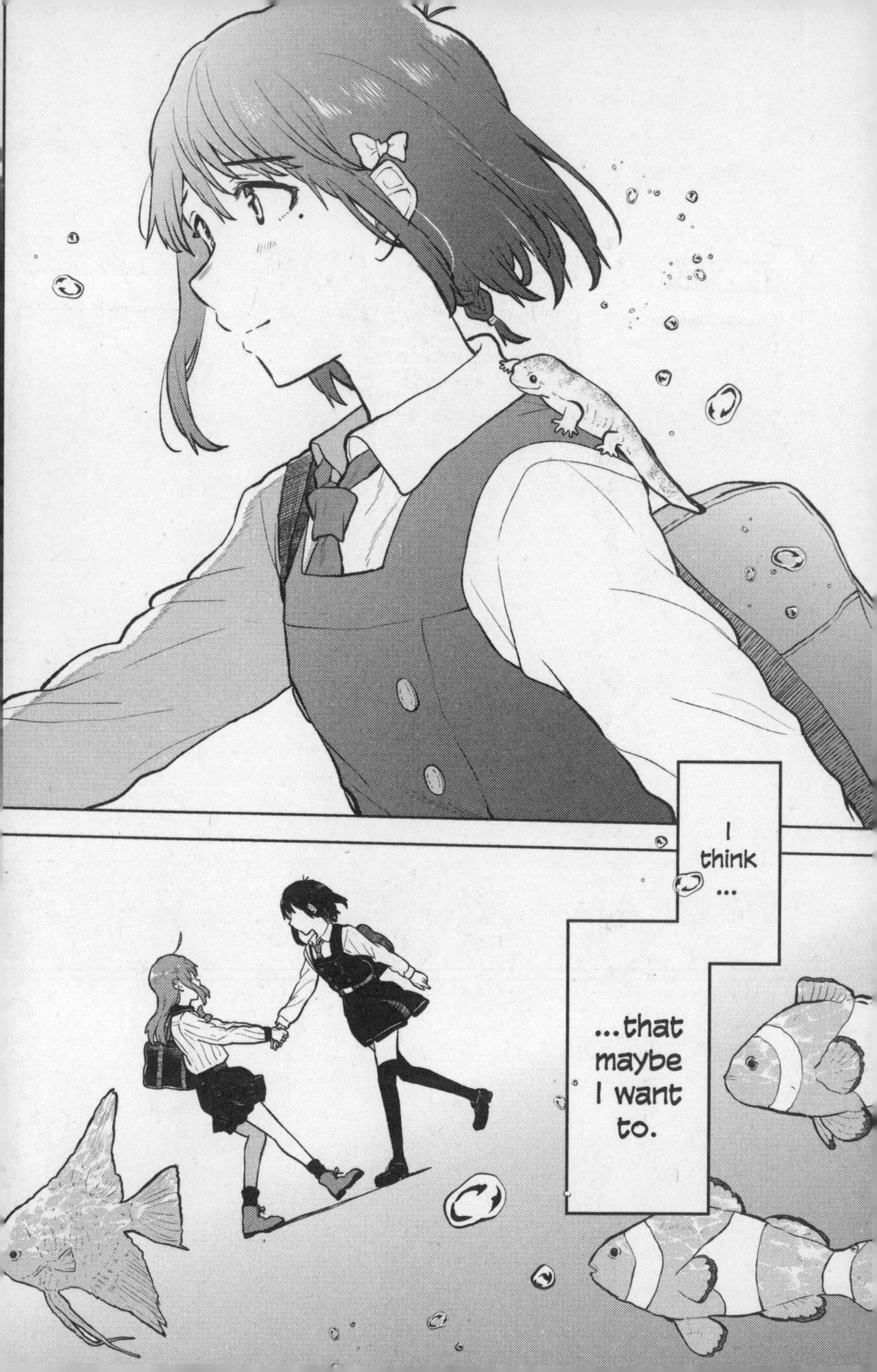
I think ...
...that maybe I want to.

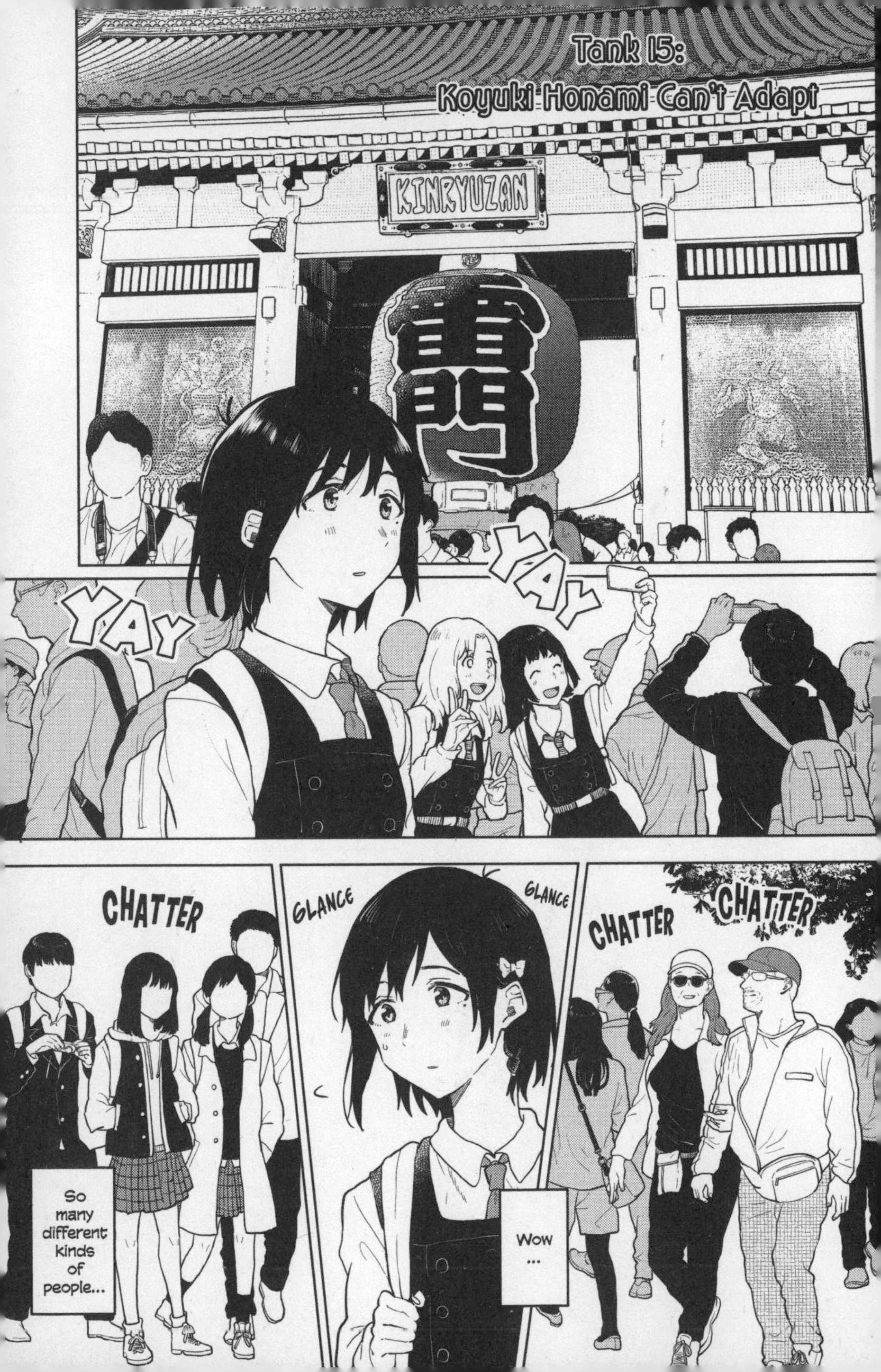
Tank 15:
Koyuki Honami Can't Adapt
KINRYUZAN
雷門
YAY
YAY
CHATTER
CHATTER
GLANCE
GLANCE
Wow ...
CHATTER
So many different kinds of people...

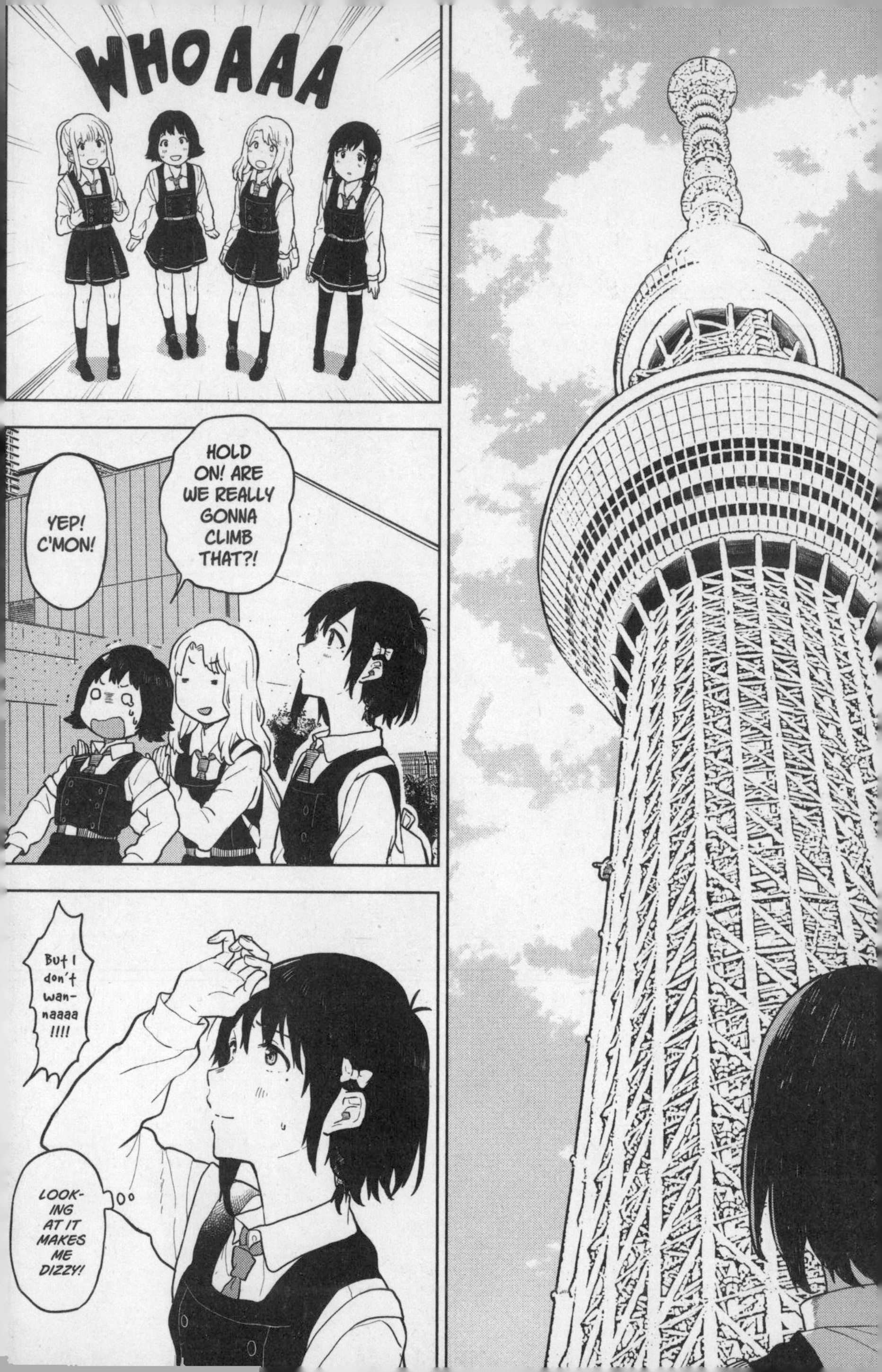
WHOAAA
HOLD ON! ARE WE REALLY GONNA CLIMB THAT?!
YEP! C'MON!
But I don't wan-naaaa!!!!
LOOK-ING AT IT MAKES ME DIZZY!

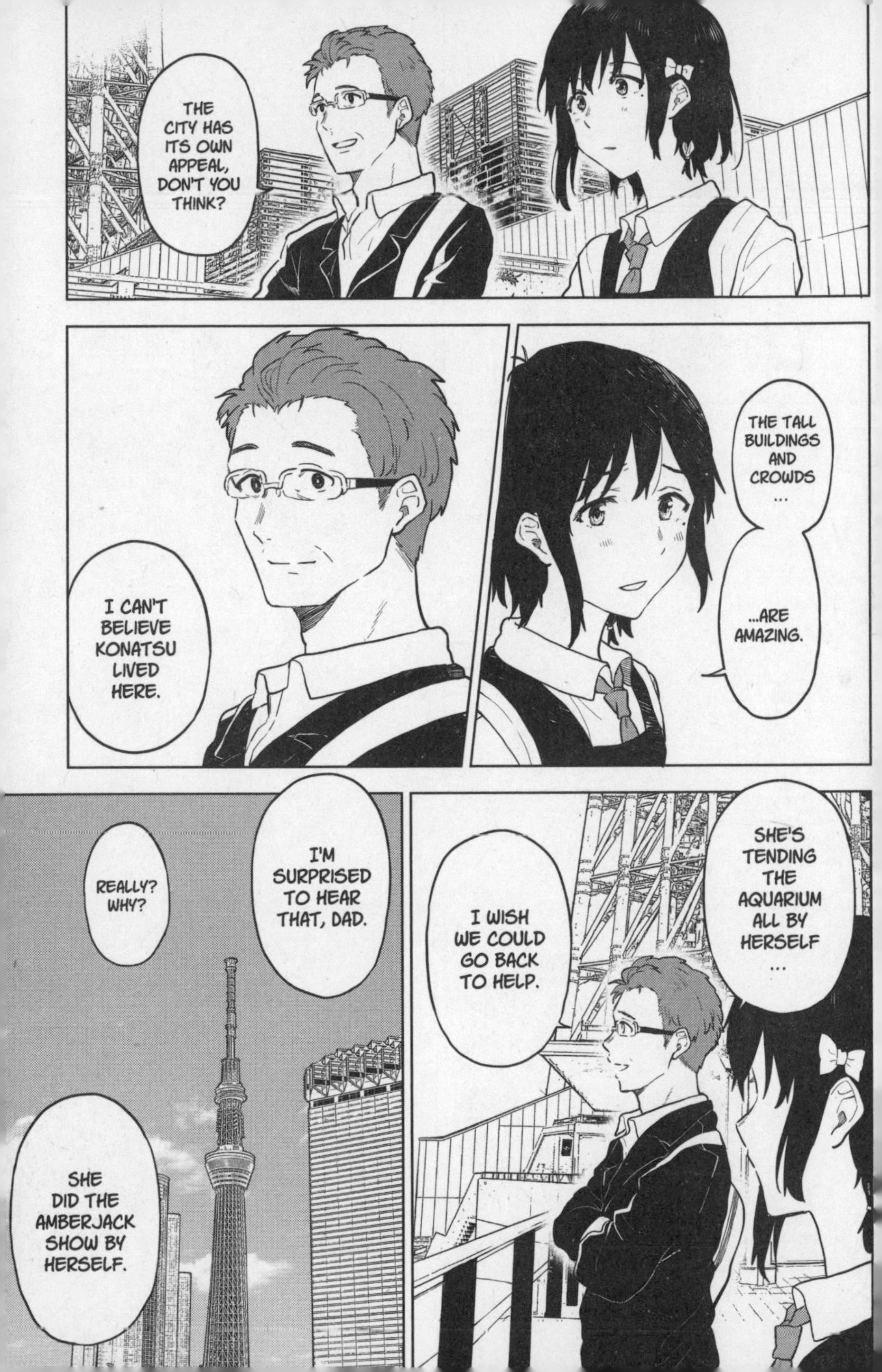
THE CITY HAS ITS OWN APPEAL, DON'T YOU THINK?
THE TALL BUILDINGS AND CROWDS...
...ARE AMAZING.
I CAN'T BELIEVE KONATSU LIVED HERE.
SHE'S TENDING THE AQUARIUM ALL BY HERSELF...
I WISH WE COULD GO BACK TO HELP.
I'M SURPRISED TO HEAR THAT, DAD.
REALLY? WHY?
SHE DID THE AMBERJACK SHOW BY HERSELF.

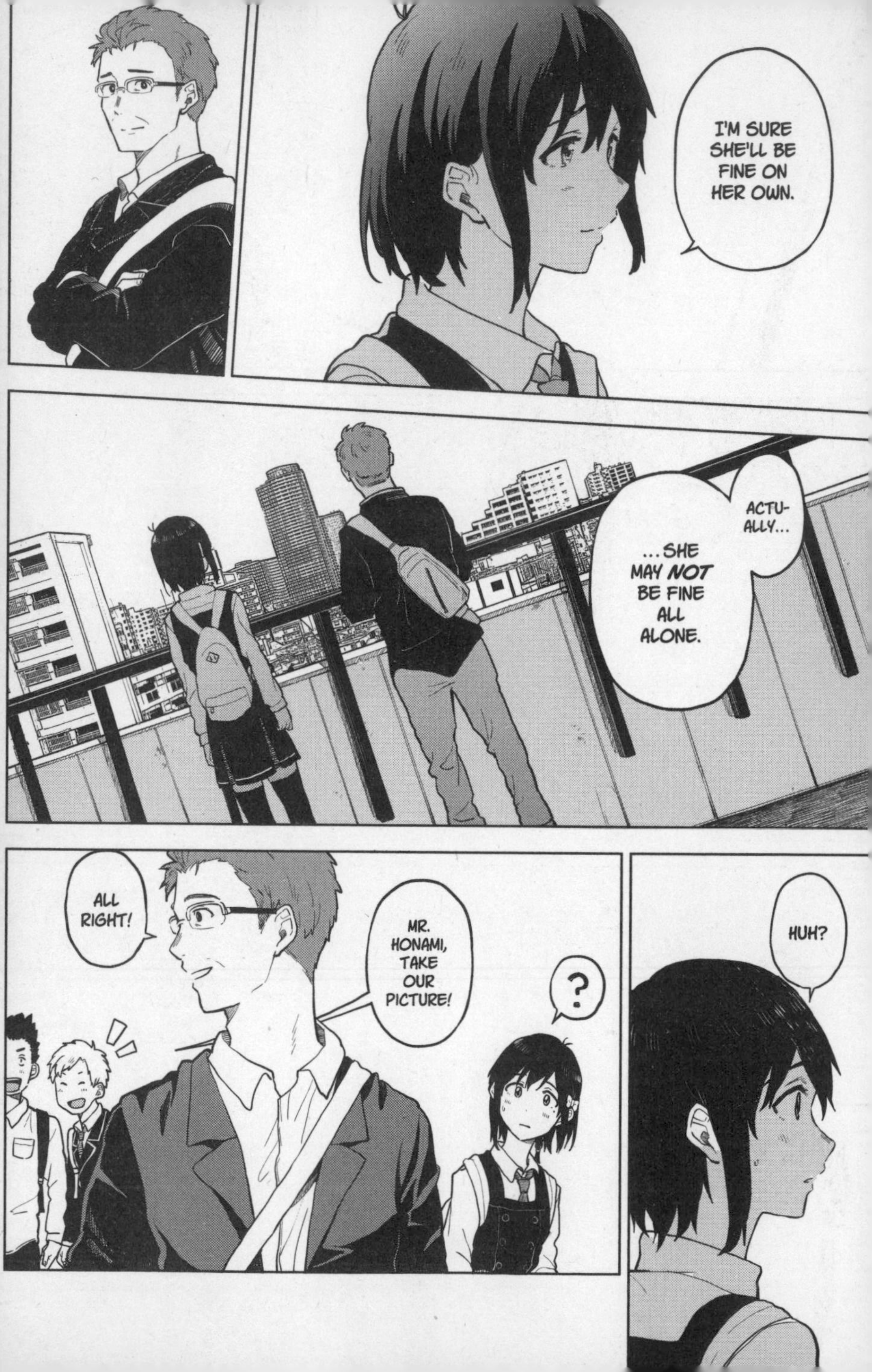

I'M SURE SHE'LL BE FINE ON HER OWN.
ACTU-ALLY...
...SHE MAY *NOT* BE FINE ALL ALONE.
HUH?
?
MR. HONAMI, TAKE OUR PICTURE!
ALL RIGHT!

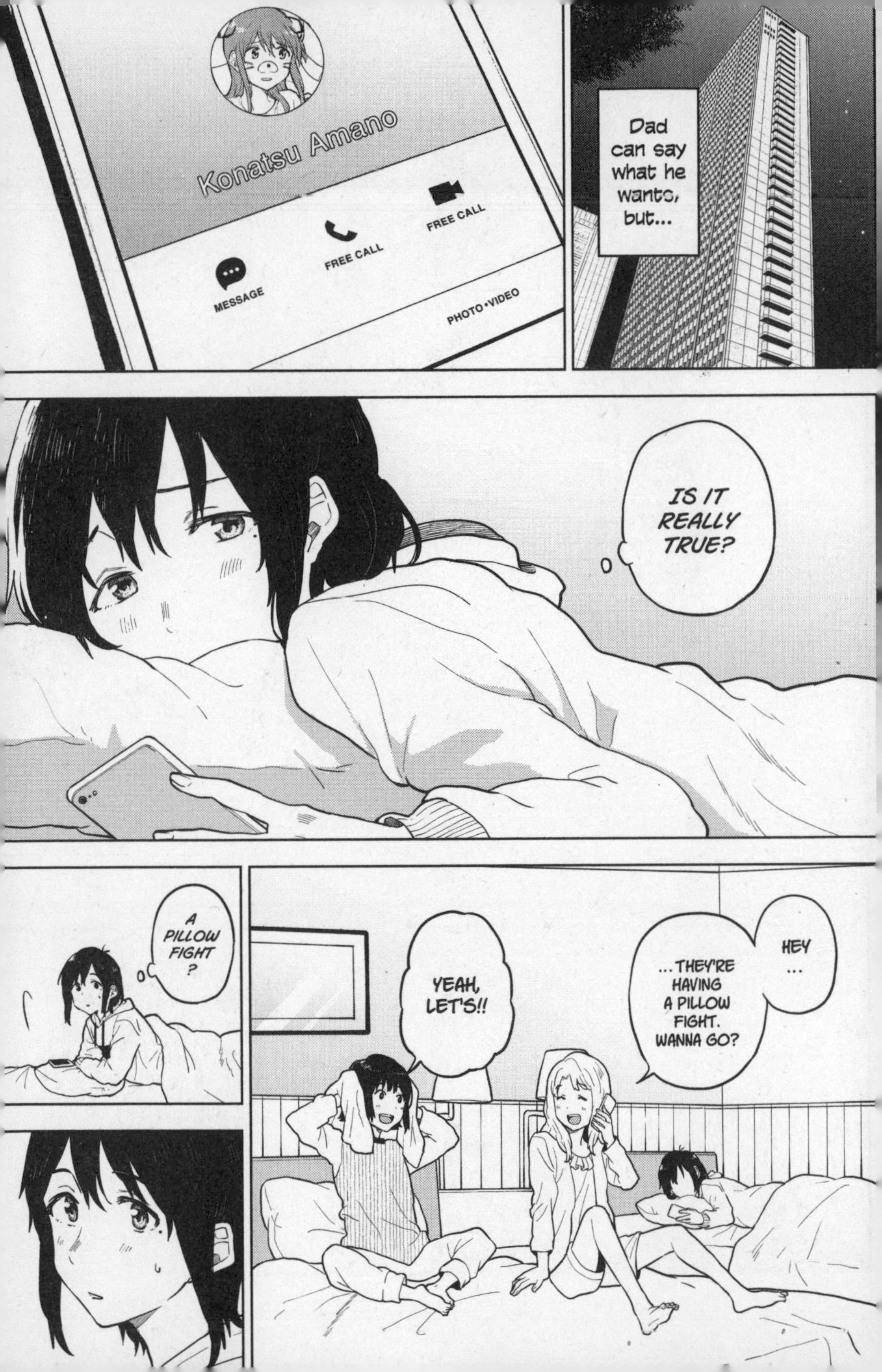
Dad can say what he wants, but...
Konatsu Amano
FREE CALL
FREE CALL
MESSAGE
PHOTO•VIDEO
IS IT REALLY TRUE?
HEY ...
...THEY'RE HAVING A PILLOW FIGHT. WANNA GO?
YEAH, LET'S!!
A PILLOW FIGHT?

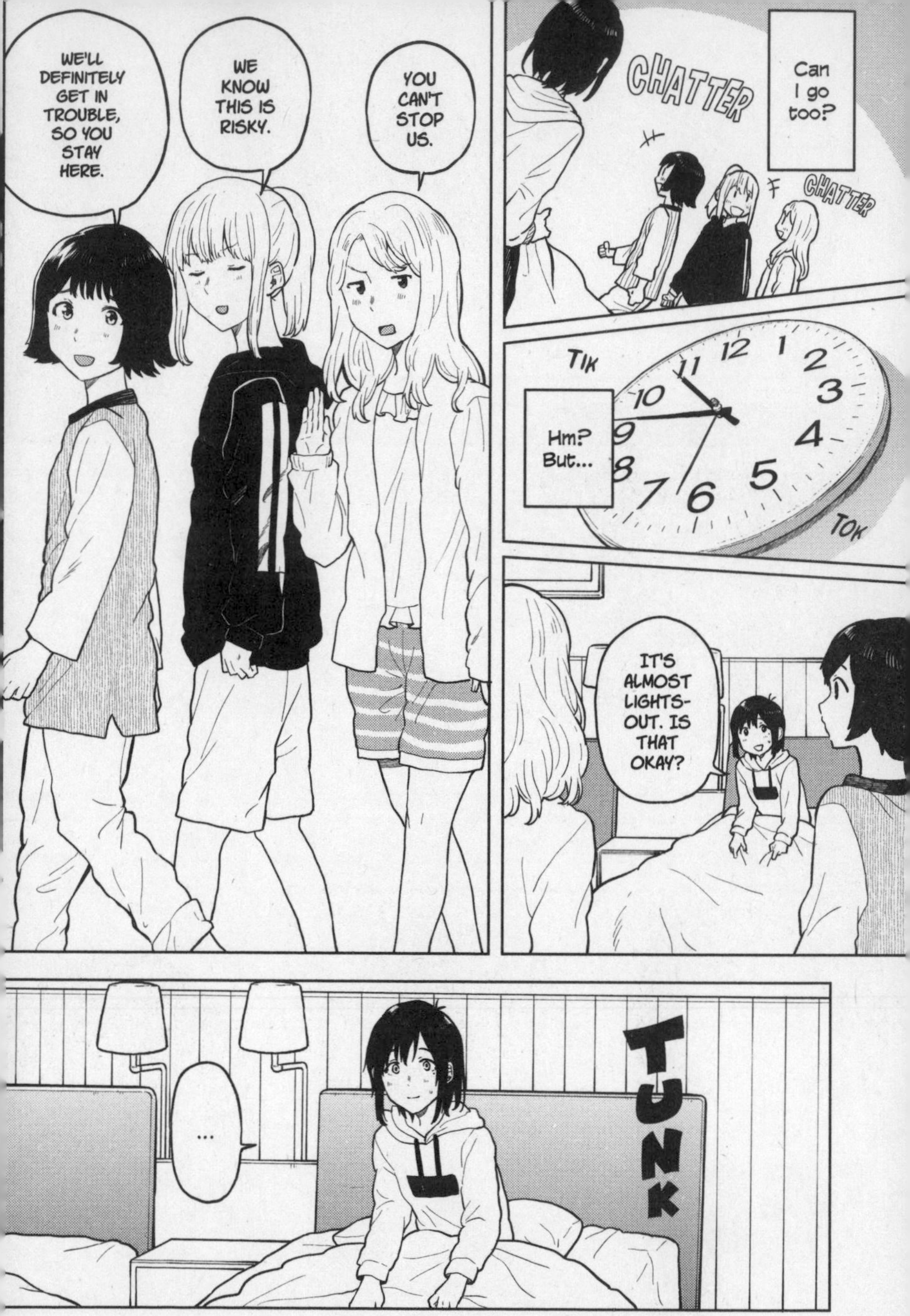
Can I go too?
CHATTER
CHATTER
TIK
Hm? But...
TOK
IT'S ALMOST LIGHTS-OUT. IS THAT OKAY?
YOU CAN'T STOP US.
WE KNOW THIS IS RISKY.
WE'LL DEFINITELY GET IN TROUBLE, SO YOU STAY HERE.
TUNK
...

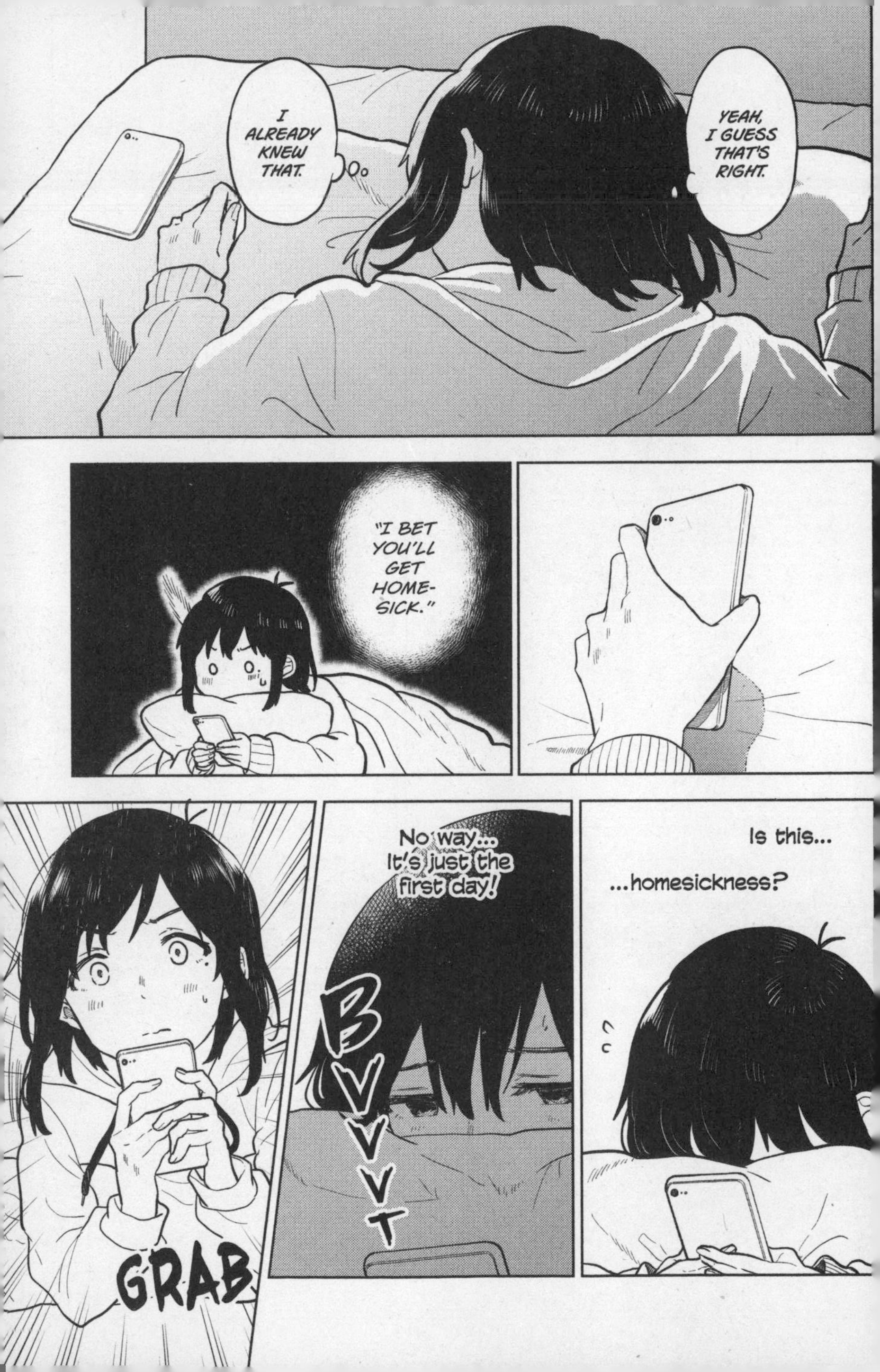
YEAH, I GUESS THAT'S RIGHT.
I ALREADY KNEW THAT.
"I BET YOU'LL GET HOME-SICK."
Is this...
...homesickness?
No way... It's just the first day!
BVVVT
GRAB

I WON'T, I WON'T!

KICK

KICK

...

Fuyuki Honami

Don't forget to bring back a souvenir for your favorite brother!

午後10:56 82%

ENTER A MESSAGE

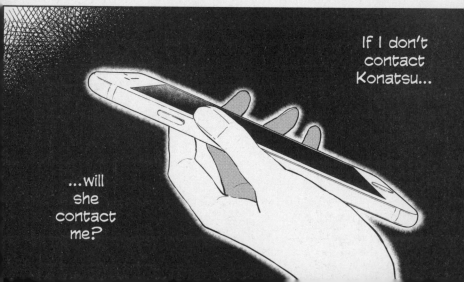

If I don't contact Konatsu...

...will she contact me?

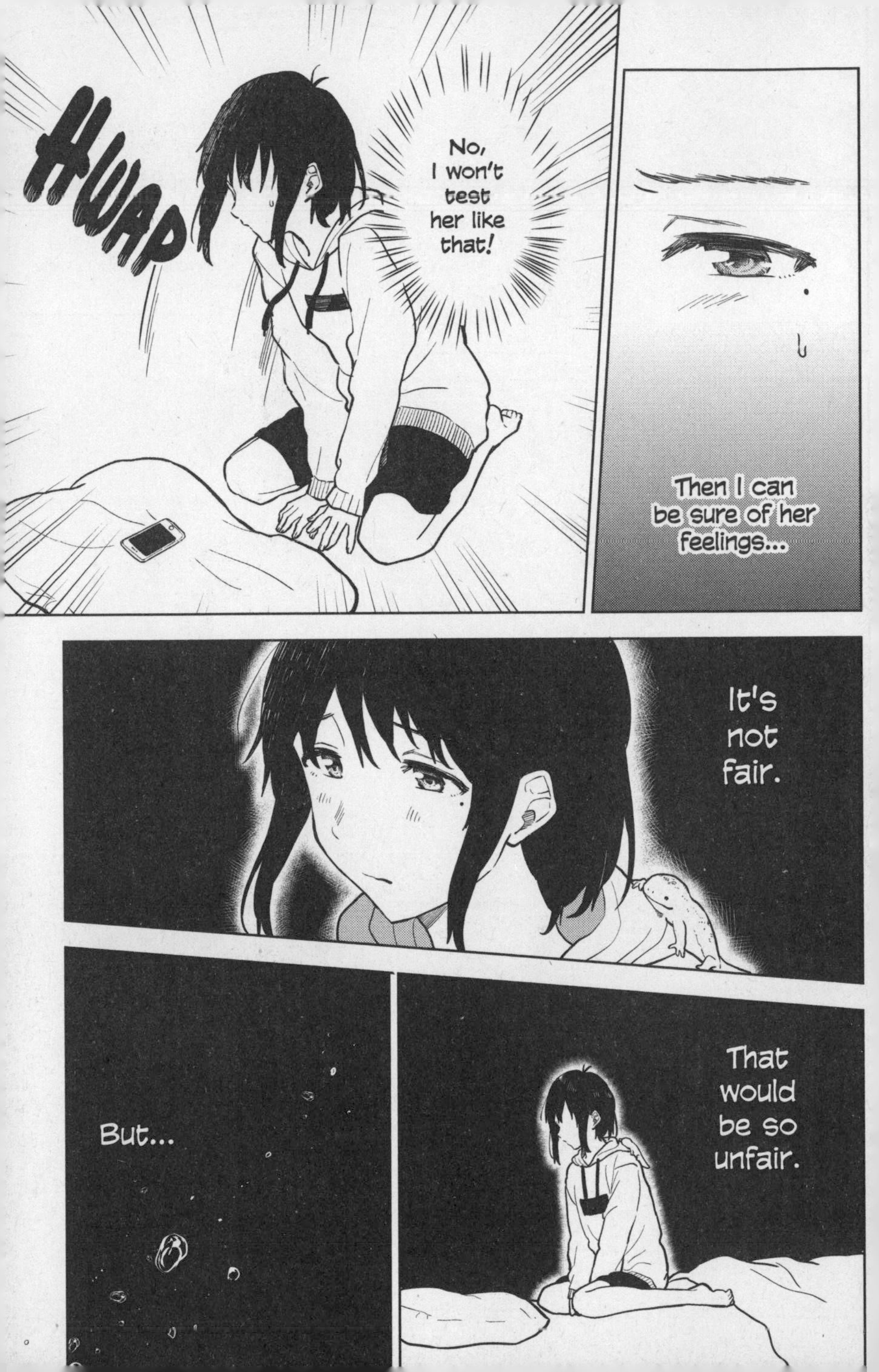
Then I can be sure of her feelings...
HWAP
No, I won't test her like that!
It's not fair.
That would be so unfair.
But...

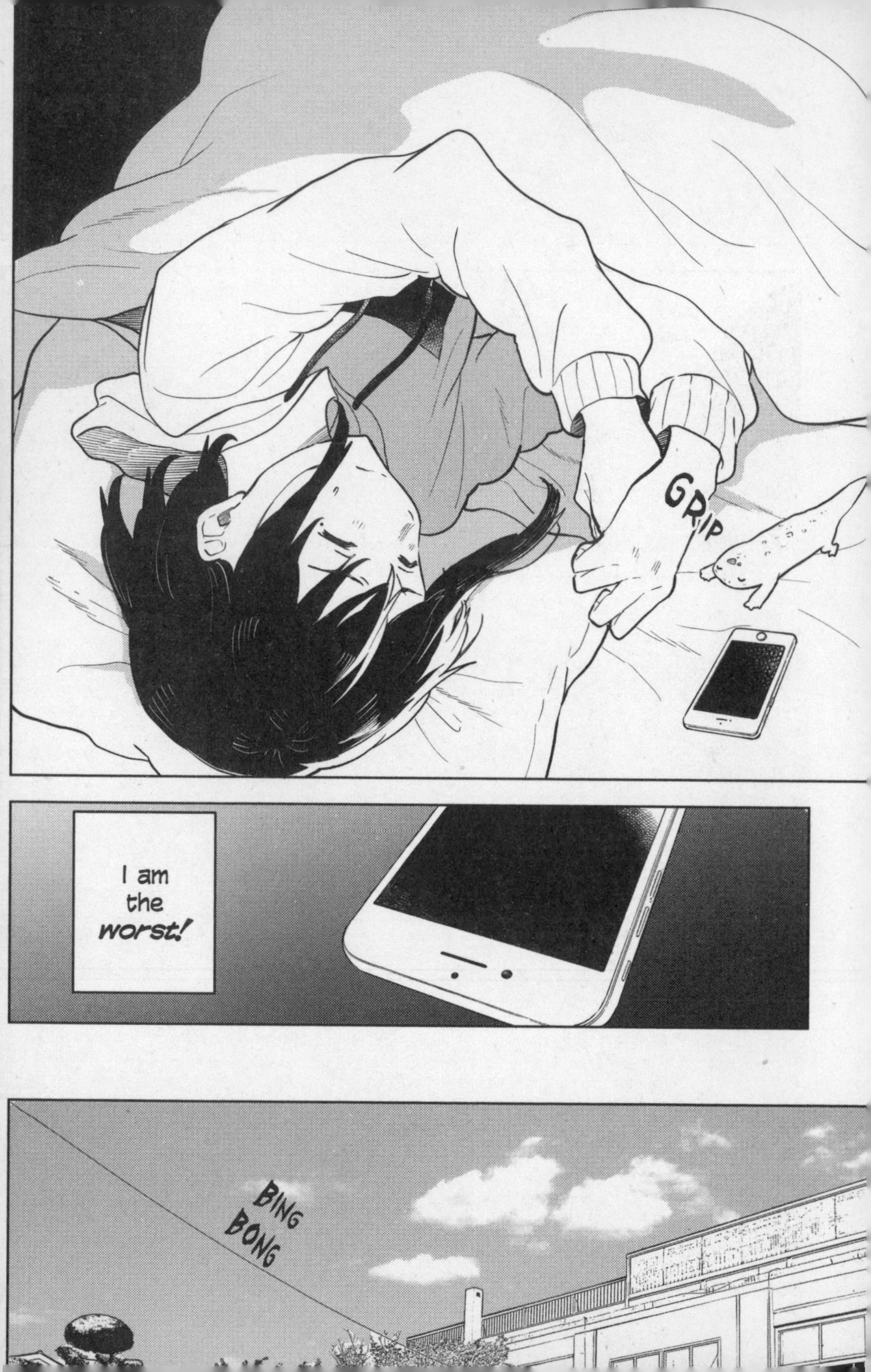
GRIP
I am the *worst!*
BING BONG

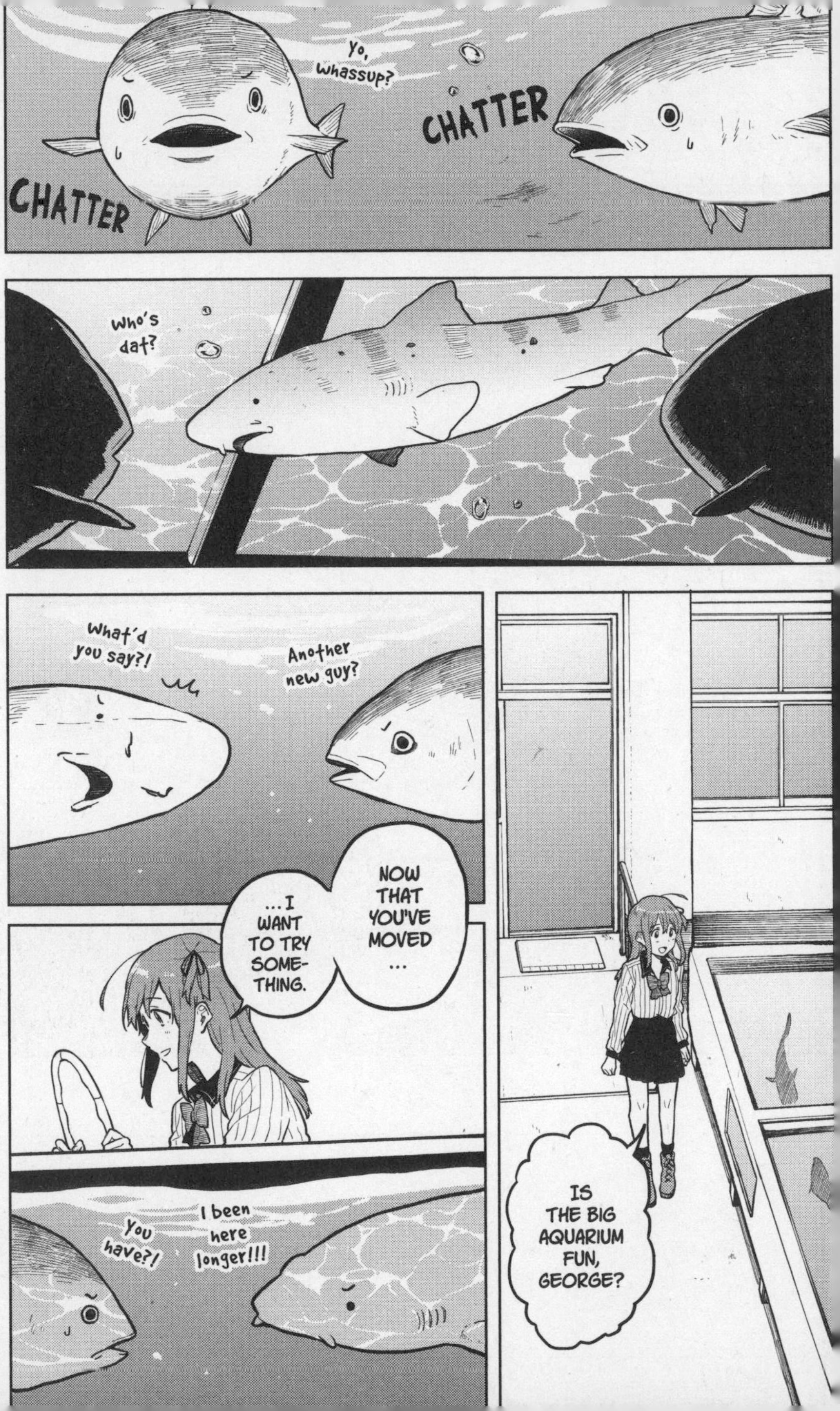
CHATTER
Yo, whassup?
CHATTER
Who's dat?
IS THE BIG AQUARIUM FUN, GEORGE?
Another new guy?
What'd you say?!
NOW THAT YOU'VE MOVED ...
...I WANT TO TRY SOME-THING.
I been here longer!!!
You have?!

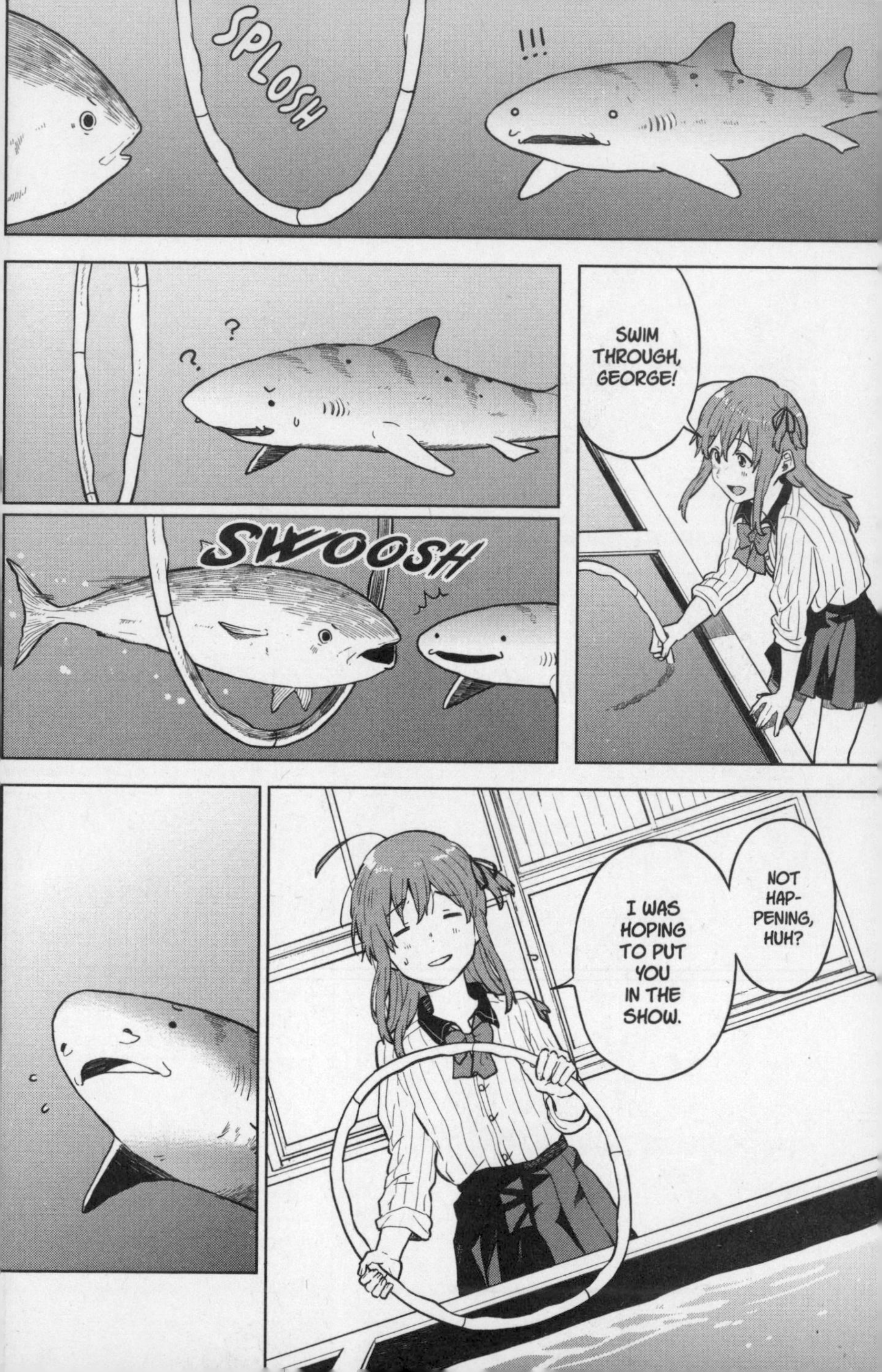
!!!
SPLOSH
SWIM THROUGH, GEORGE!
? ?
SWOOSH
NOT HAP-PENING, HUH?
I WAS HOPING TO PUT YOU IN THE SHOW.

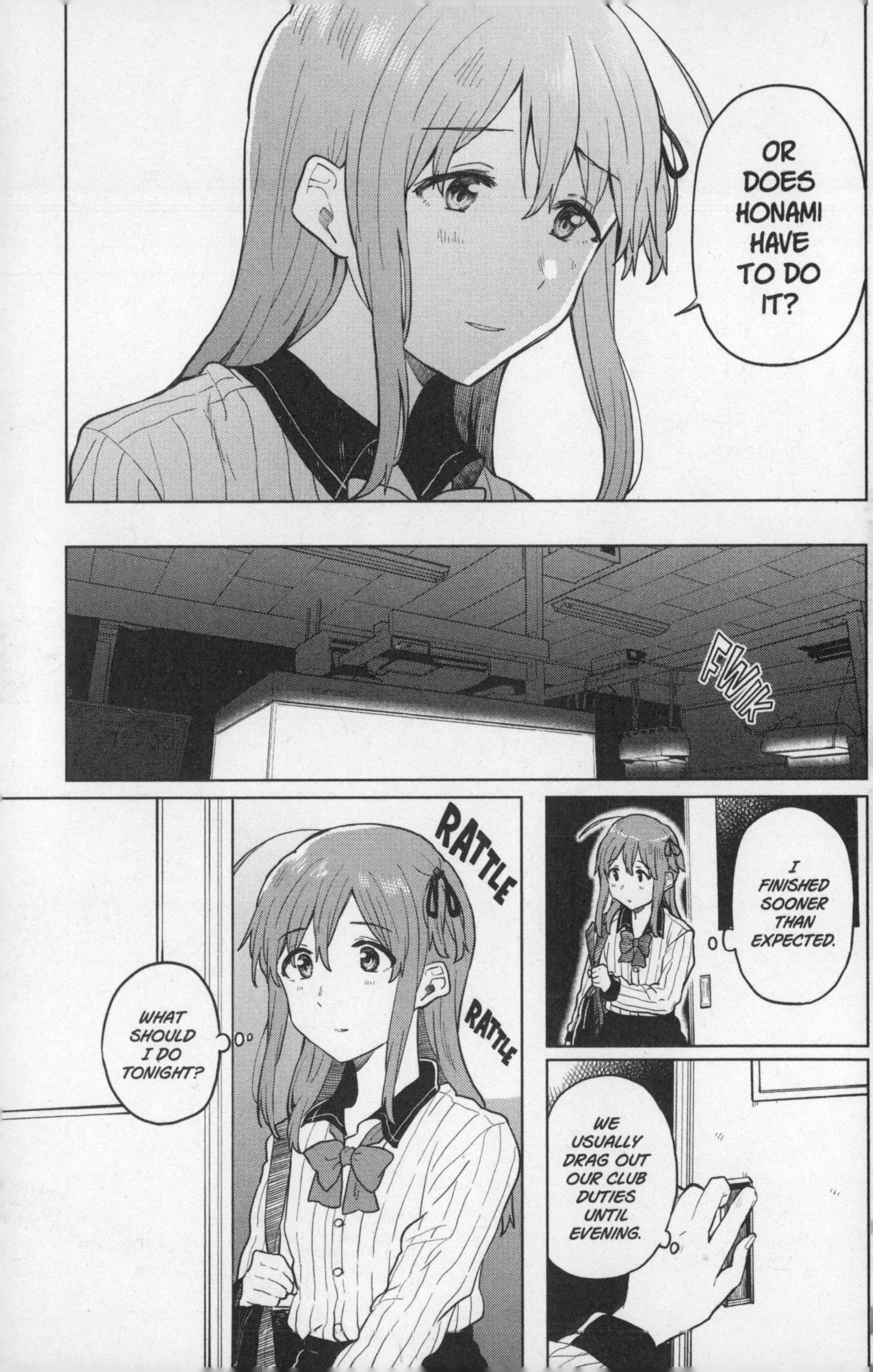
OR DOES HONAMI HAVE TO DO IT?
FWIK
I FINISHED SOONER THAN EXPECTED.
WE USUALLY DRAG OUT OUR CLUB DUTIES UNTIL EVENING.
RATTLE
RATTLE
WHAT SHOULD I DO TONIGHT?

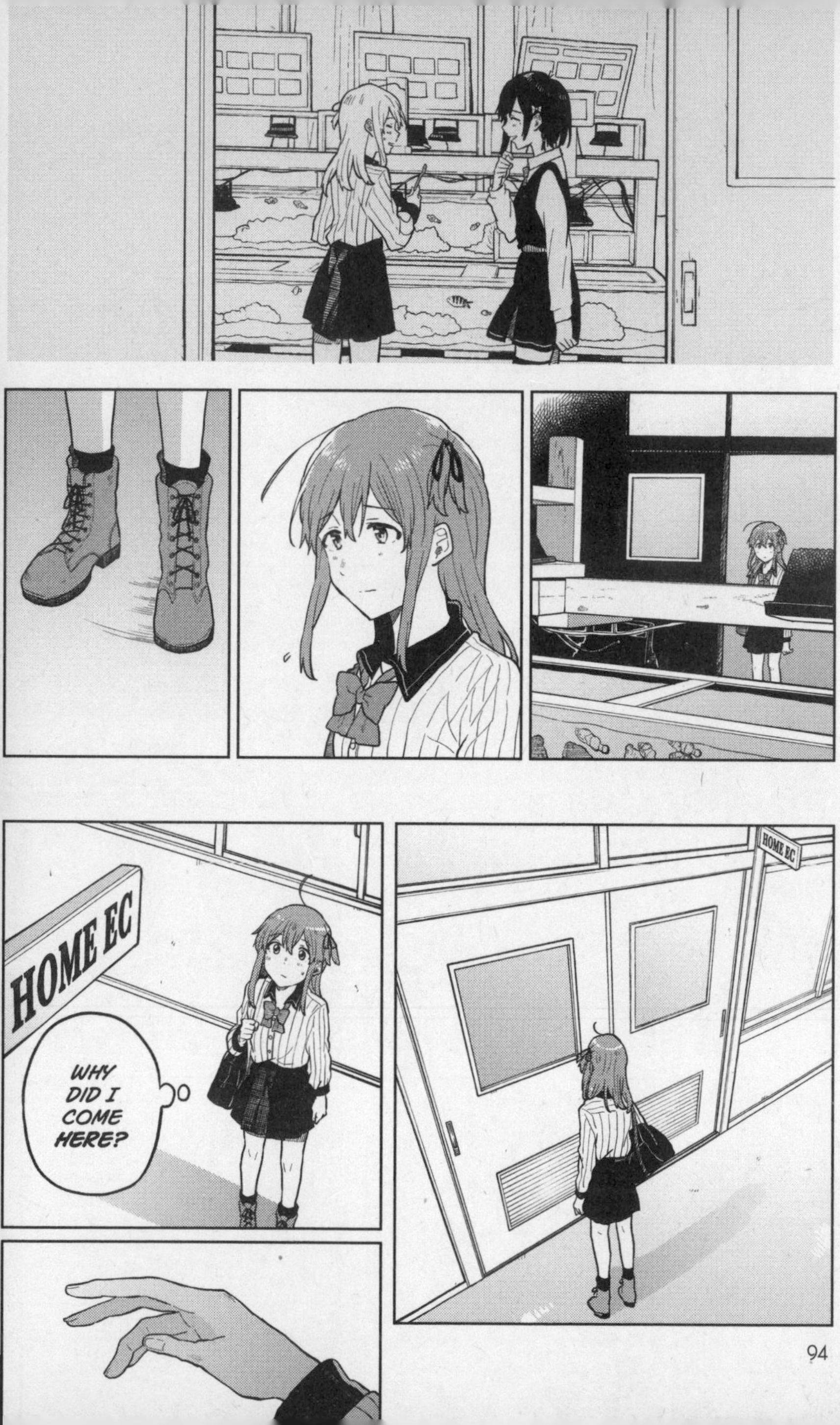
HOME EC
HOME EC
WHY DID I COME HERE?

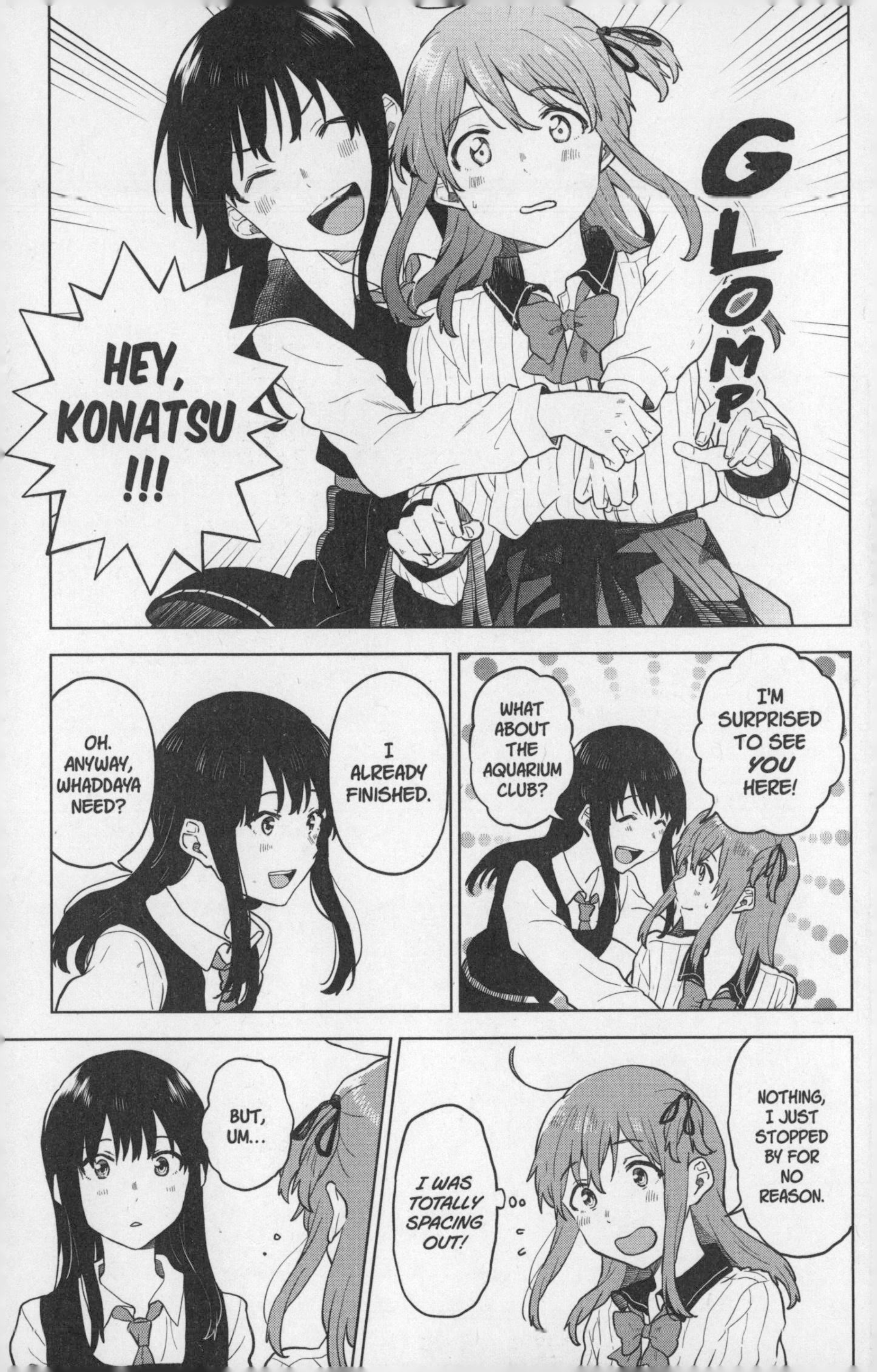
GLOMP
HEY, KONATSU!!!
I'M SURPRISED TO SEE *YOU* HERE!
WHAT ABOUT THE AQUARIUM CLUB?
I ALREADY FINISHED.
OH. ANYWAY, WHADDAYA NEED?
NOTHING, I JUST STOPPED BY FOR NO REASON.
I WAS TOTALLY SPACING OUT!
BUT, UM...

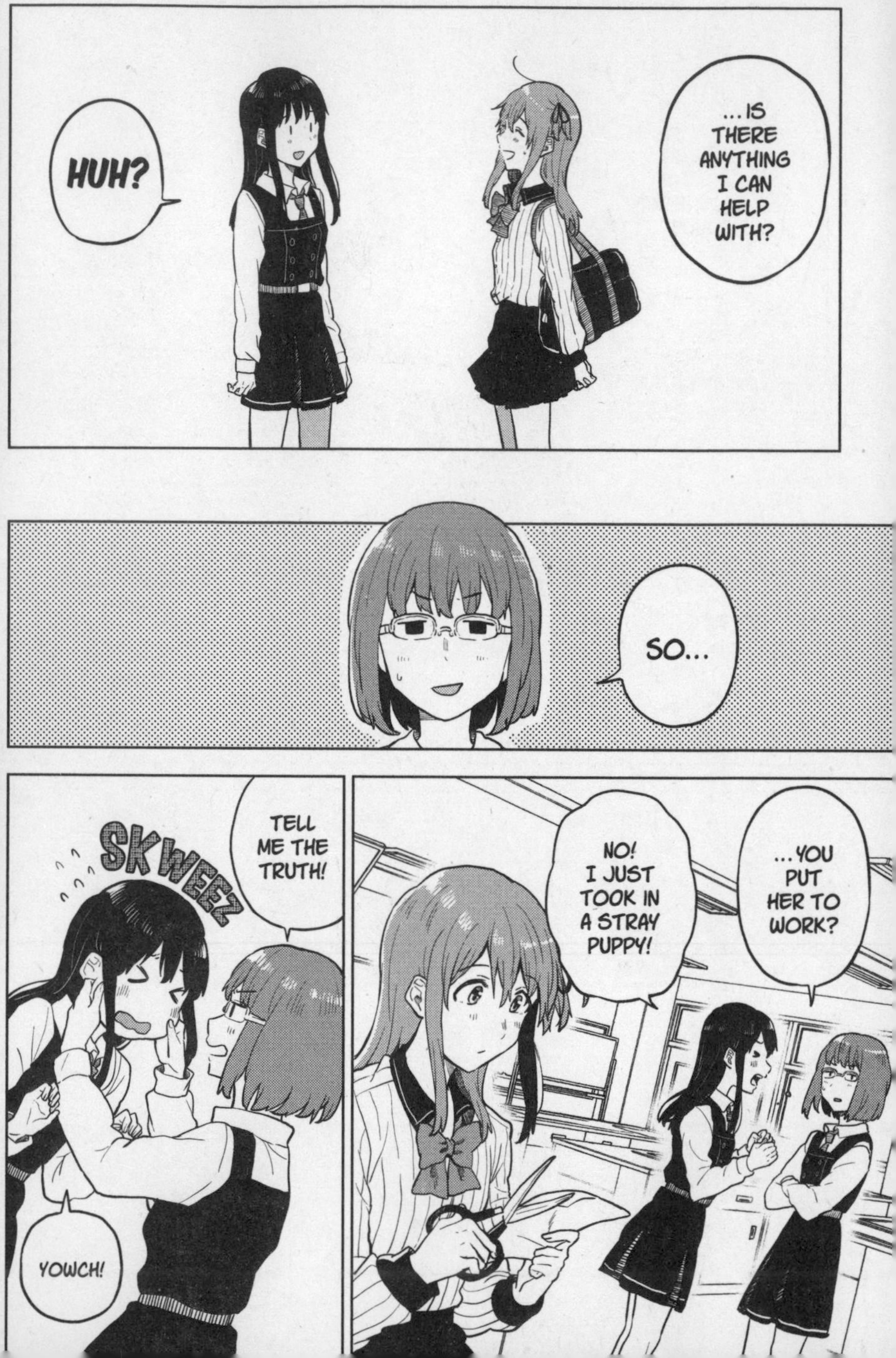
...IS THERE ANYTHING I CAN HELP WITH?
HUH?
SO...
...YOU PUT HER TO WORK?
NO! I JUST TOOK IN A STRAY PUPPY!
TELL ME THE TRUTH!
SKWEEZ
YOWCH!

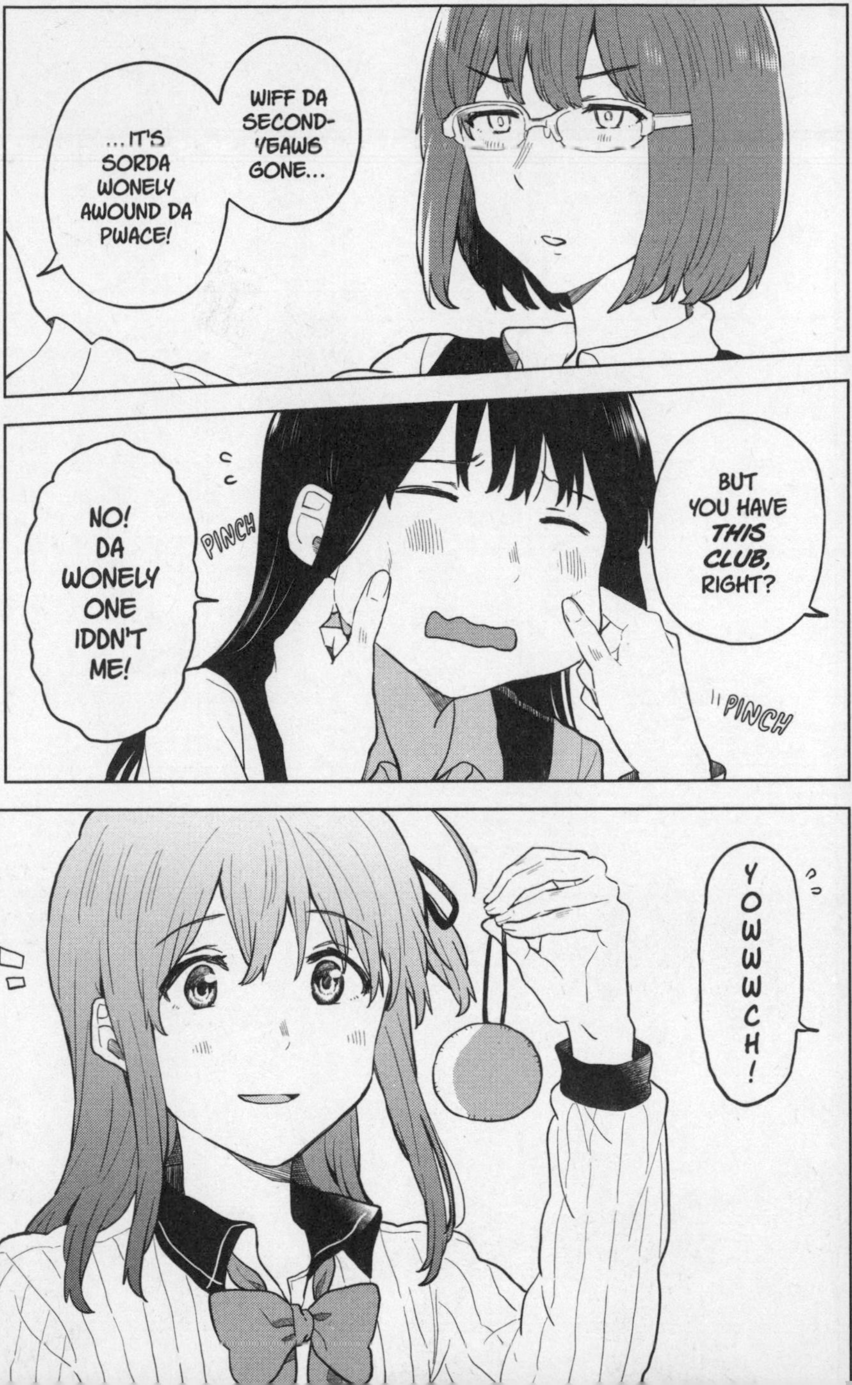
WIFF DA SECOND-YEAWS GONE...
...IT'S SORDA WONELY AWOUND DA PWACE!
BUT YOU HAVE *THIS CLUB*, RIGHT?
PINCH
PINCH
NO! DA WONELY ONE IDDN'T ME!
YOWWWCH!

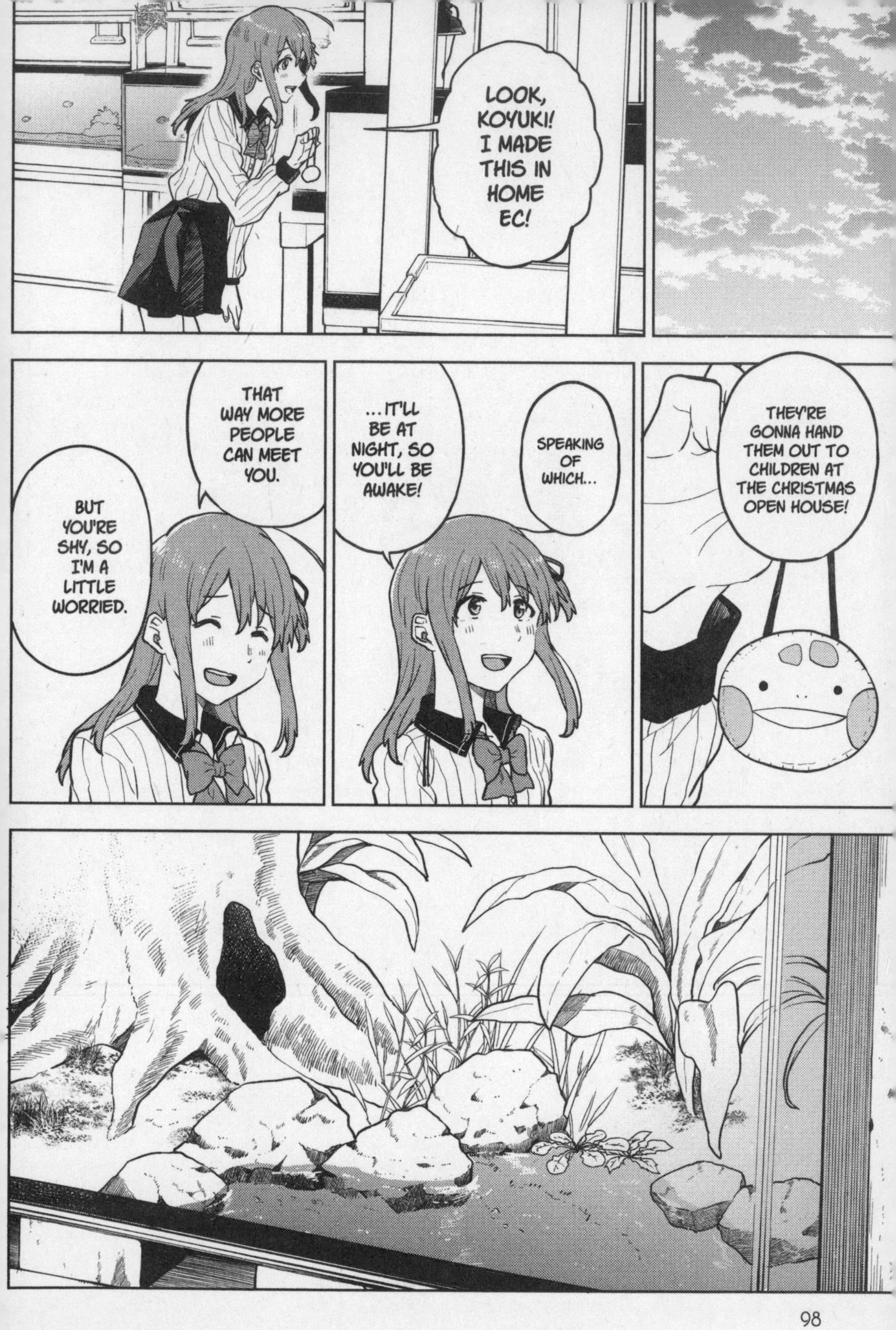
LOOK, KOYUKI! I MADE THIS IN HOME EC!
THEY'RE GONNA HAND THEM OUT TO CHILDREN AT THE CHRISTMAS OPEN HOUSE!
SPEAKING OF WHICH...
...IT'LL BE AT NIGHT, SO YOU'LL BE AWAKE!
THAT WAY MORE PEOPLE CAN MEET YOU.
BUT YOU'RE SHY, SO I'M A LITTLE WORRIED.

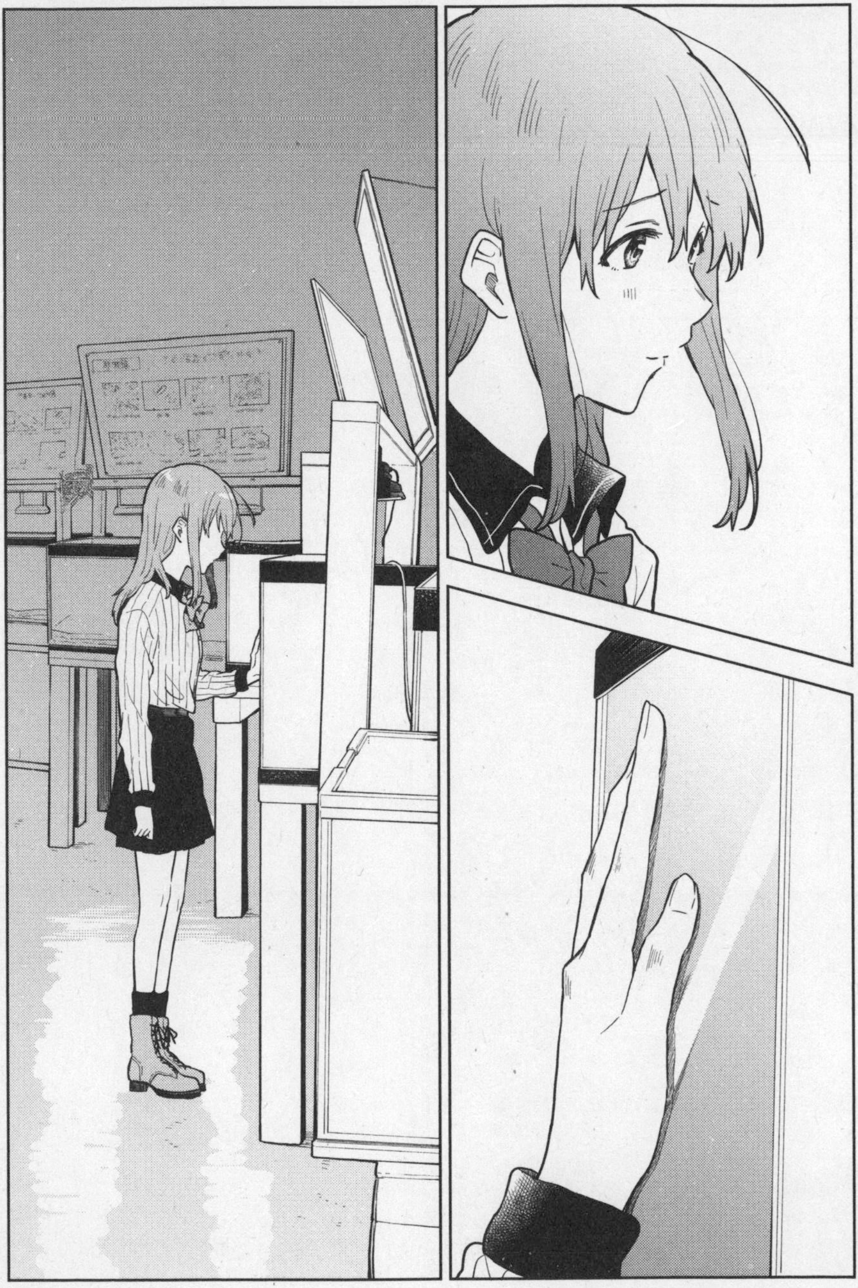

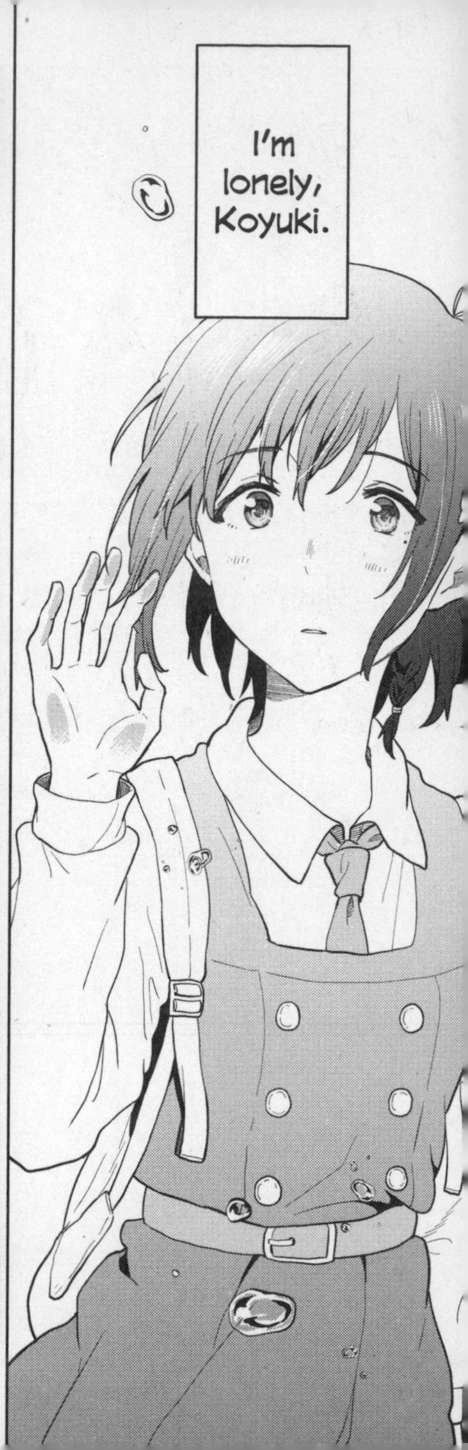
I'm lonely, Koyuki.
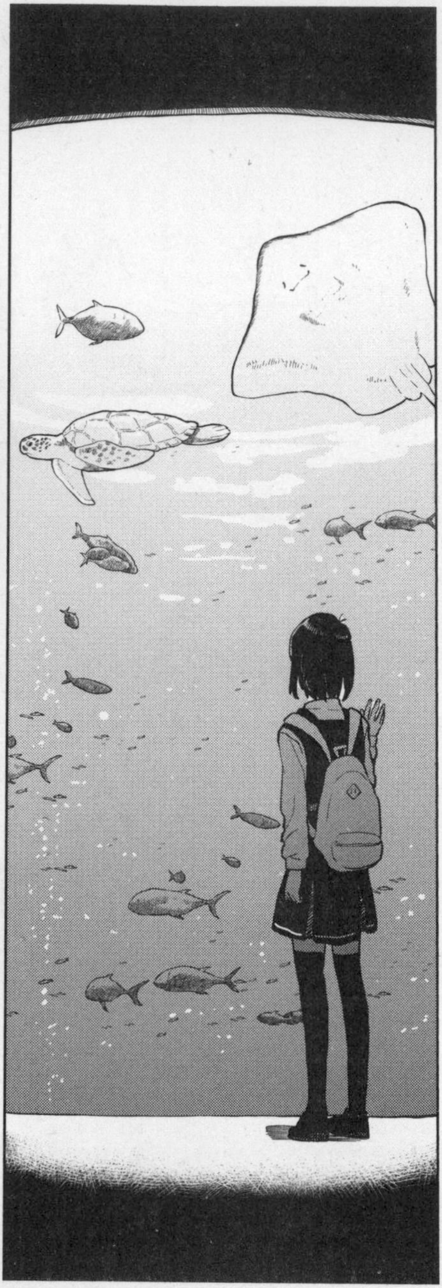

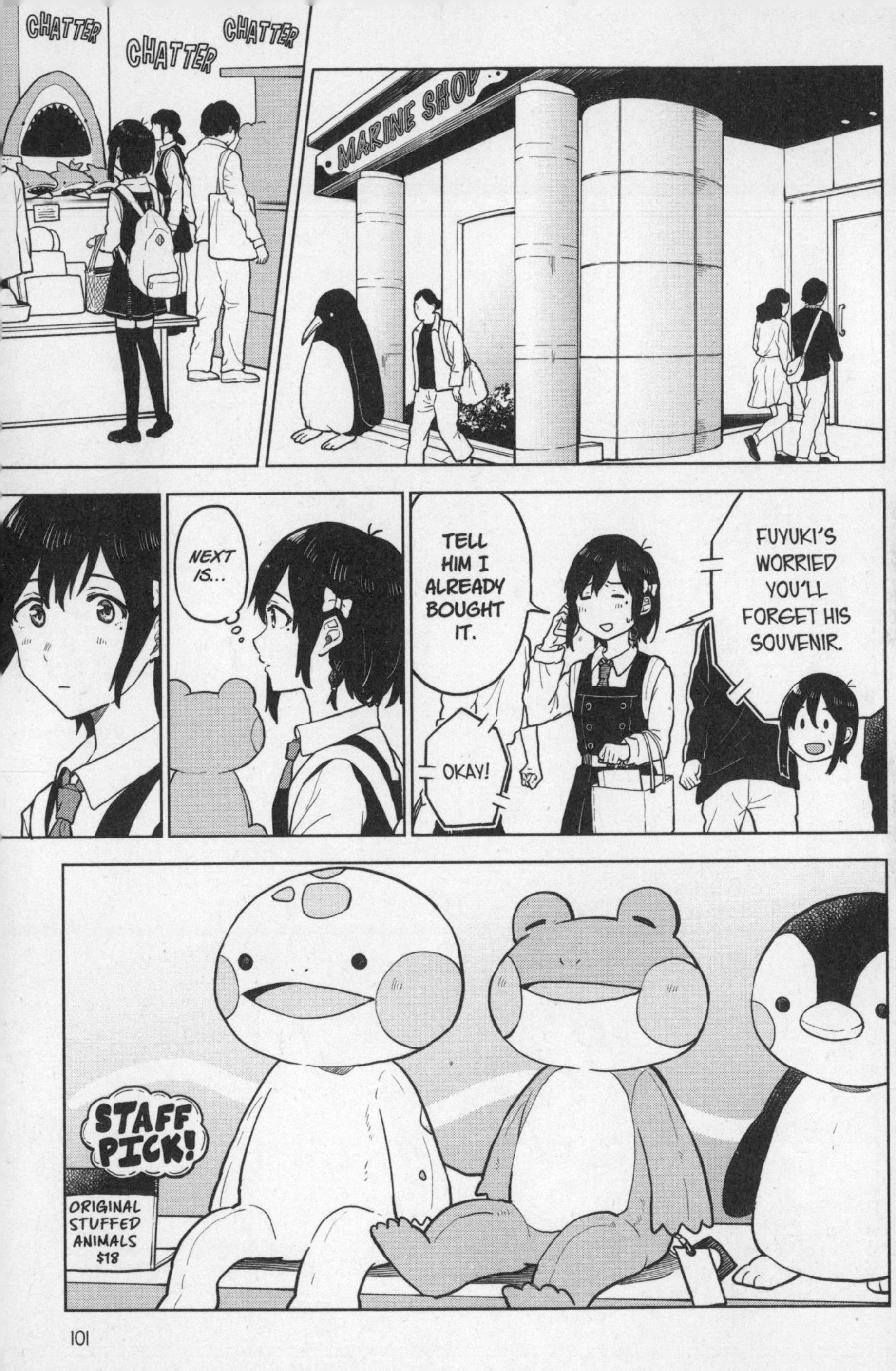
MARINE SHOP
CHATTER
CHATTER
CHATTER
FUYUKI'S WORRIED YOU'LL FORGET HIS SOUVENIR.
TELL HIM I ALREADY BOUGHT IT.
OKAY!
NEXT IS...
STAFF PICK!
ORIGINAL STUFFED ANIMALS $18

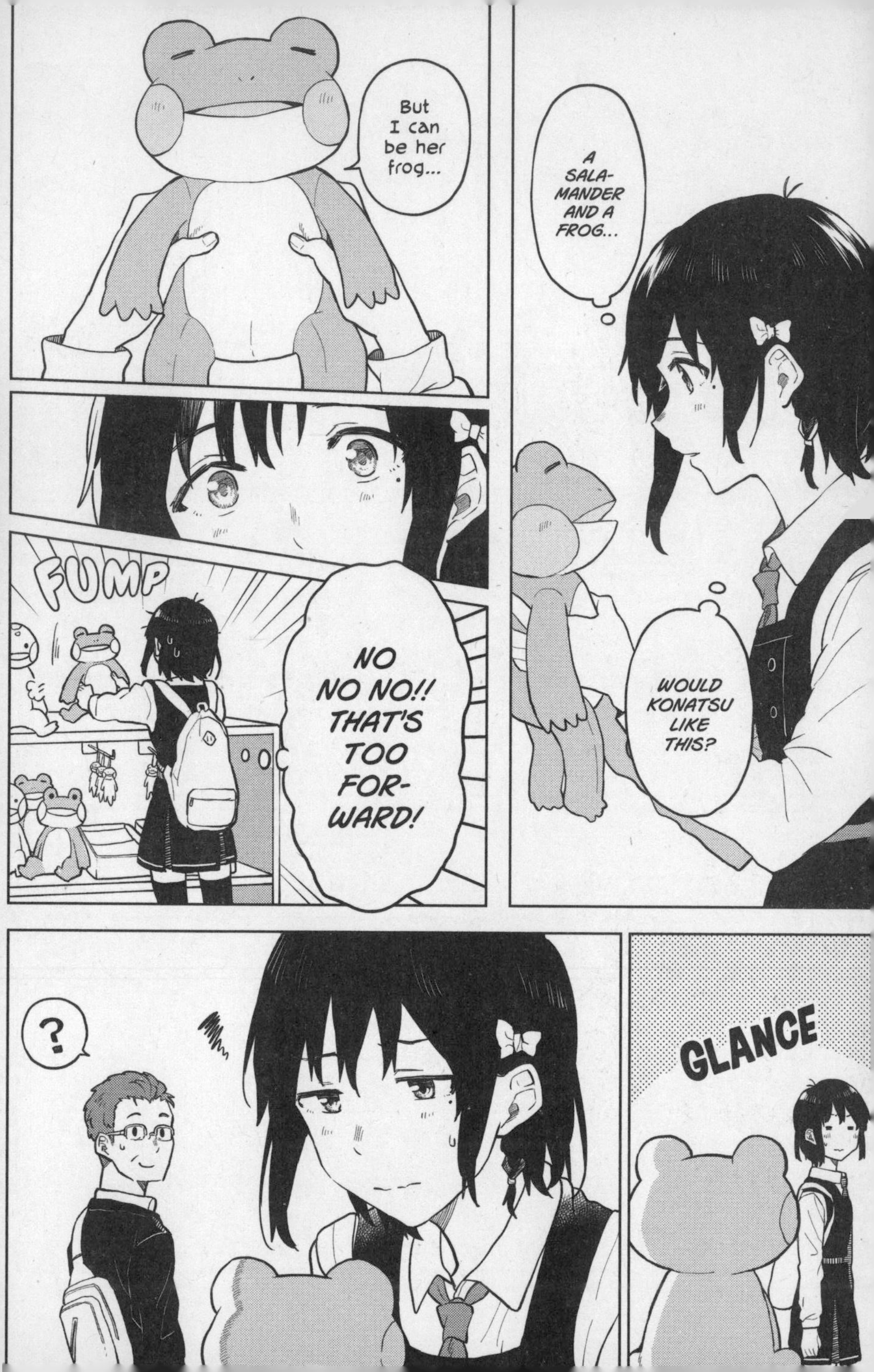
A SALAMANDER AND A FROG...
WOULD KONATSU LIKE THIS?
But I can be her frog...
FUMP
NO NO NO!! THAT'S TOO FORWARD!
GLANCE
?

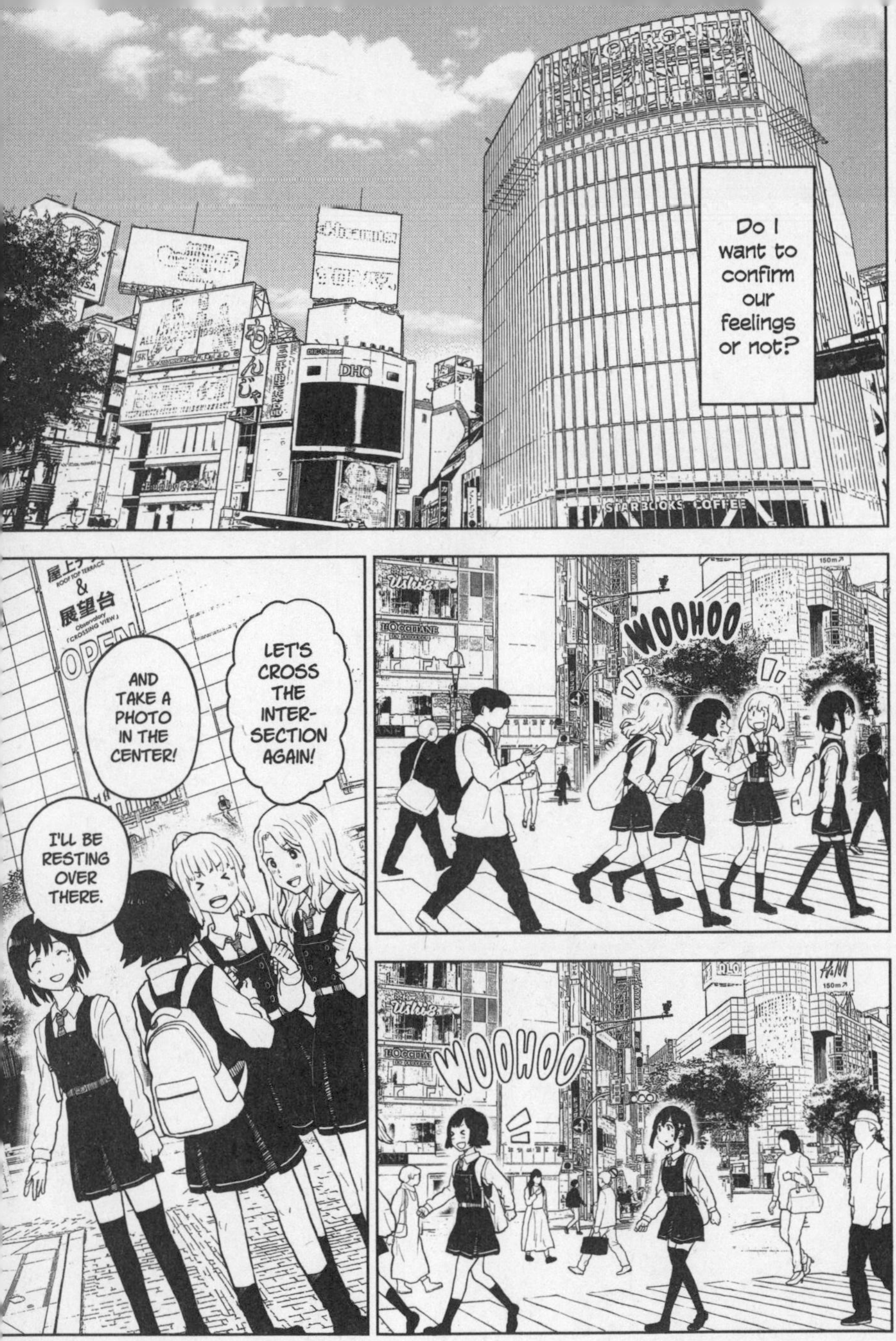
Do I want to confirm our feelings or not?
STARBOOKS COFFEE
WOOHOO
WOOHOO
LET'S CROSS THE INTER-SECTION AGAIN!
AND TAKE A PHOTO IN THE CENTER!
I'LL BE RESTING OVER THERE.

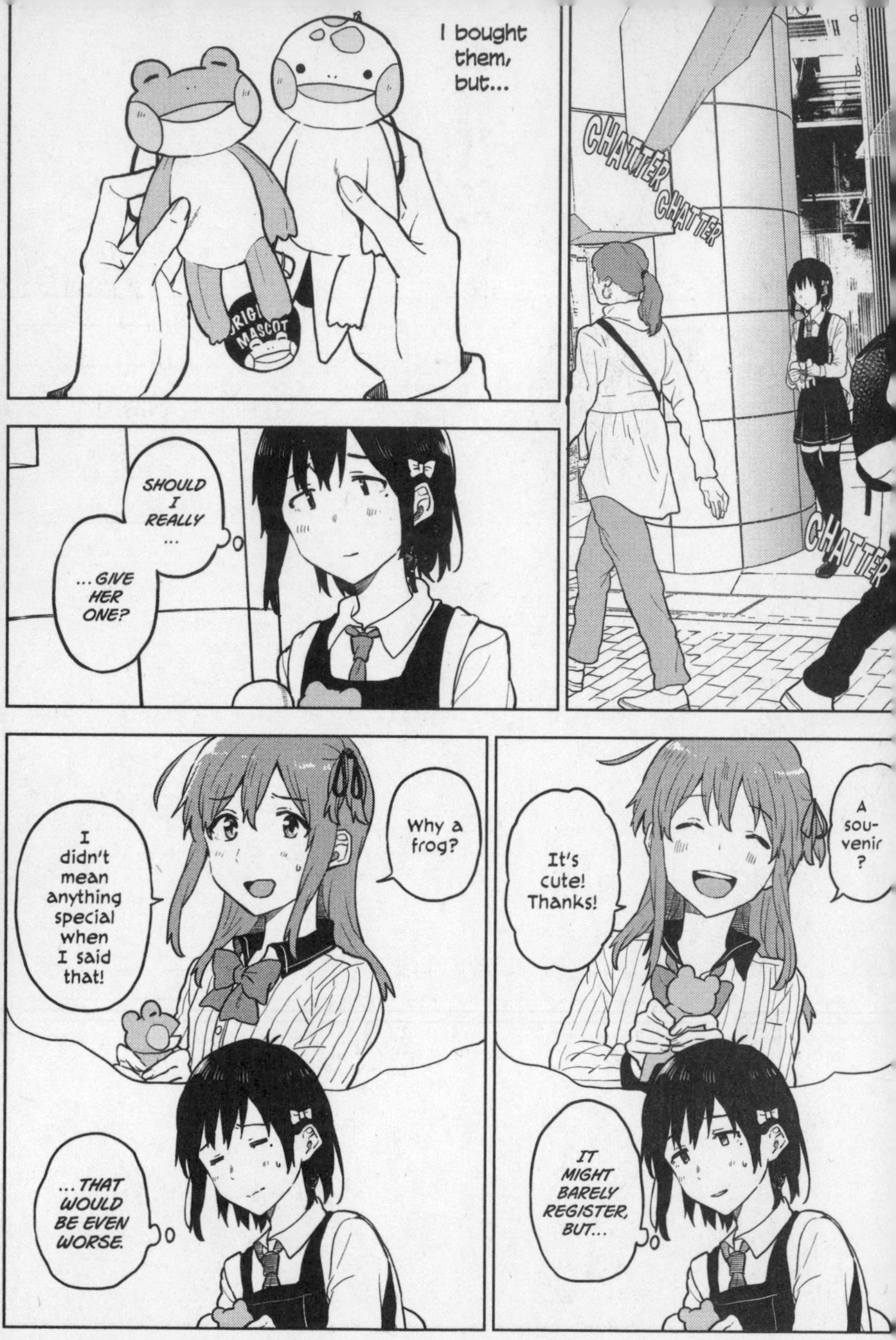

CHATTER CHATTER
CHATTER
I bought them, but...
MASCOT
SHOULD I REALLY ...
...GIVE HER ONE?
A sou-venir?
It's cute! Thanks!
IT MIGHT BARELY REGISTER, BUT...
Why a frog?
I didn't mean anything special when I said that!
...THAT WOULD BE EVEN WORSE.

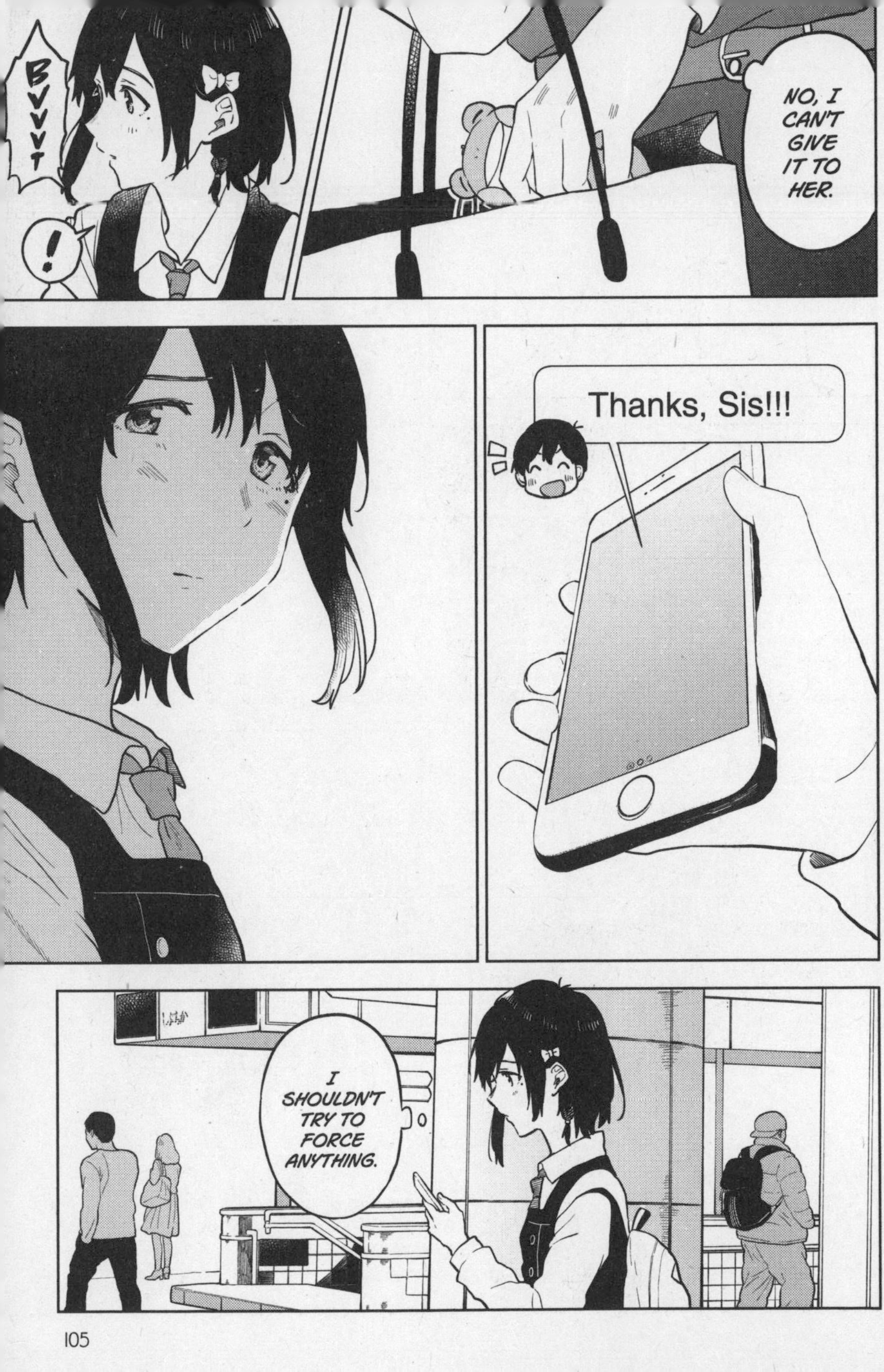
NO, I CAN'T GIVE IT TO HER.
BVVVT
!
Thanks, Sis!!!
I SHOULDN'T TRY TO FORCE ANYTHING.

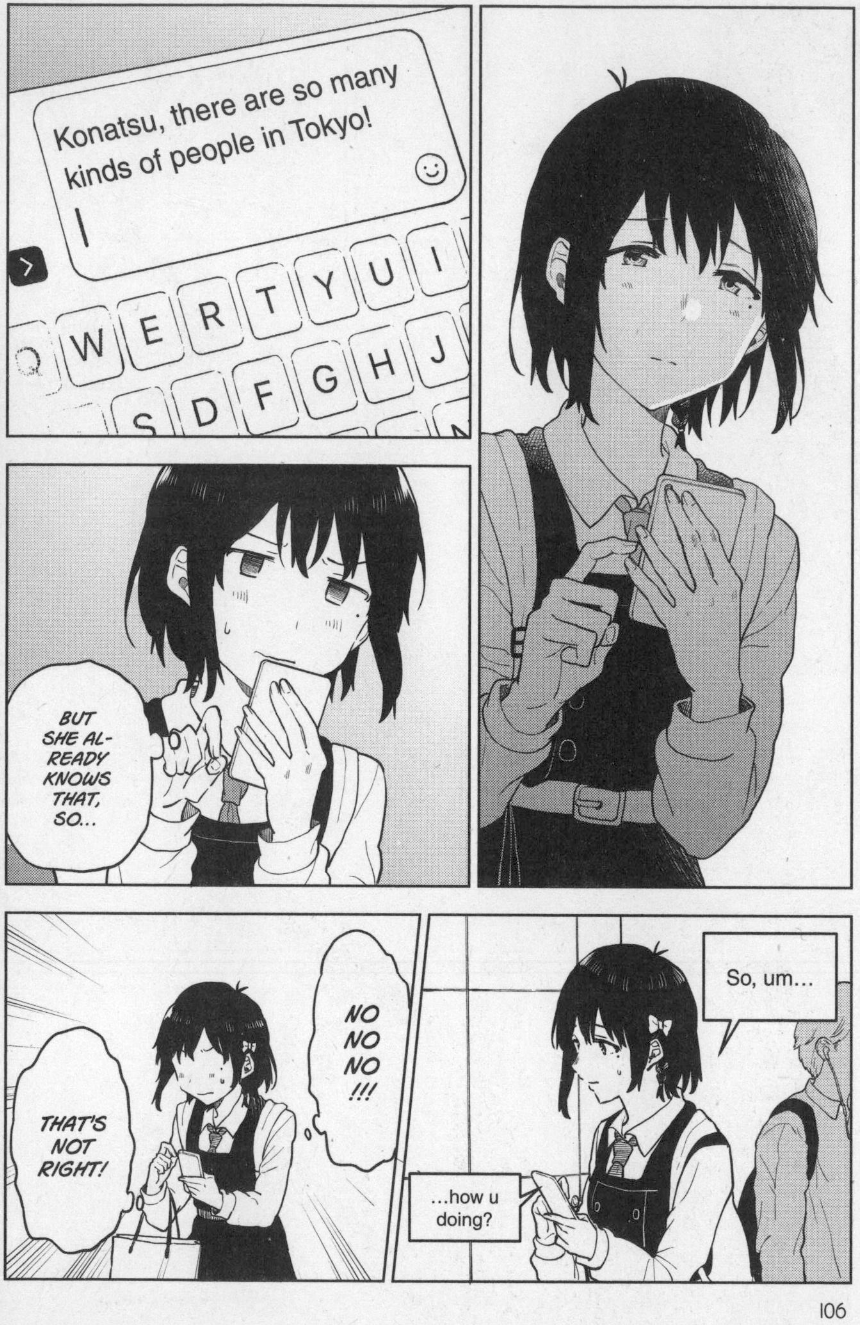
Konatsu, there are so many kinds of people in Tokyo!
BUT SHE AL-READY KNOWS THAT, SO...
So, um…
…how u doing?
NO NO NO !!!
THAT'S NOT RIGHT!

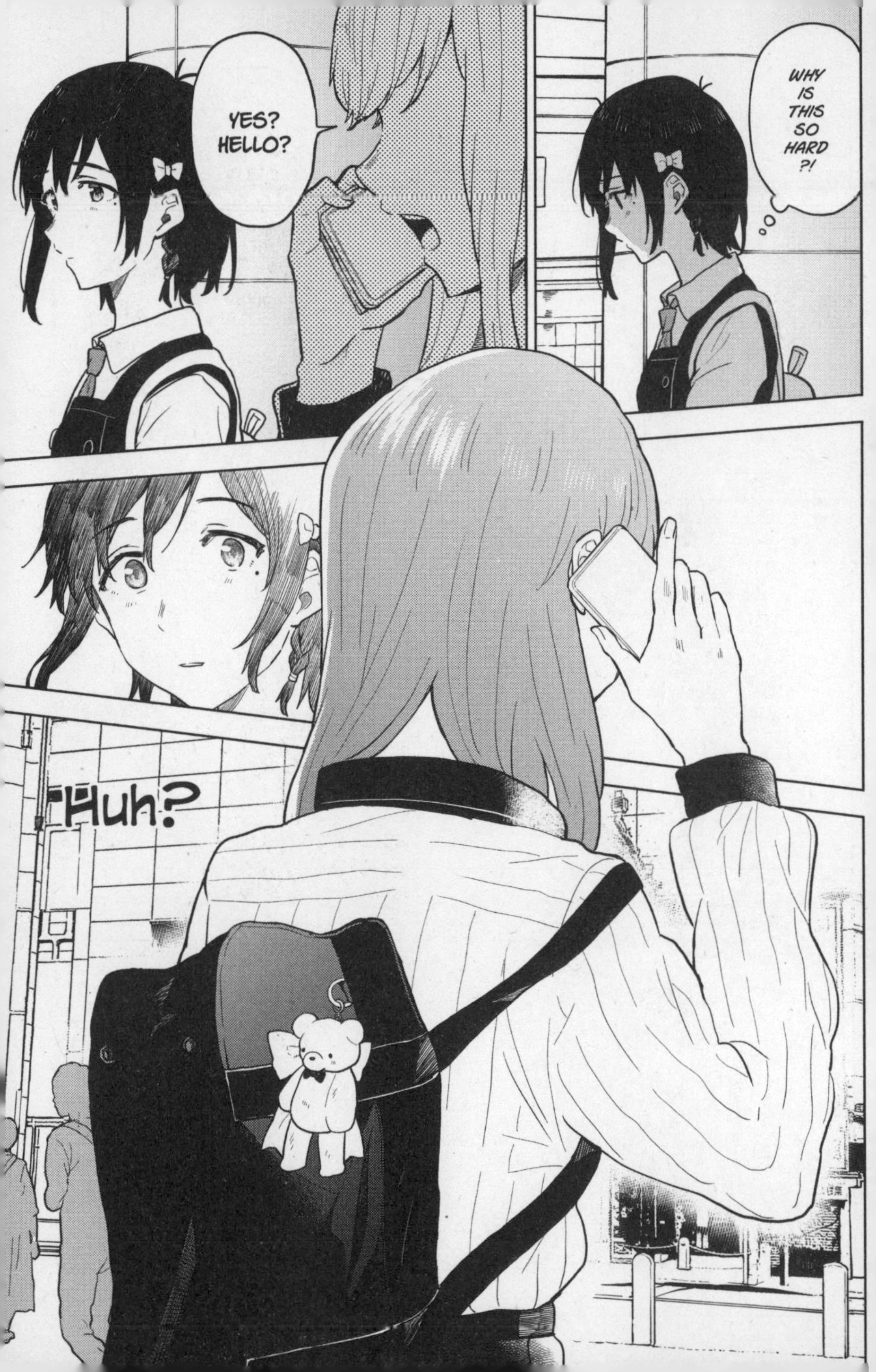
WHY IS THIS SO HARD ?!
YES? HELLO?
Huh?

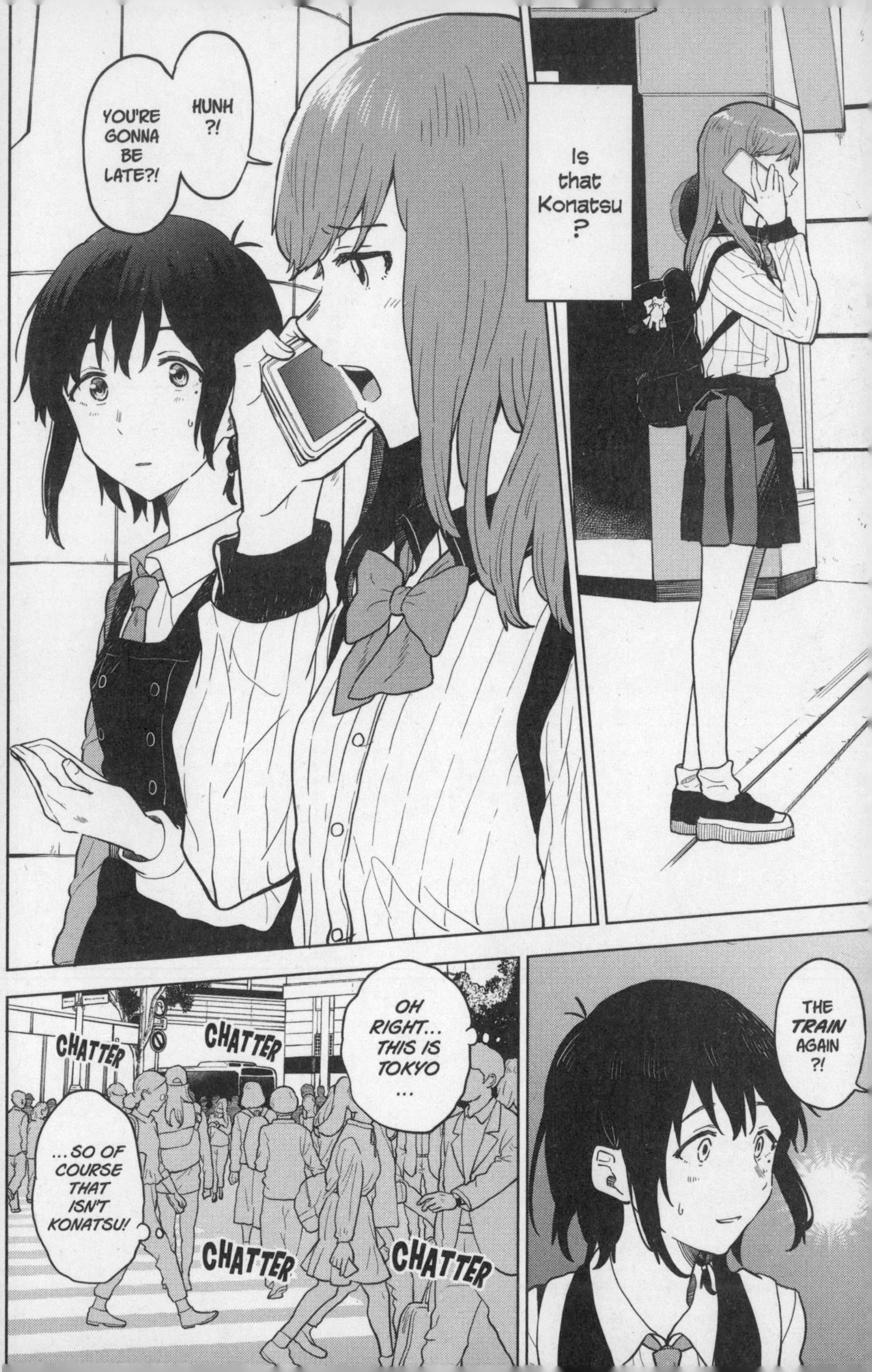
Is that Konatsu ?
HUNH ?!
YOU'RE GONNA BE LATE?!
THE TRAIN AGAIN ?!
OH RIGHT... THIS IS TOKYO ...
CHATTER
CHATTER
...SO OF COURSE THAT ISN'T KONATSU!
CHATTER
CHATTER

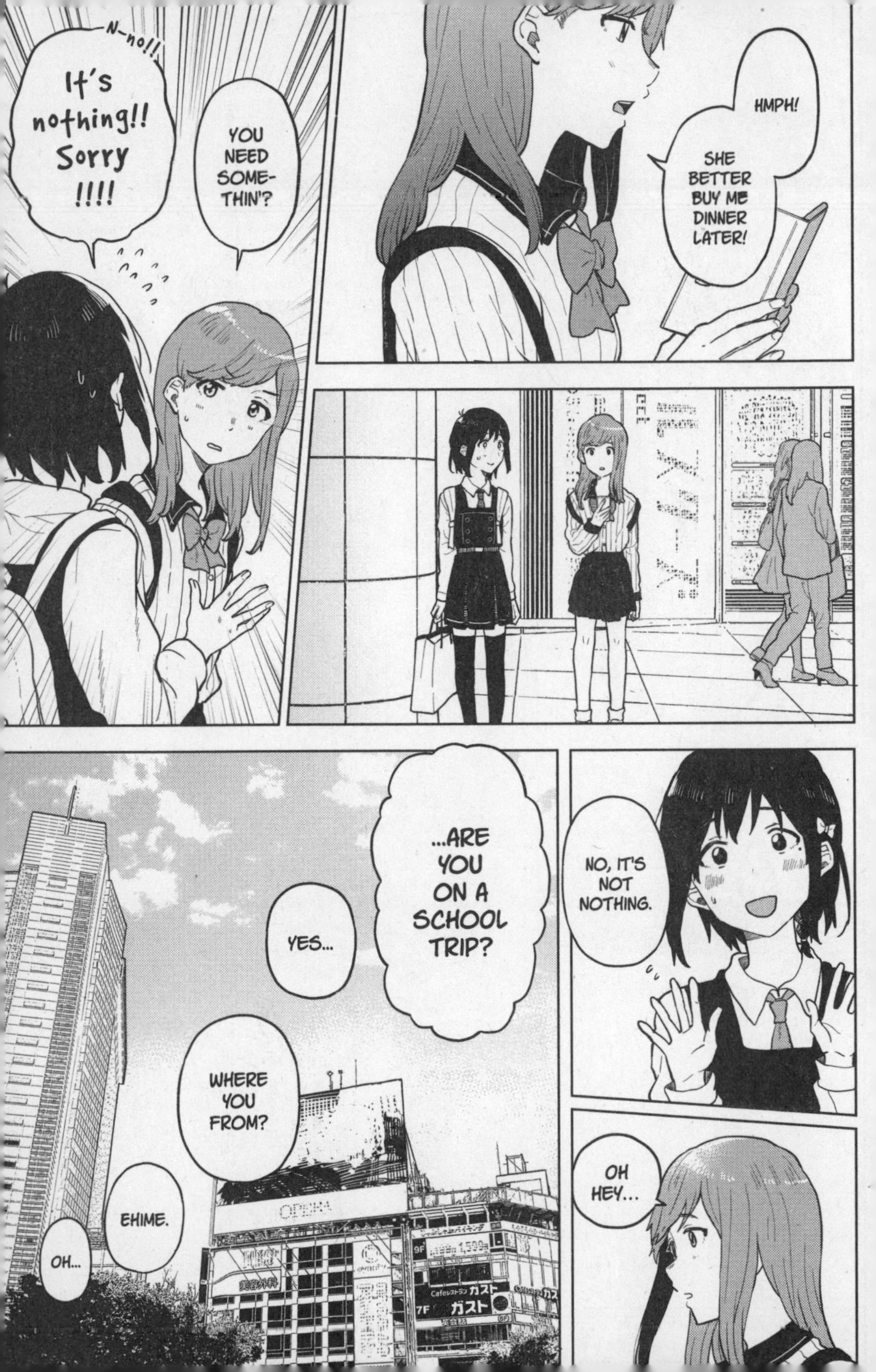
HMPH!
SHE BETTER BUY ME DINNER LATER!
YOU NEED SOMETHIN'?
N-no!!
It's nothing!! Sorry!!!!
NO, IT'S NOT NOTHING.
OH HEY...
...ARE YOU ON A SCHOOL TRIP?
YES...
WHERE YOU FROM?
EHIME.
OH...

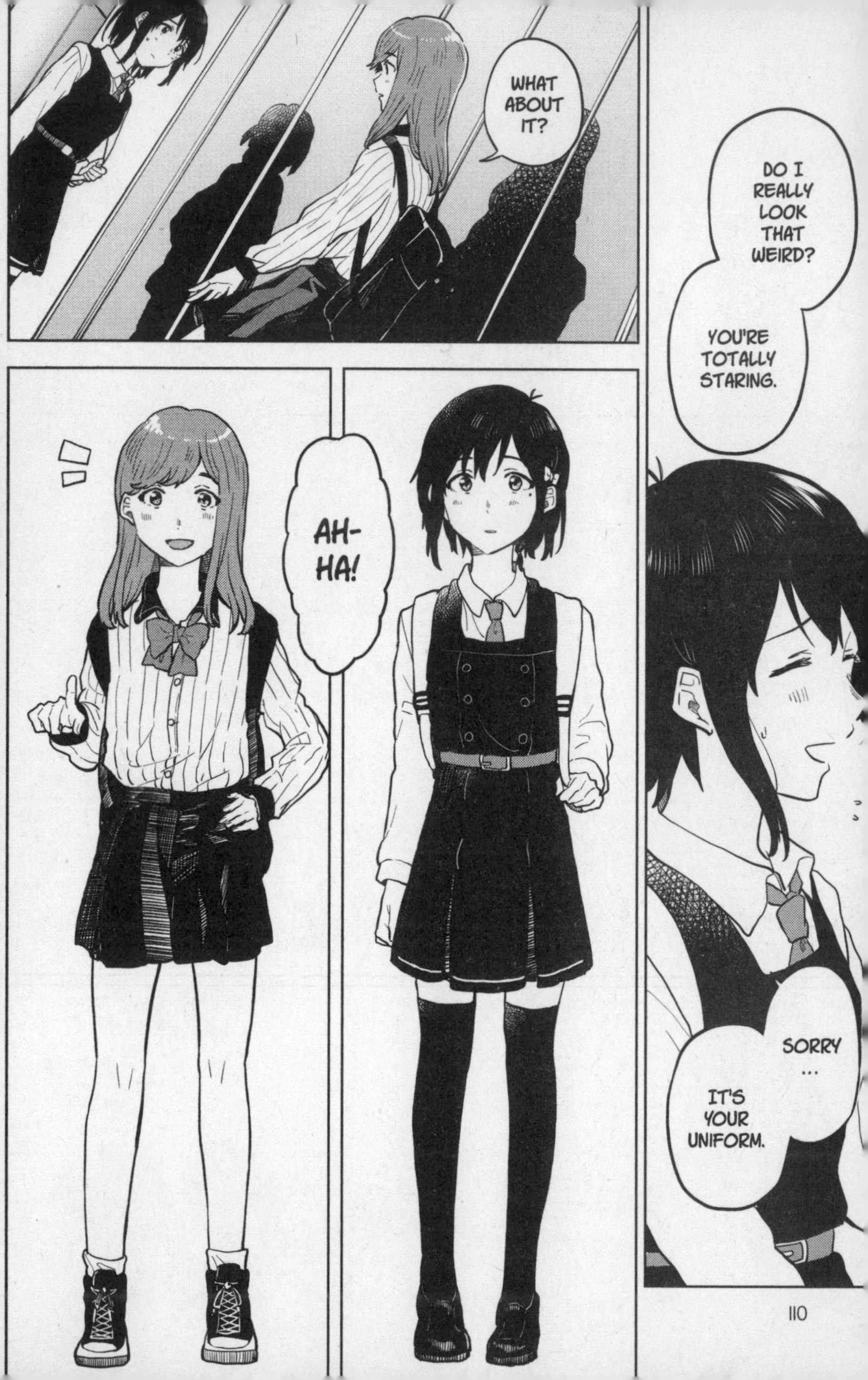

DO I REALLY LOOK THAT WEIRD?
YOU'RE TOTALLY STARING.
SORRY ...
IT'S YOUR UNIFORM.
WHAT ABOUT IT?
AH-HA!

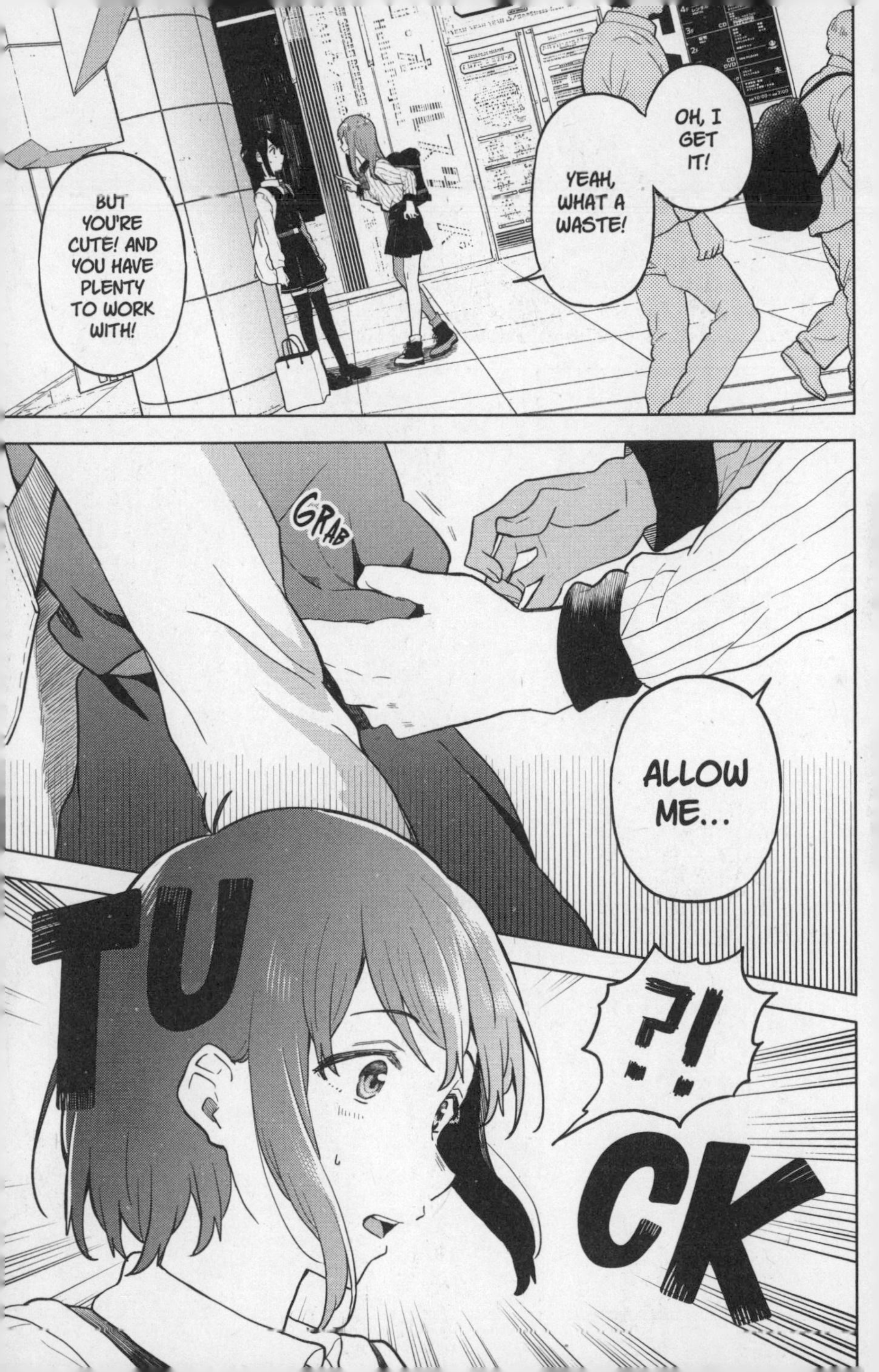
OH, I GET IT!
YEAH, WHAT A WASTE!
BUT YOU'RE CUTE! AND YOU HAVE PLENTY TO WORK WITH!
GRAB
ALLOW ME...
TUCK
?!

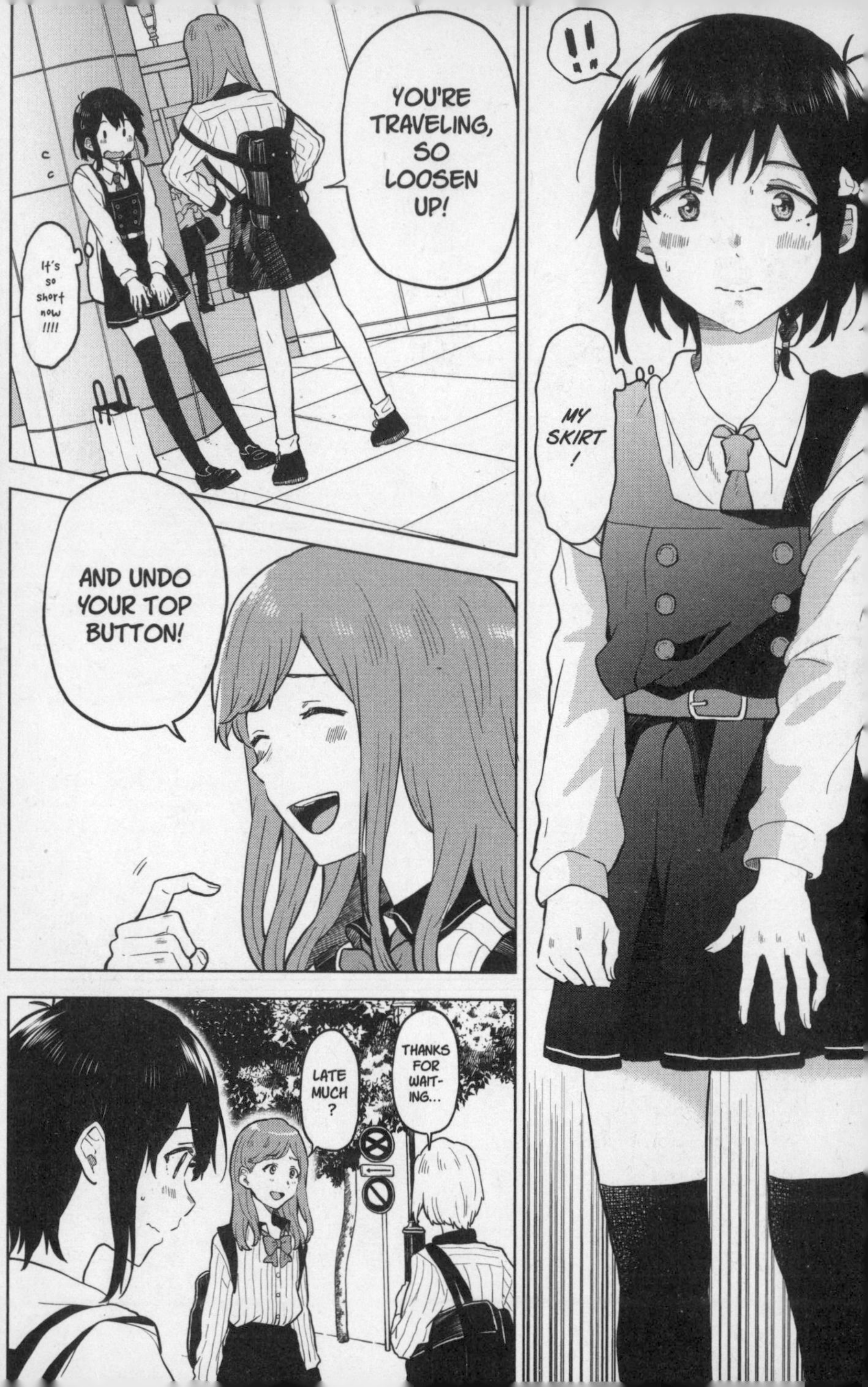
!!
MY SKIRT!
YOU'RE TRAVELING, SO LOOSEN UP!
It's so short now !!!!
AND UNDO YOUR TOP BUTTON!
THANKS FOR WAIT-ING...
LATE MUCH?

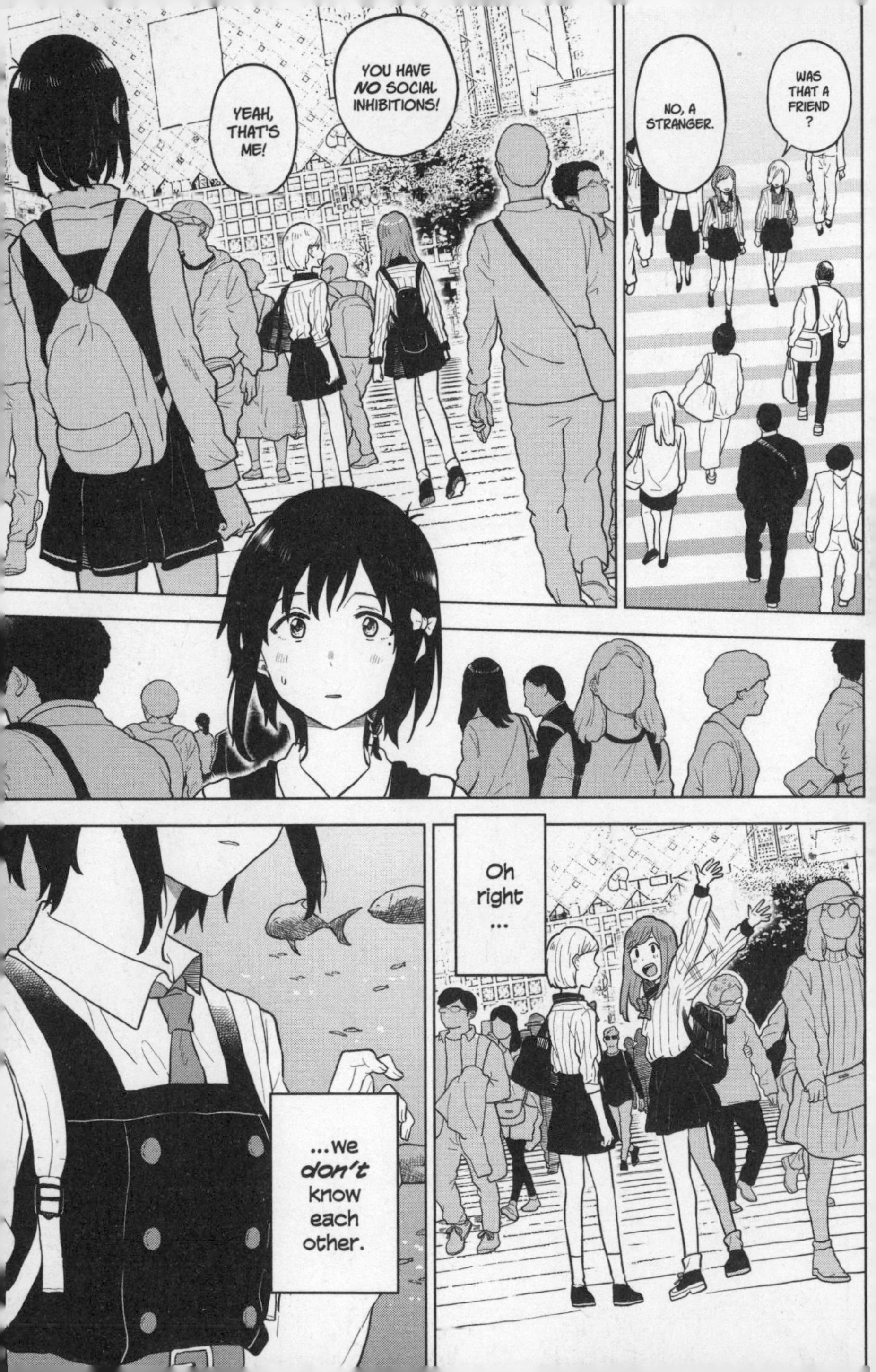
WAS THAT A FRIEND?
NO, A STRANGER.
YOU HAVE *NO* SOCIAL INHIBITIONS!
YEAH, THAT'S ME!
Oh right ...
...we *don't* know each other.

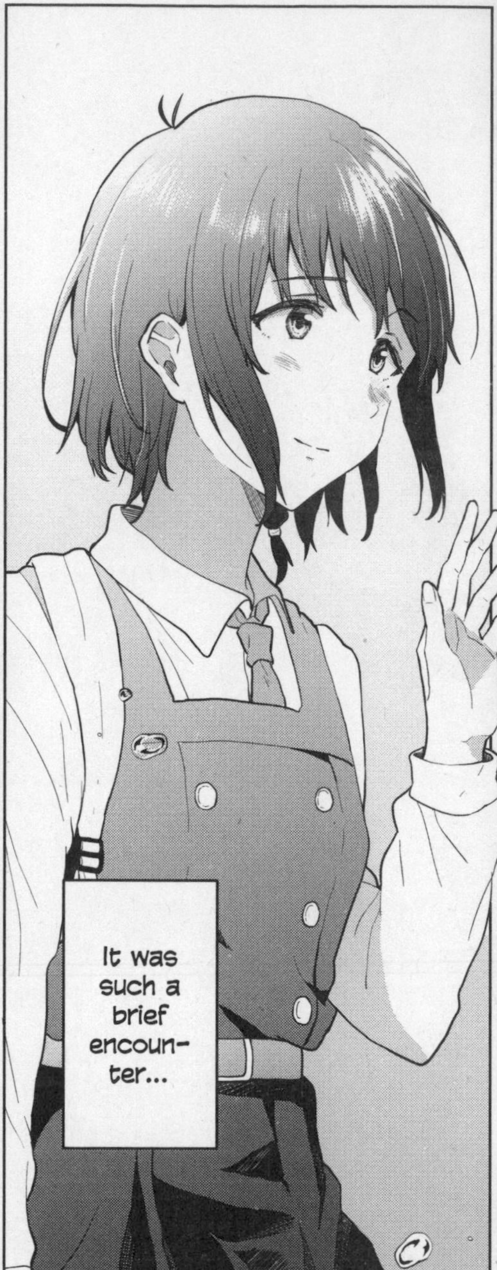
It was such a brief encounter...

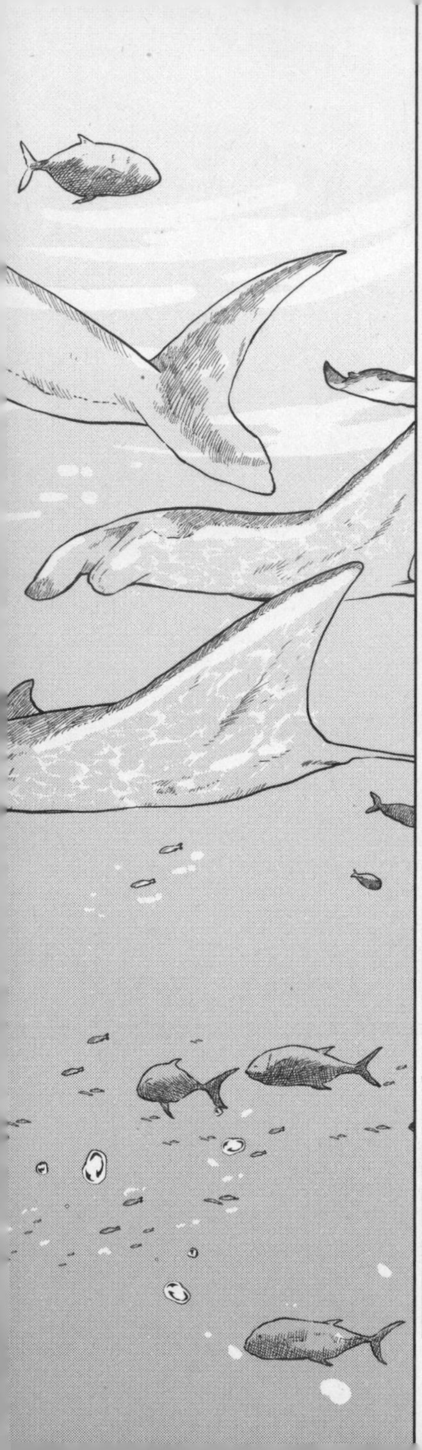

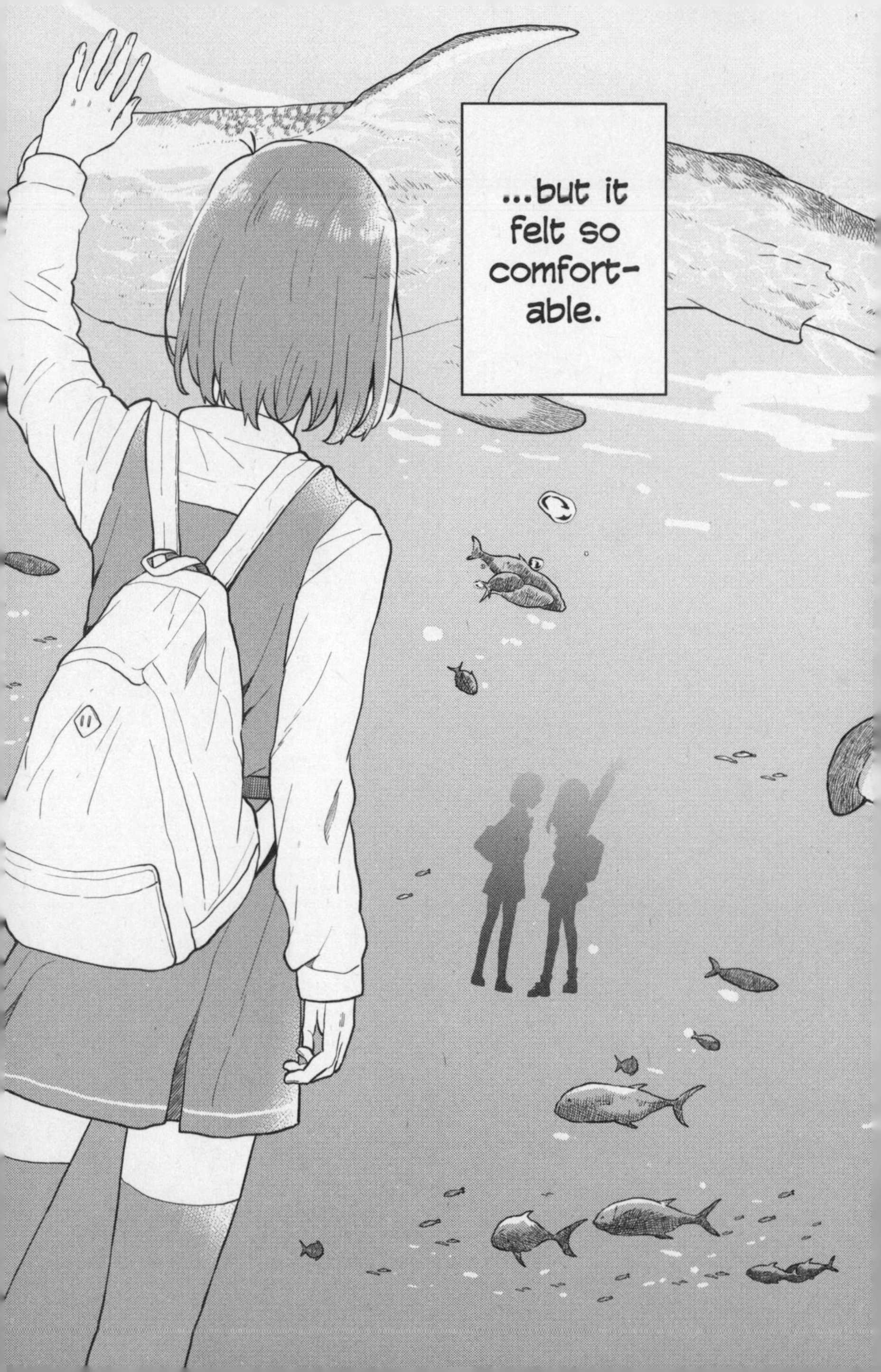
...but it felt so comfort-able.

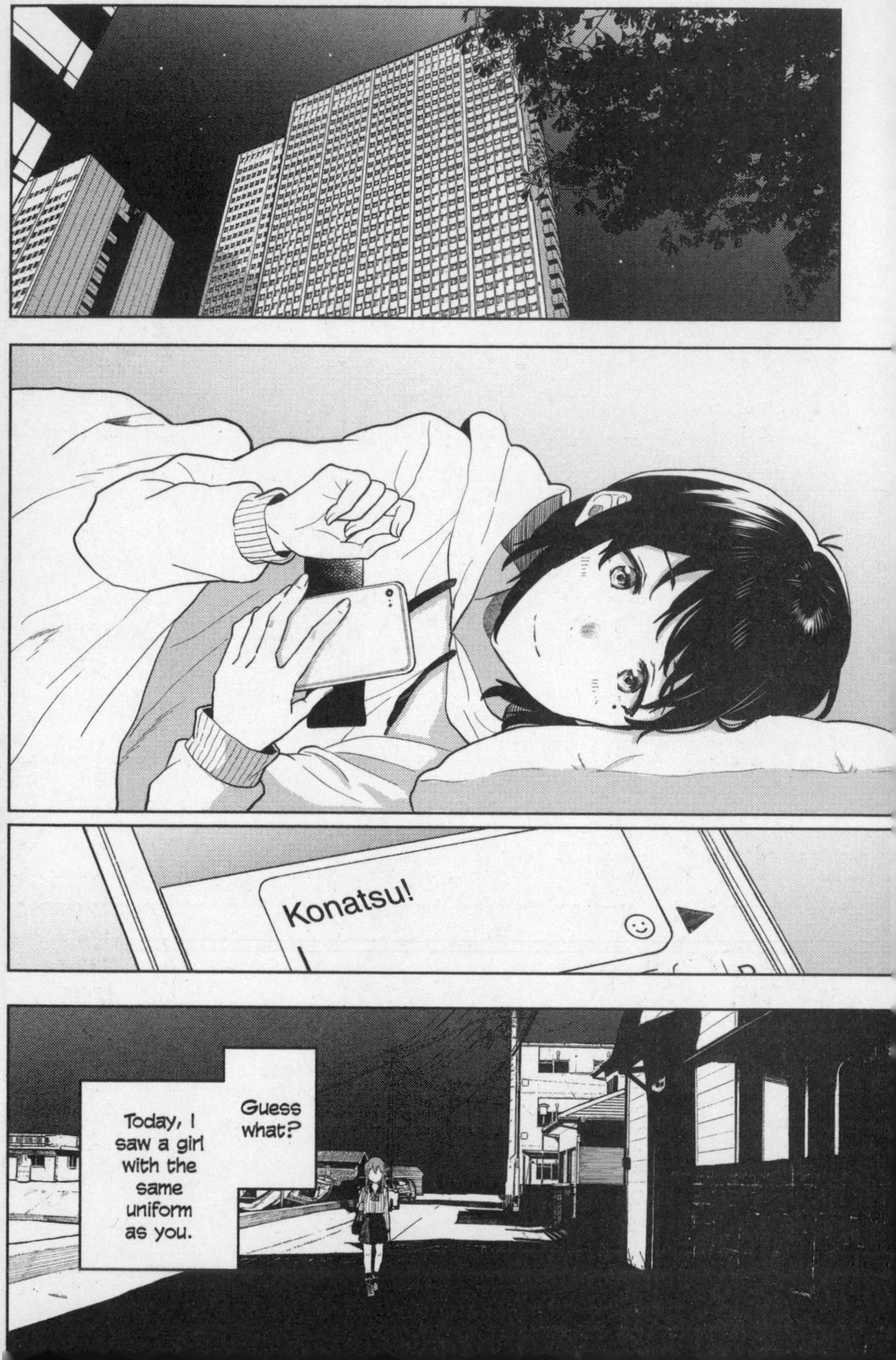
Konatsu!
Guess what?
Today, I saw a girl with the same uniform as you.

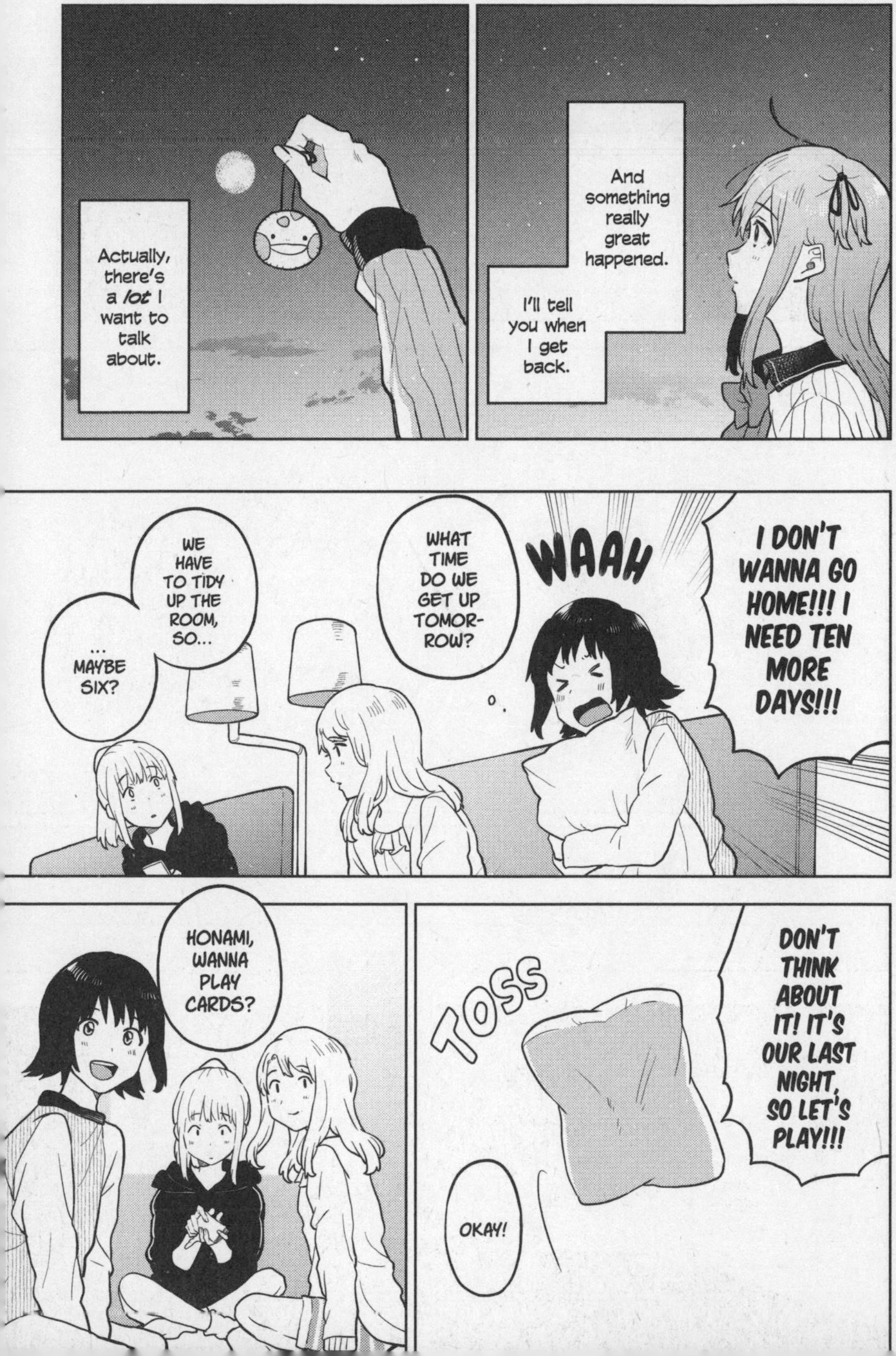
And something really great happened.
I'll tell you when I get back.
Actually, there's a *lot* I want to talk about.
I DON'T WANNA GO HOME!!! I NEED TEN MORE DAYS!!!
WAAH
WHAT TIME DO WE GET UP TOMOR-ROW?
WE HAVE TO TIDY UP THE ROOM, SO...
... MAYBE SIX?
DON'T THINK ABOUT IT! IT'S OUR LAST NIGHT, SO LET'S PLAY!!!
TOSS
OKAY!
HONAMI, WANNA PLAY CARDS?

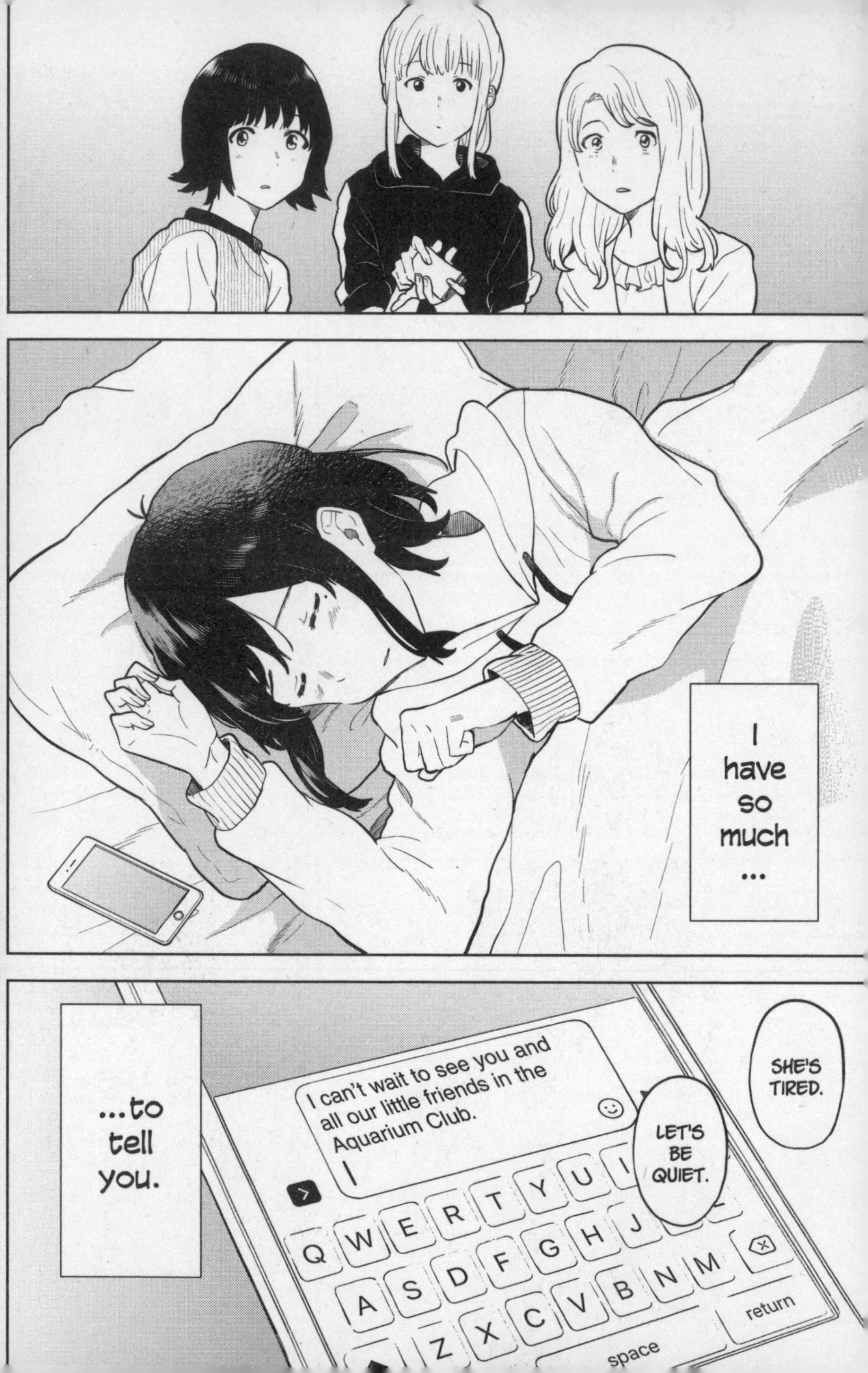
I have so much...
SHE'S TIRED.
LET'S BE QUIET.
I can't wait to see you and all our little friends in the Aquarium Club.
...to tell you.

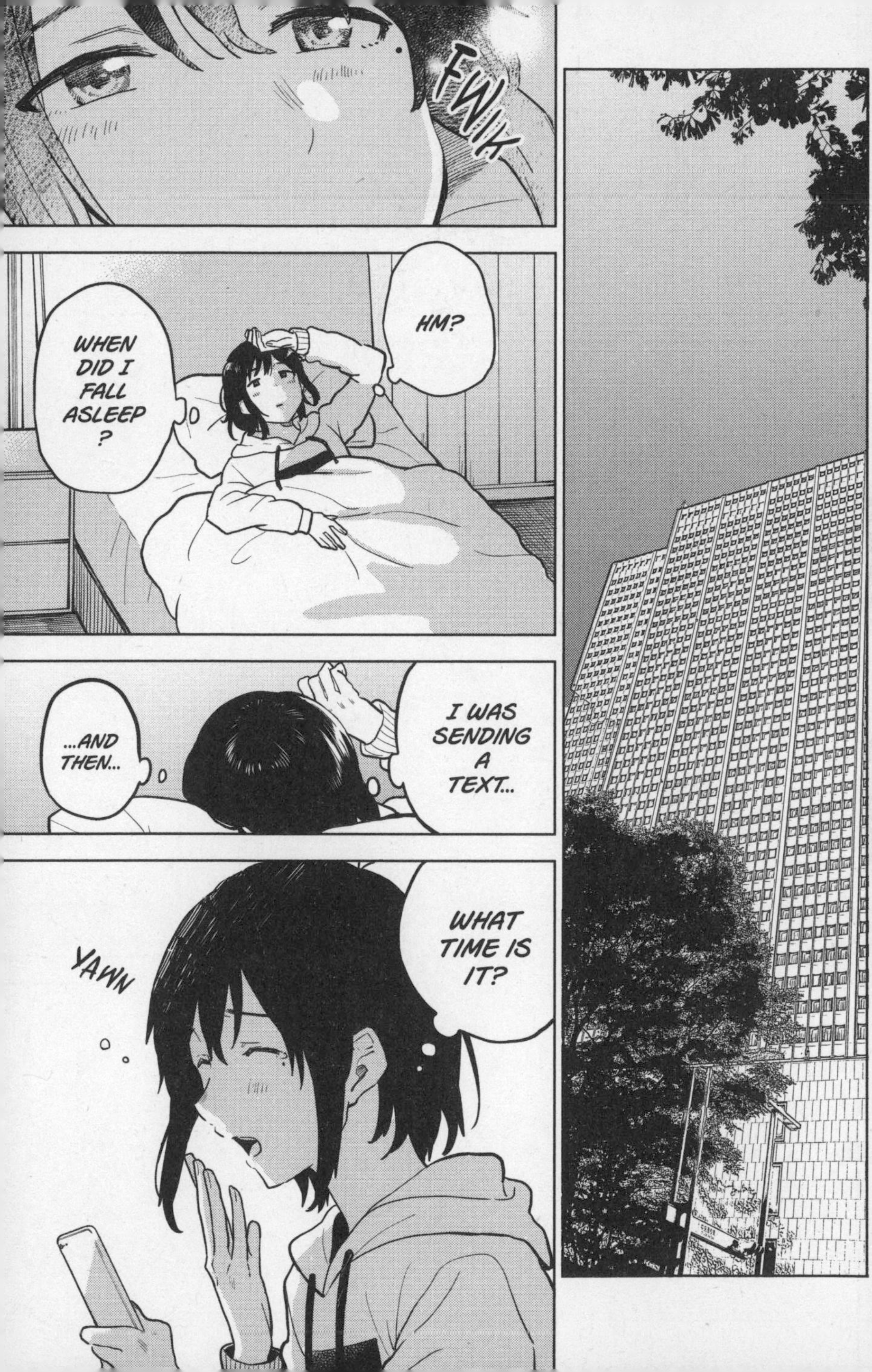
FWIP
HM?
WHEN DID I FALL ASLEEP?
I WAS SENDING A TEXT...
...AND THEN...
WHAT TIME IS IT?
YAWN

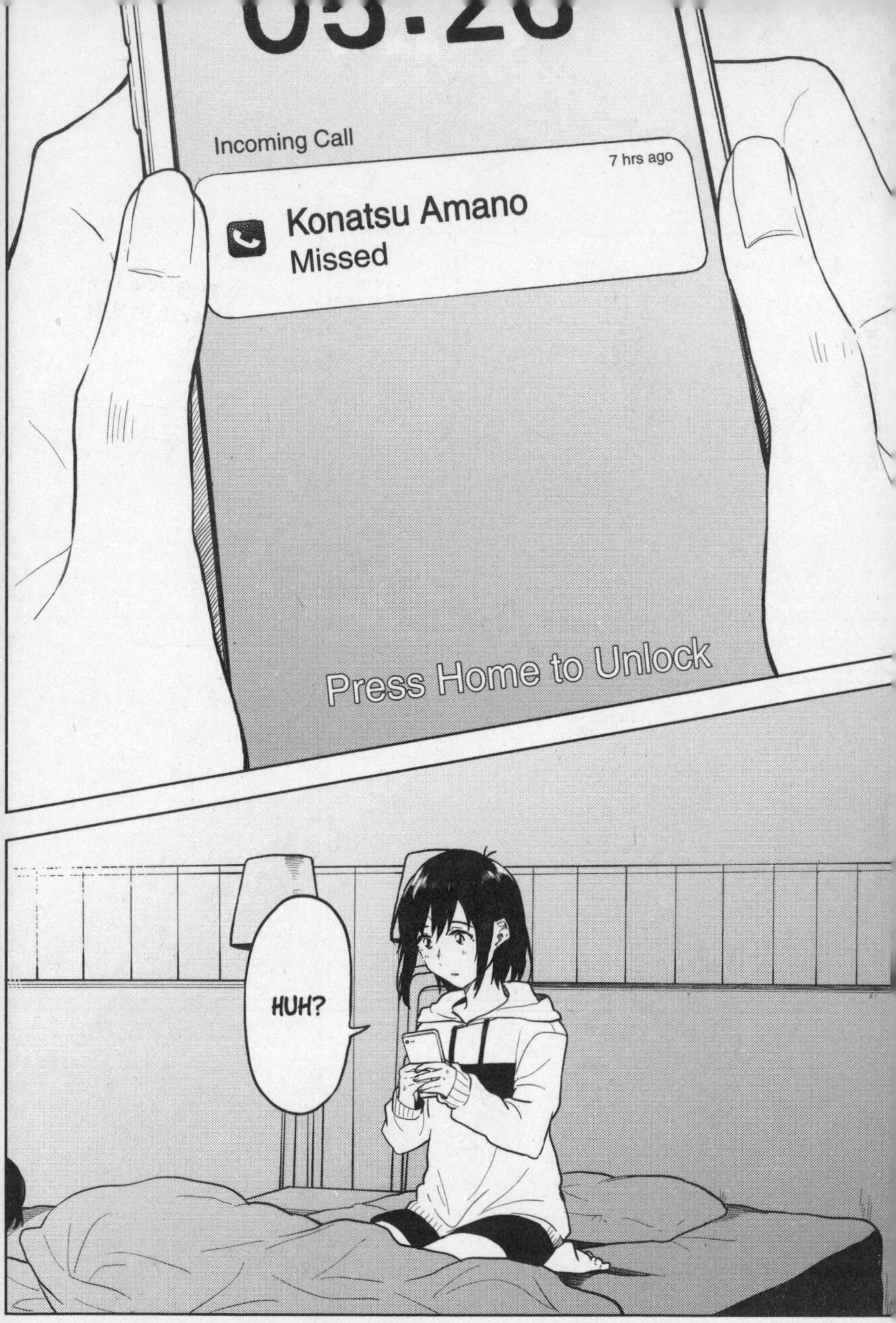
Incoming Call
7 hrs ago
Konatsu Amano
Missed
Press Home to Unlock
HUH?

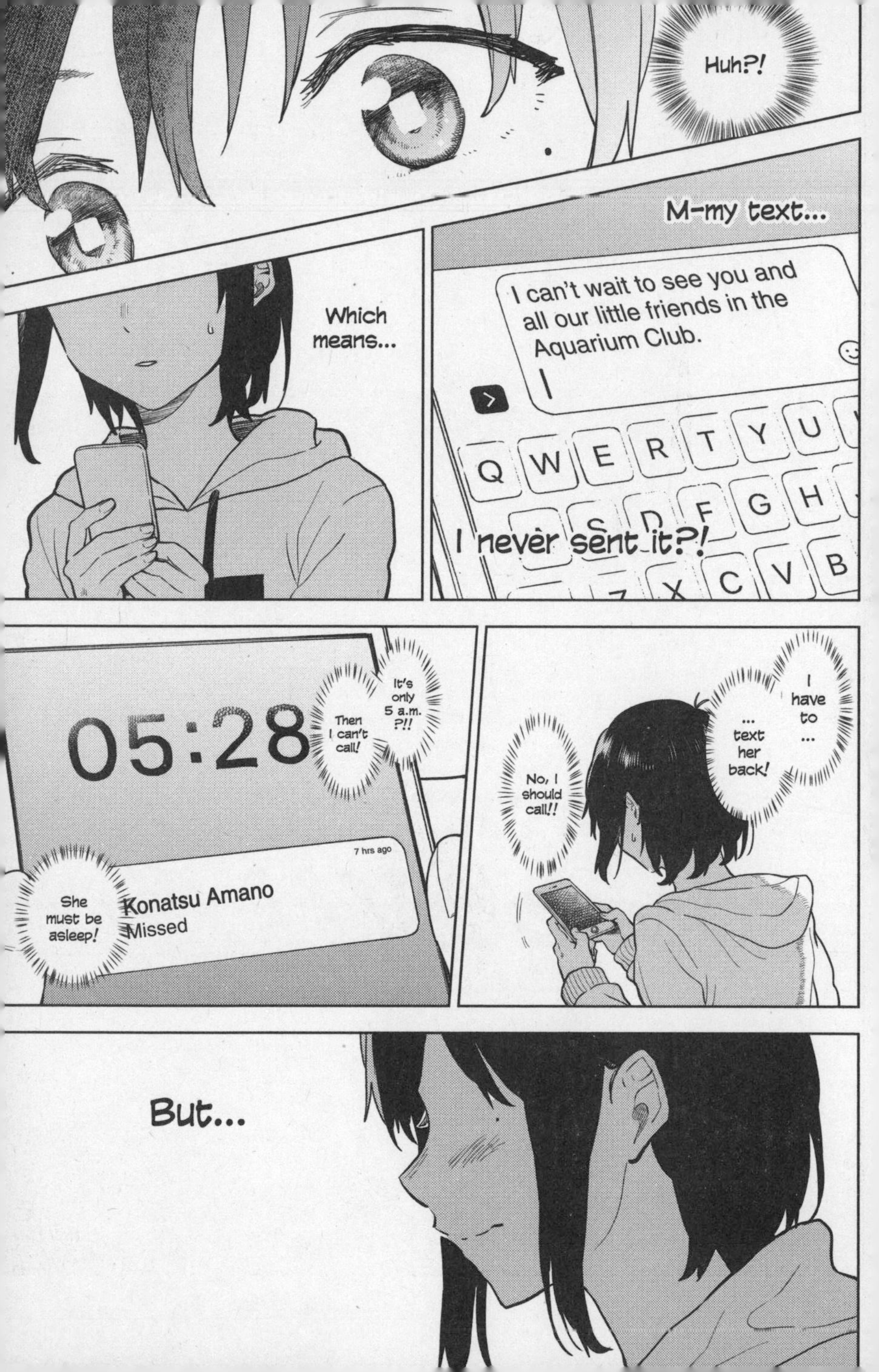

Huh?!
M-my text...
I can't wait to see you and all our little friends in the Aquarium Club.
I never sent it?!
Which means...
I have to ... text her back!
No, I should call!!
05:28
It's only 5 a.m. ?!!
Then I can't call!
7 hrs ago
Konatsu Amano
Missed
She must be asleep!
But...

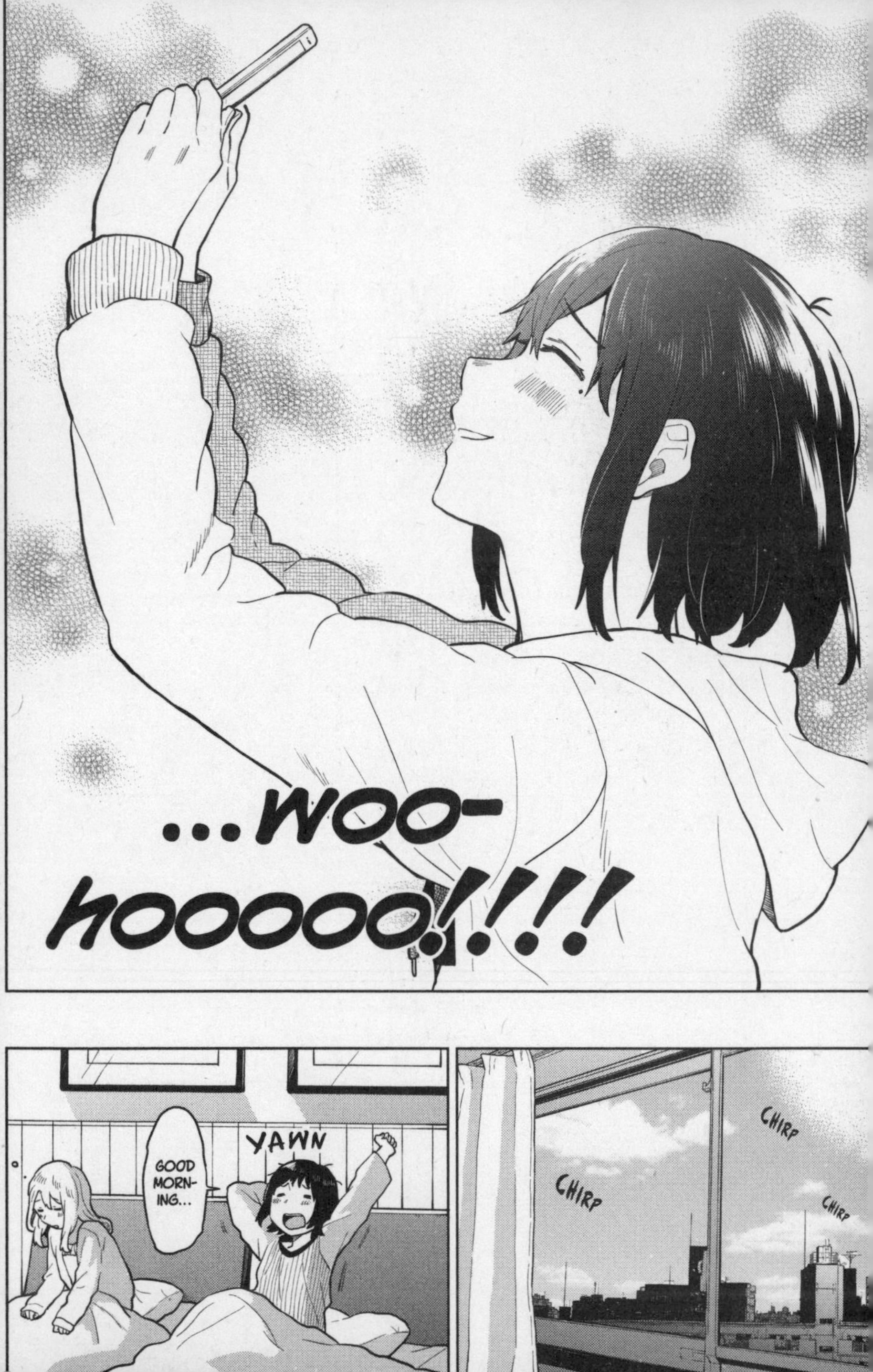
...WOO-HOOOOOO!!!!
CHIRP
CHIRP
CHIRP
YAWN
GOOD MORNING...

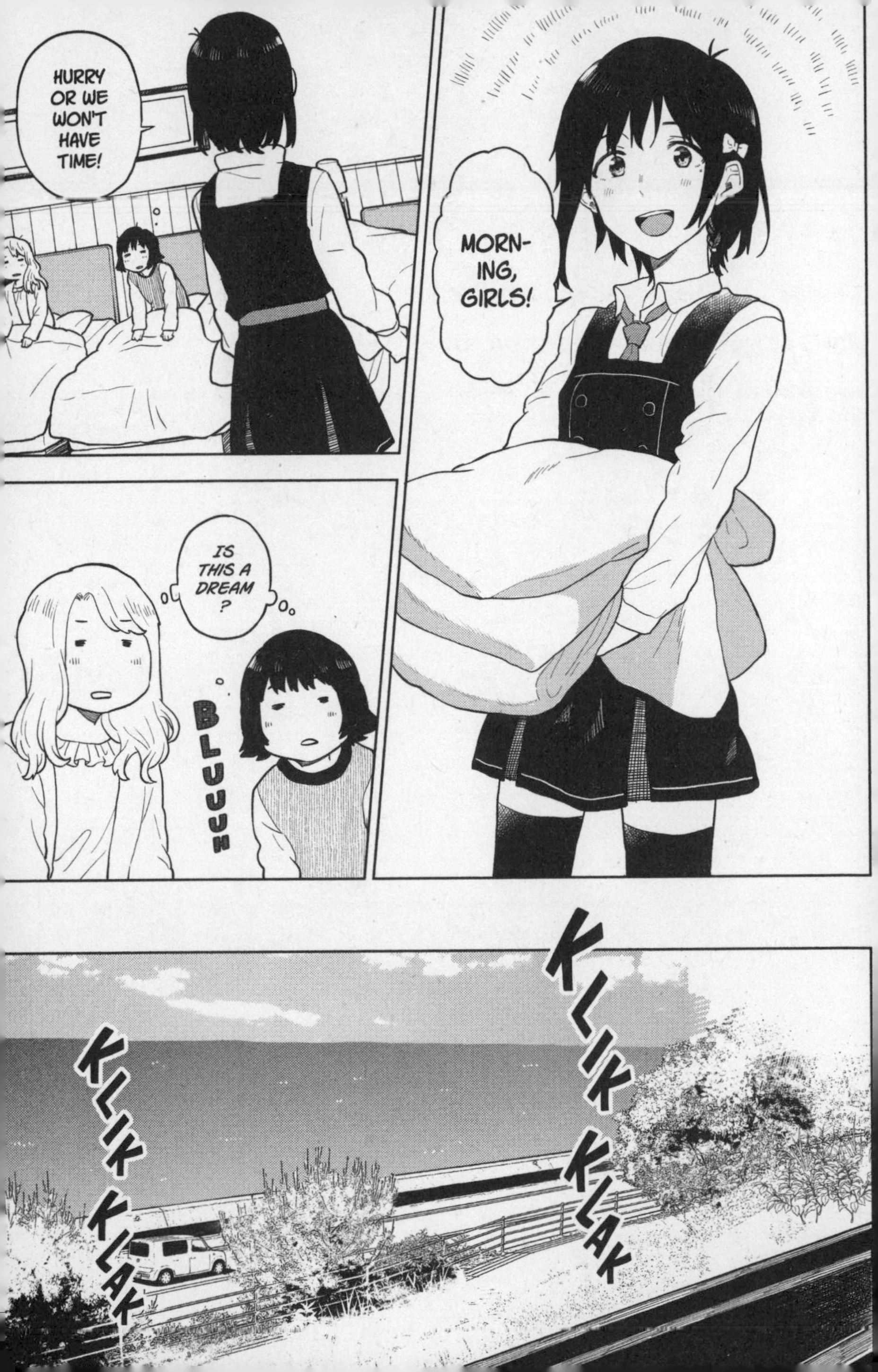
MORNING, GIRLS!
HURRY OR WE WON'T HAVE TIME!
IS THIS A DREAM?
BLUUUH
KLIK KLAK
KLIK KLAK

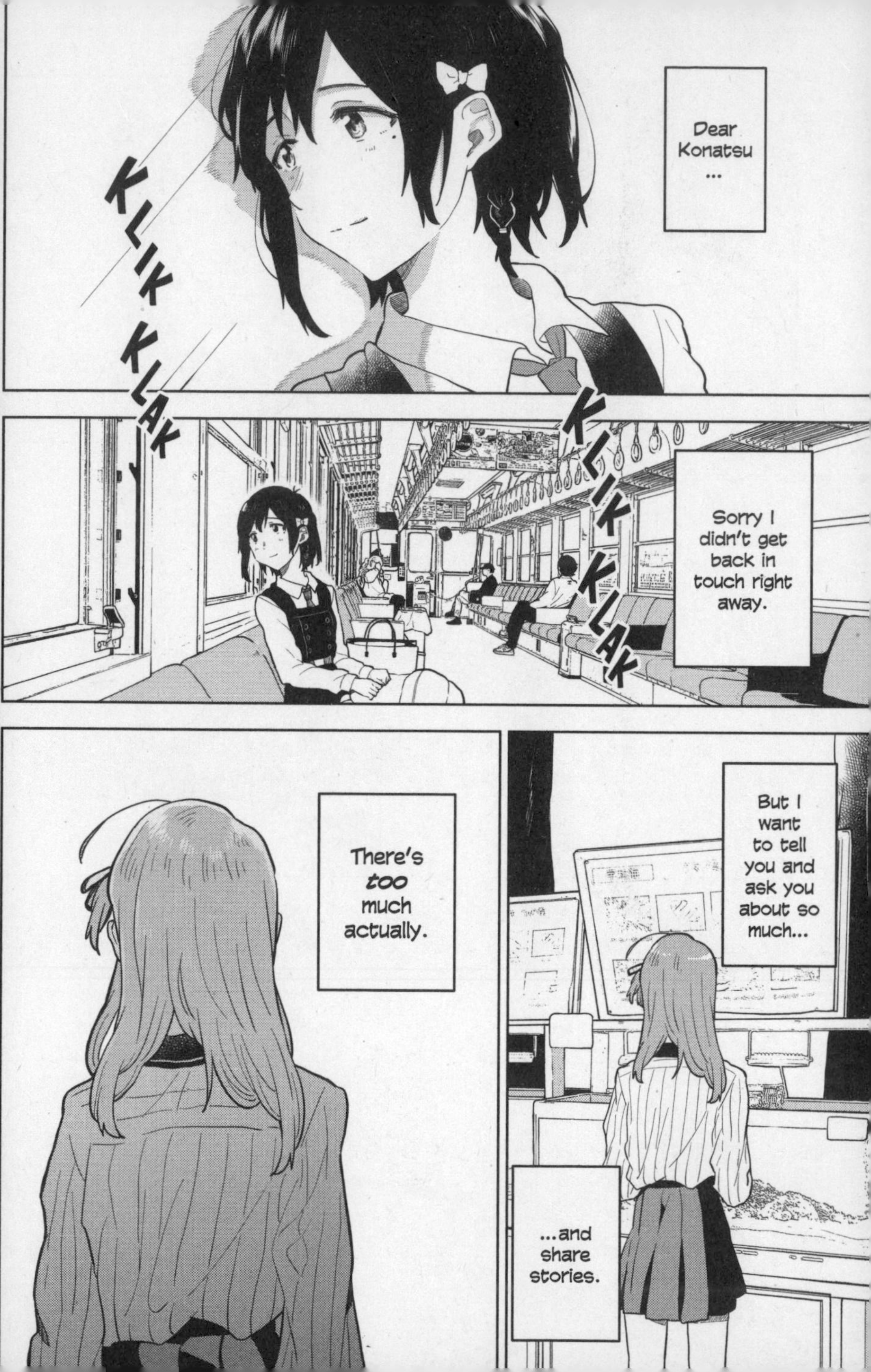
Dear Konatsu ...
KLIK KLAK
Sorry I didn't get back in touch right away.
KLIK KLAK
But I want to tell you and ask you about so much...
...and share stories.
There's *too* much actually.

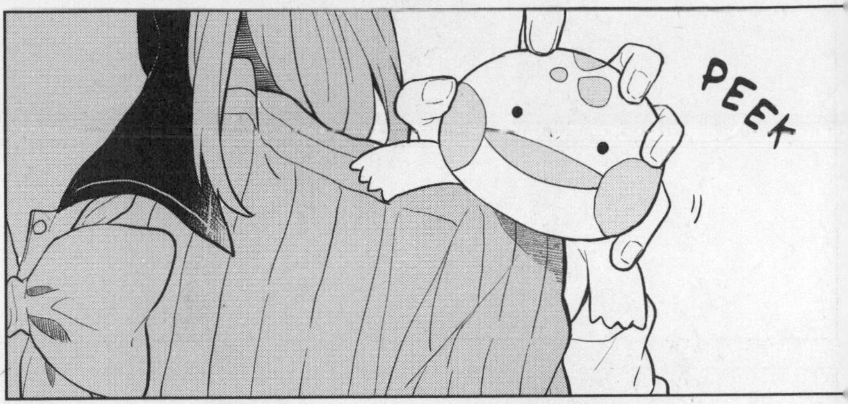
PEEK
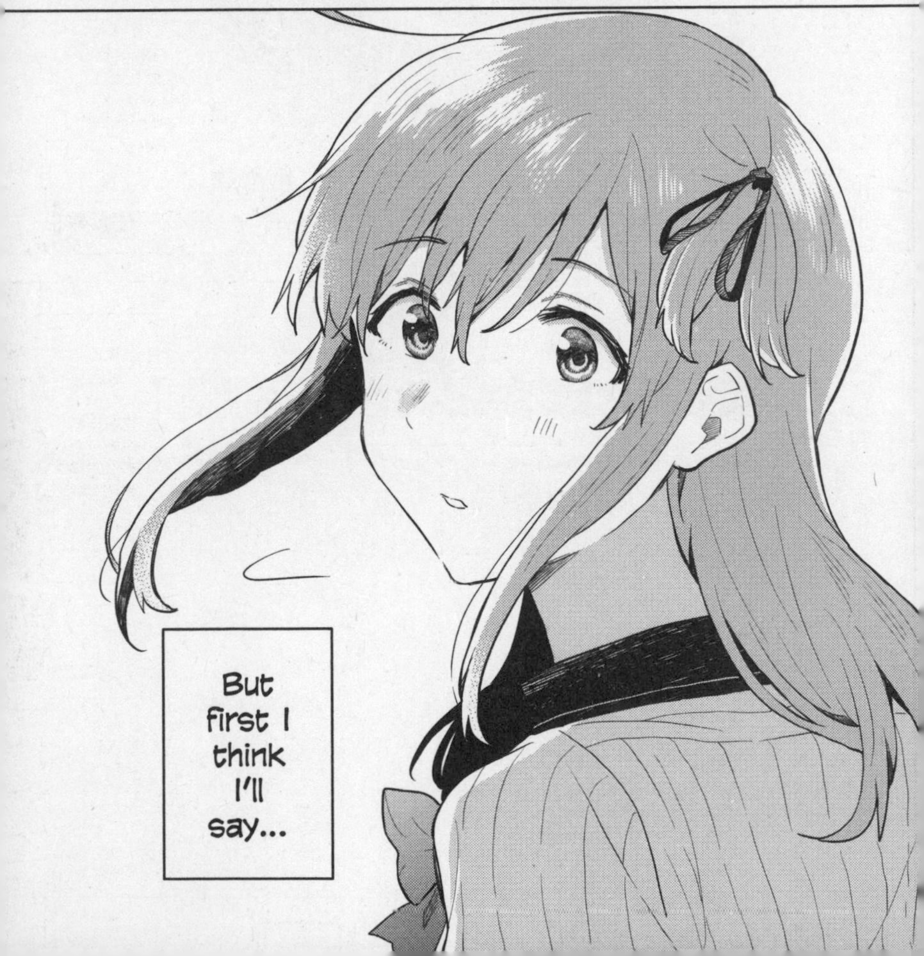
But first I think I'll say...

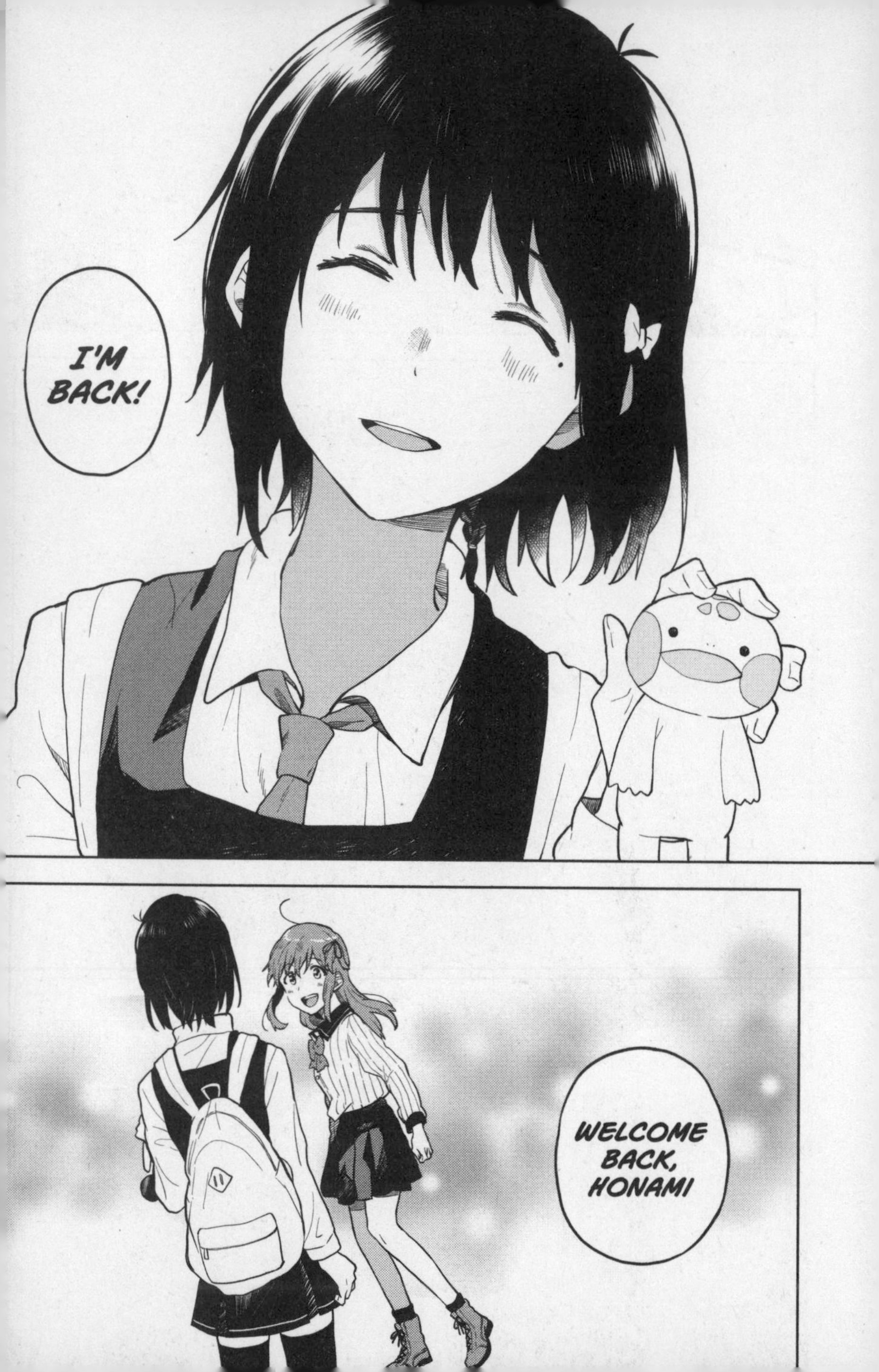
I'M BACK!
WELCOME BACK, HONAMI

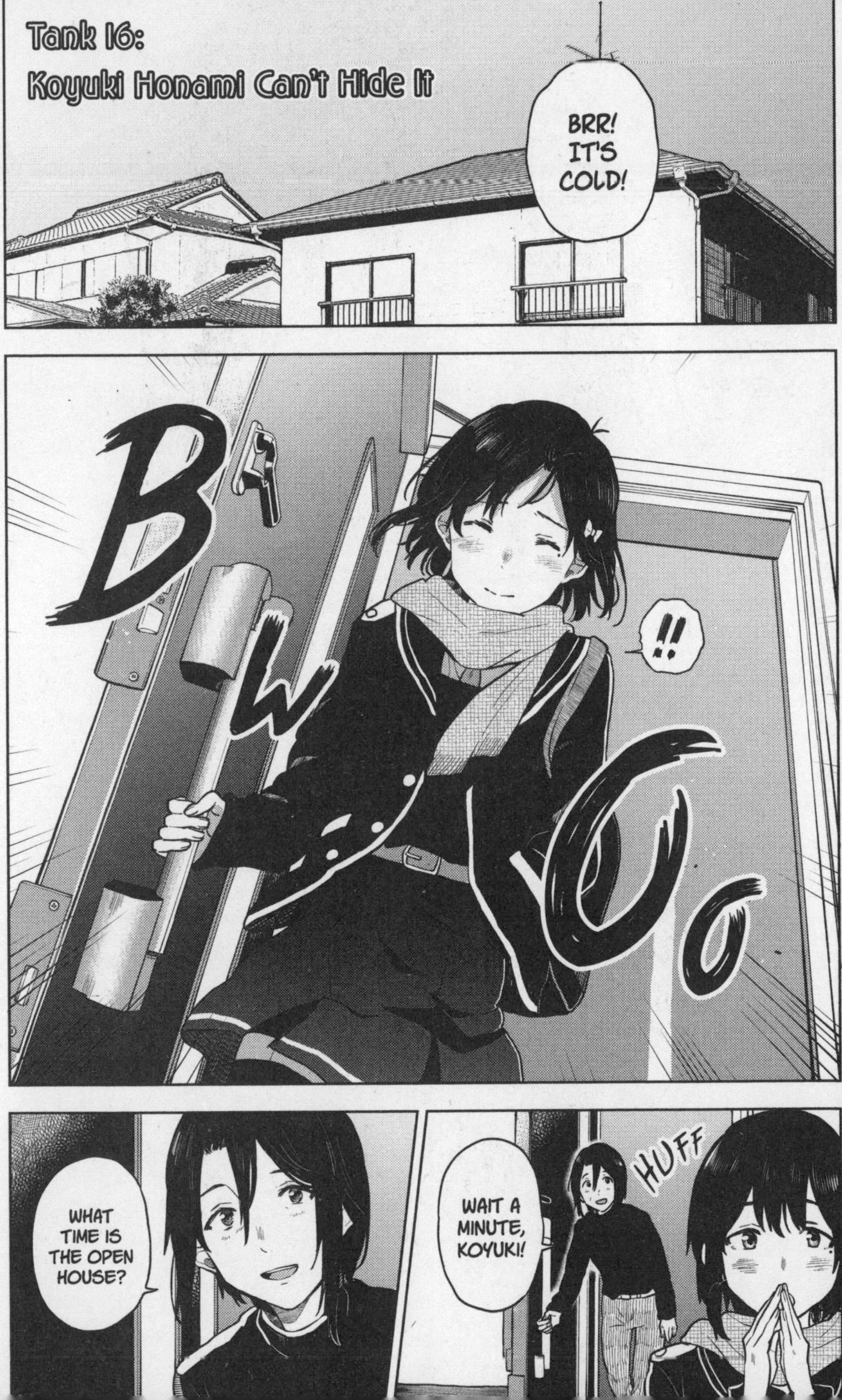
Tank 16:
Koyuki Honami Can't Hide It
BRR! IT'S COLD!
BWOO
!!
HUFF
WAIT A MINUTE, KOYUKI!
WHAT TIME IS THE OPEN HOUSE?

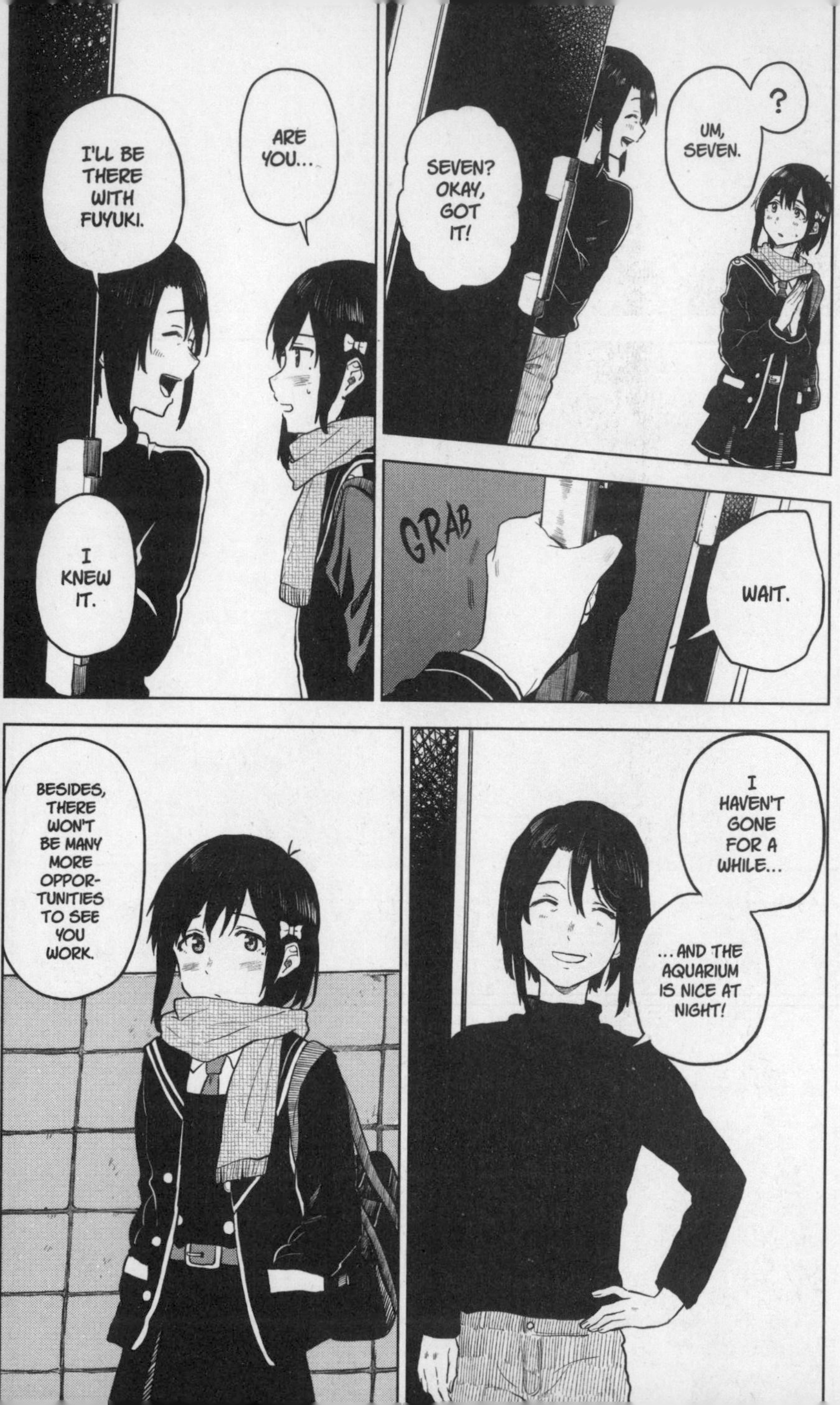
?
UM, SEVEN.
SEVEN? OKAY, GOT IT!
WAIT.
GRAB
ARE YOU...
I'LL BE THERE WITH FUYUKI.
I KNEW IT.
I HAVEN'T GONE FOR A WHILE...
...AND THE AQUARIUM IS NICE AT NIGHT!
BESIDES, THERE WON'T BE MANY MORE OPPOR-TUNITIES TO SEE YOU WORK.

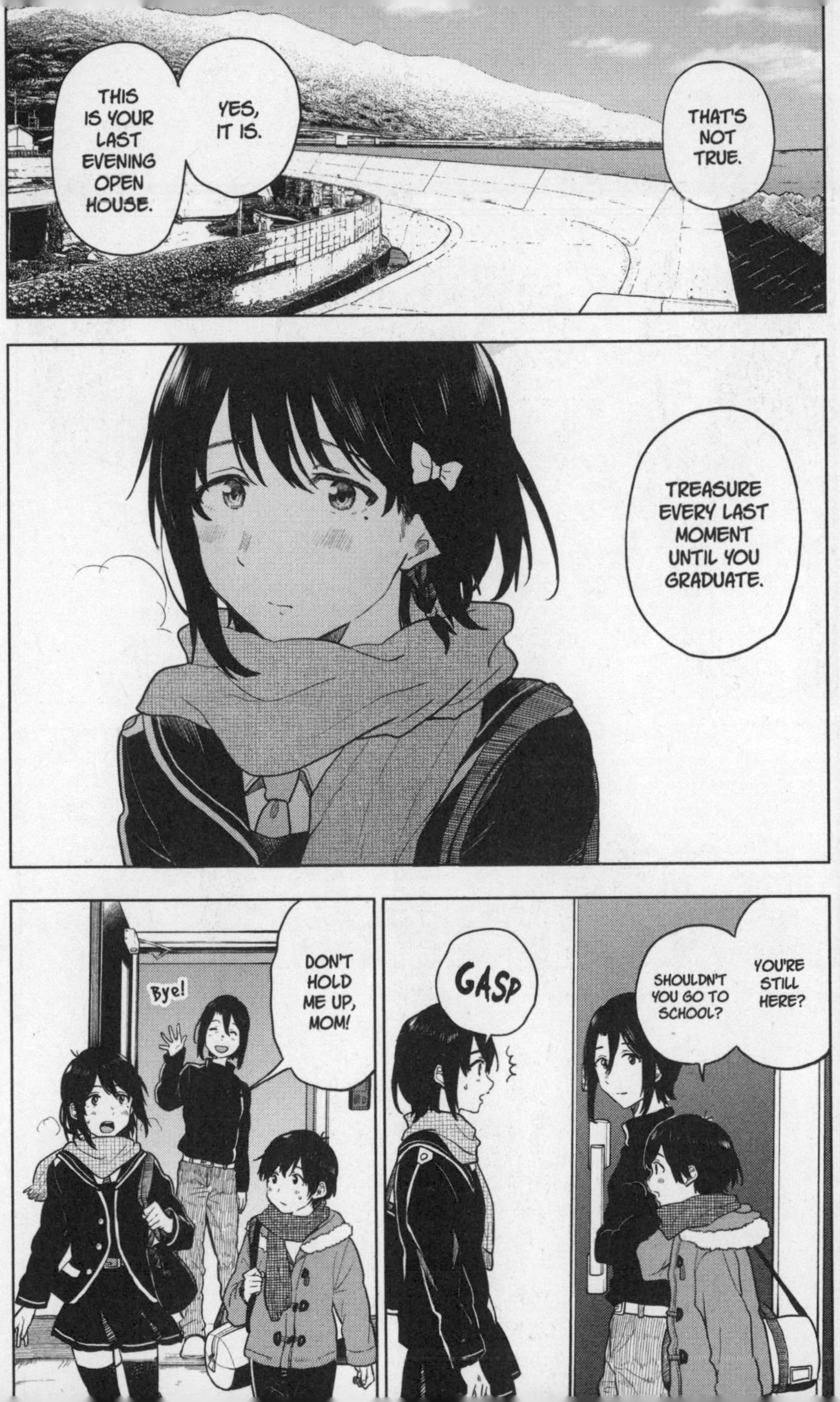
THAT'S NOT TRUE.
YES, IT IS.
THIS IS YOUR LAST EVENING OPEN HOUSE.
TREASURE EVERY LAST MOMENT UNTIL YOU GRADUATE.
YOU'RE STILL HERE?
SHOULDN'T YOU GO TO SCHOOL?
GASP
DON'T HOLD ME UP, MOM!
Bye!

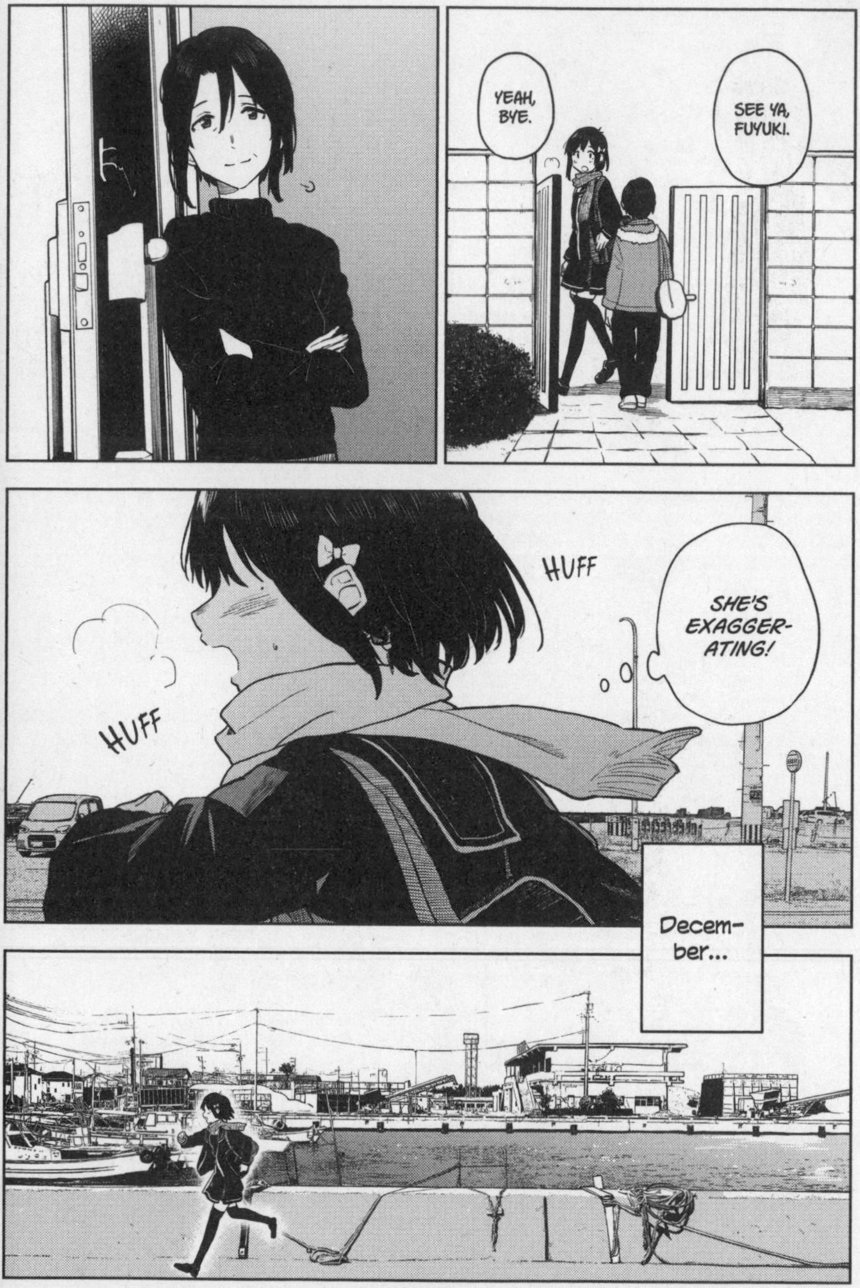
SEE YA, FUYUKI.
YEAH, BYE.
HUFF
SHE'S EXAGGER-ATING!
HUFF
Decem-ber...

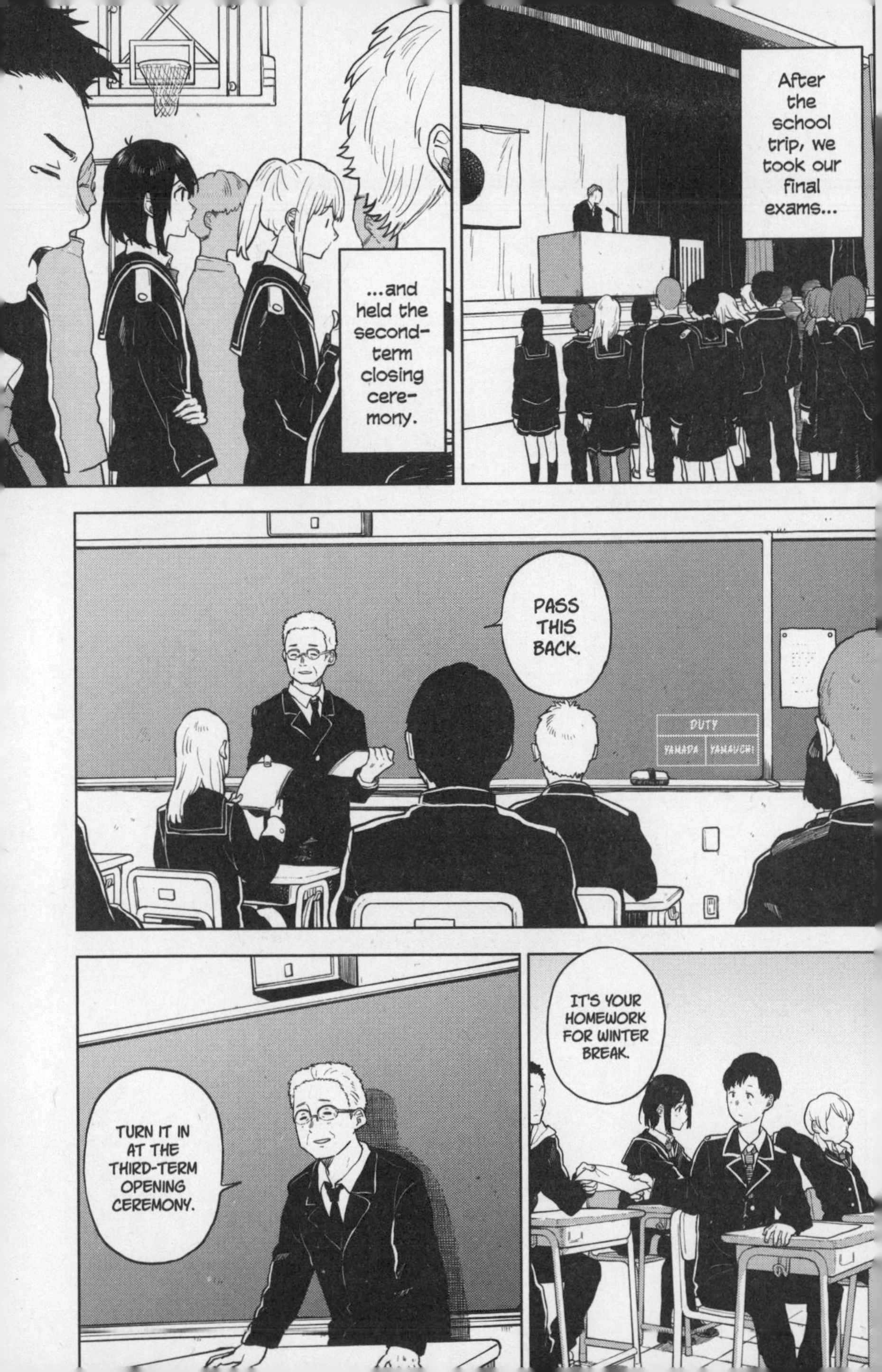
After the school trip, we took our final exams...
...and held the second-term closing ceremony.
PASS THIS BACK.
DUTY
YAMADA
YAMAUCHI
IT'S YOUR HOMEWORK FOR WINTER BREAK.
TURN IT IN AT THE THIRD-TERM OPENING CEREMONY.

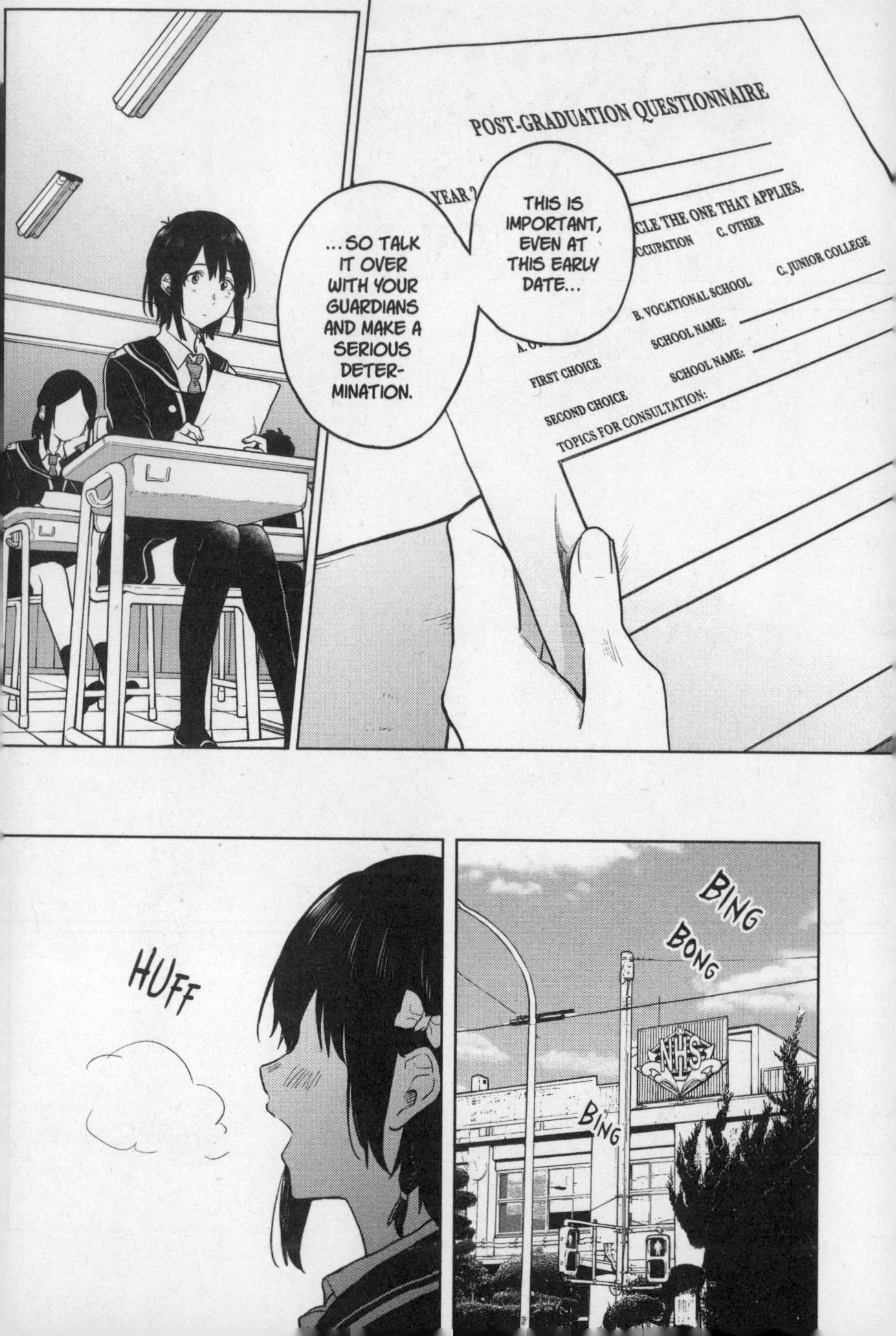
POST-GRADUATION QUESTIONNAIRE
YEAR
CLE THE ONE THAT APPLIES.
CCUPATION C. OTHER
B. VOCATIONAL SCHOOL C. JUNIOR COLLEGE
SCHOOL NAME:
FIRST CHOICE
SECOND CHOICE SCHOOL NAME:
TOPICS FOR CONSULTATION:
THIS IS IMPORTANT, EVEN AT THIS EARLY DATE...
...SO TALK IT OVER WITH YOUR GUARDIANS AND MAKE A SERIOUS DETER-MINATION.
BING BONG
BING
NHS
HUFF

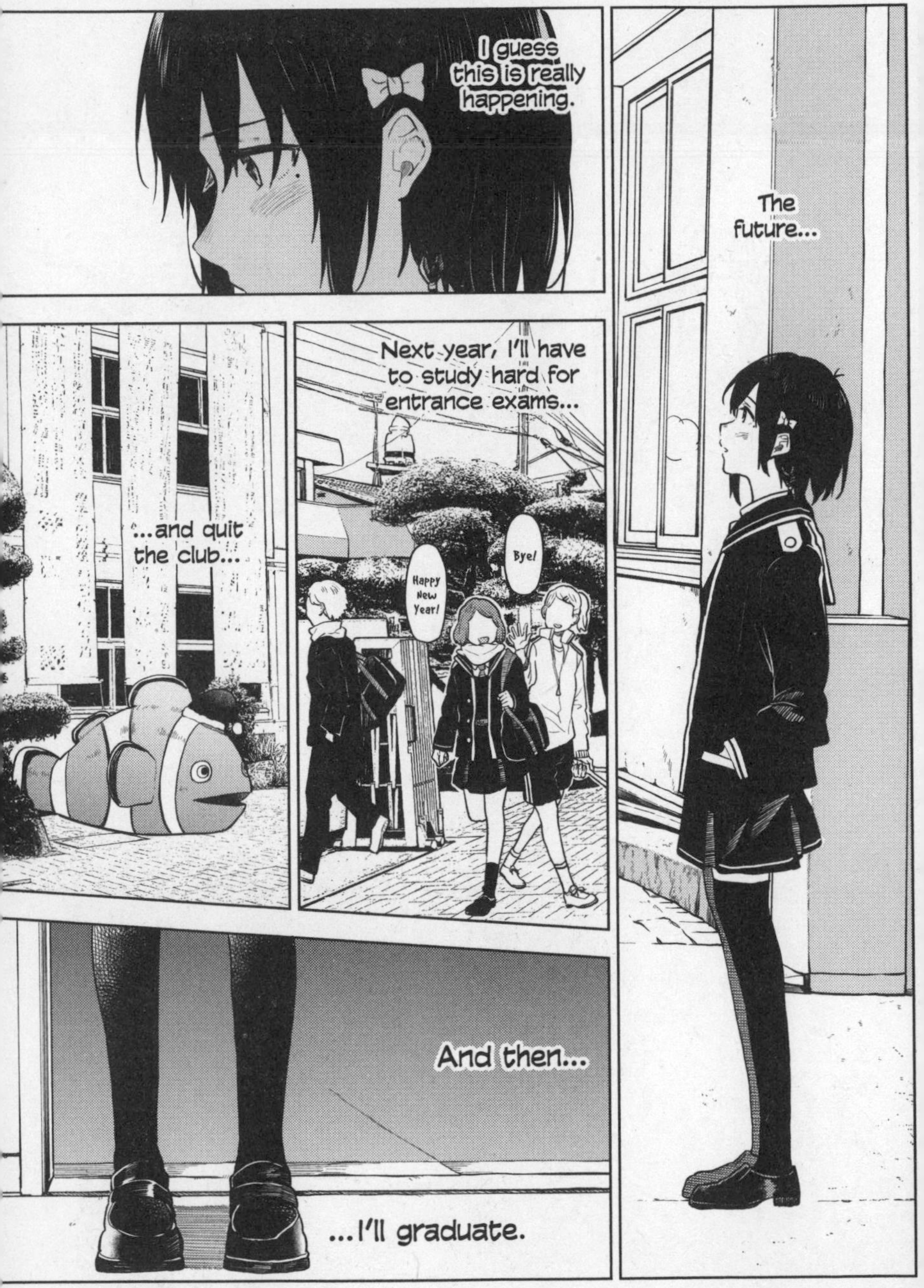
The future...
I guess this is really happening.
Next year, I'll have to study hard for entrance exams...
Bye!
Happy New Year!
...and quit the club...
And then...
...I'll graduate.

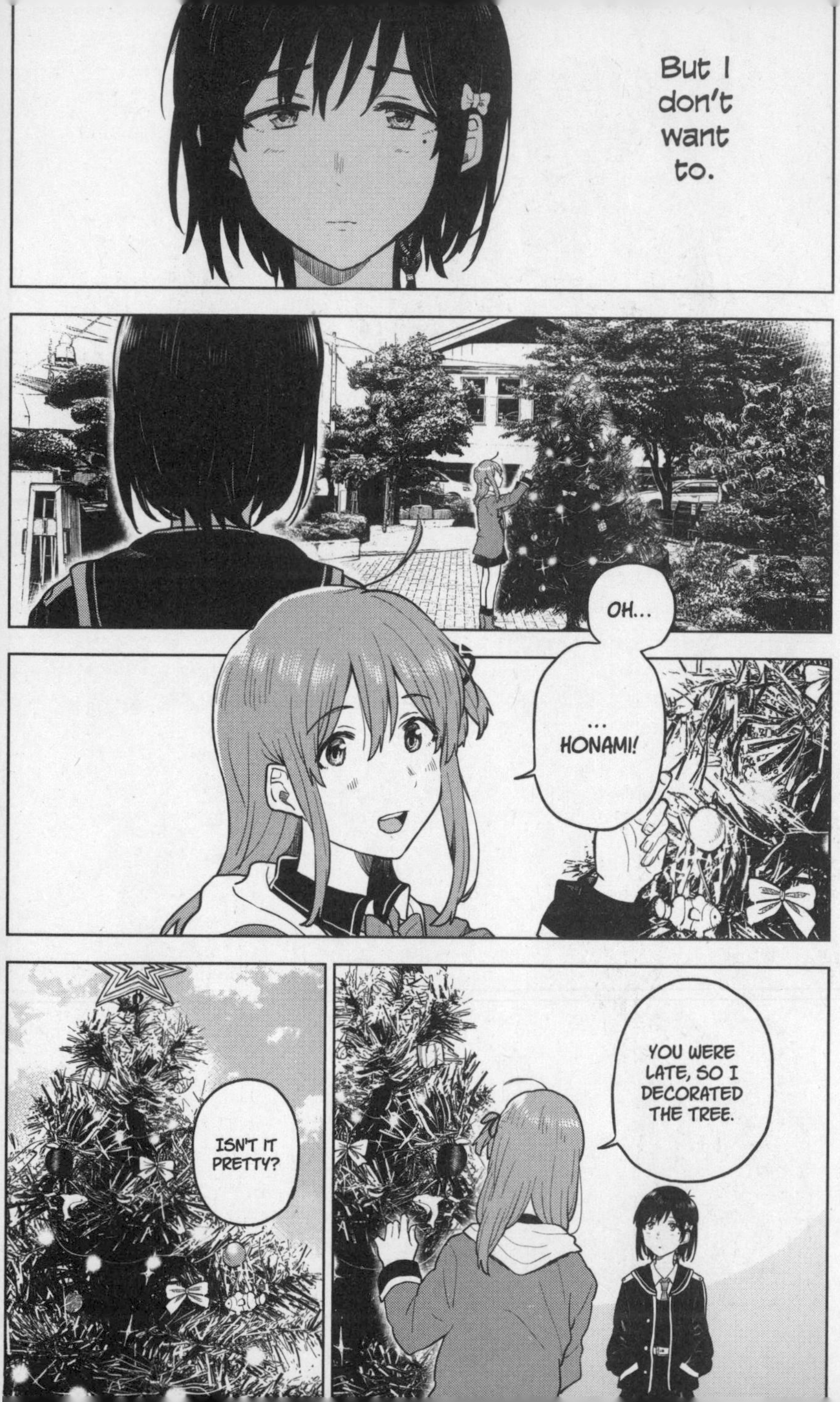
But I don't want to.
OH...
... HONAMI!
YOU WERE LATE, SO I DECORATED THE TREE.
ISN'T IT PRETTY?

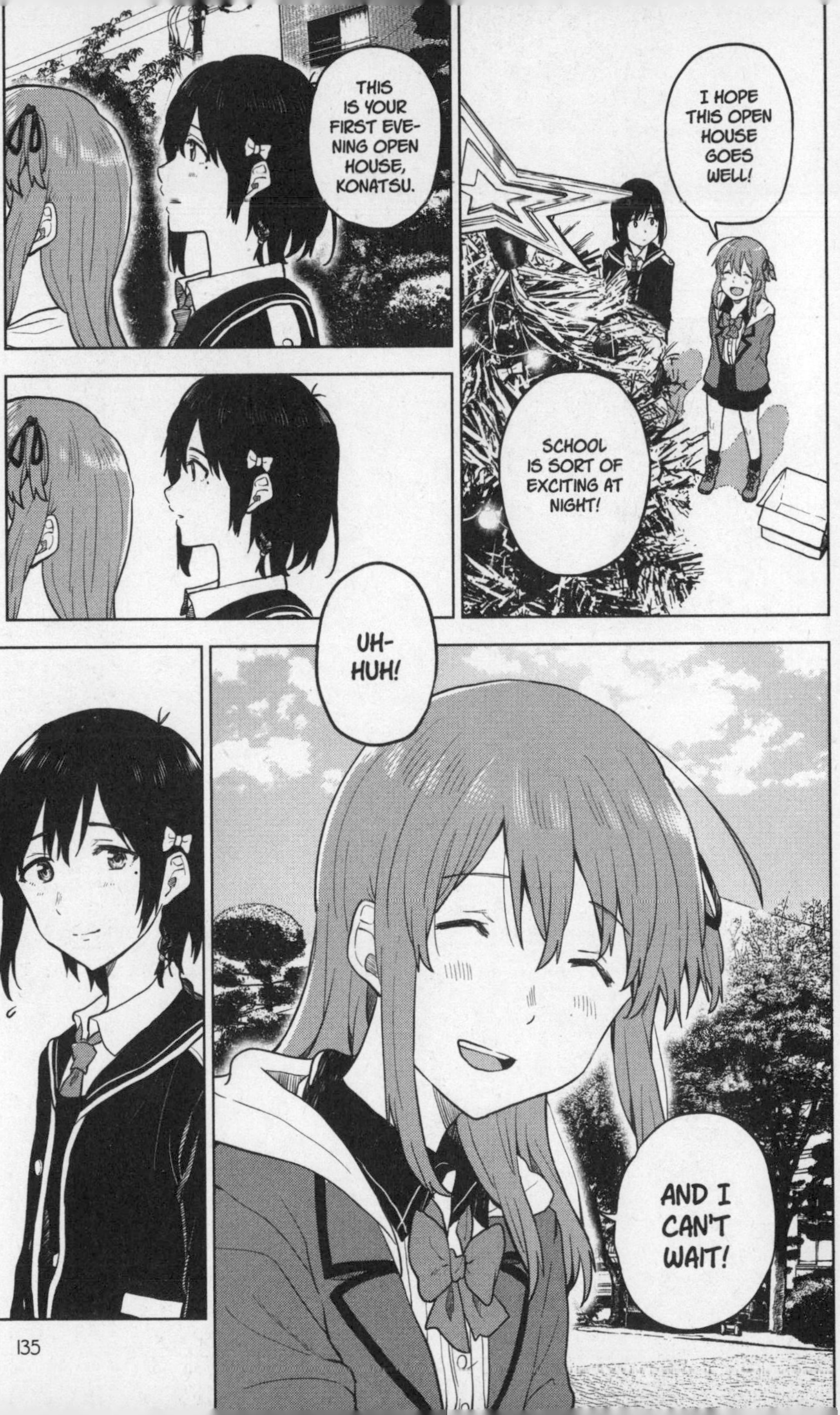
I HOPE THIS OPEN HOUSE GOES WELL!
SCHOOL IS SORT OF EXCITING AT NIGHT!
THIS IS YOUR FIRST EVENING OPEN HOUSE, KONATSU.
UH-HUH!
AND I CAN'T WAIT!

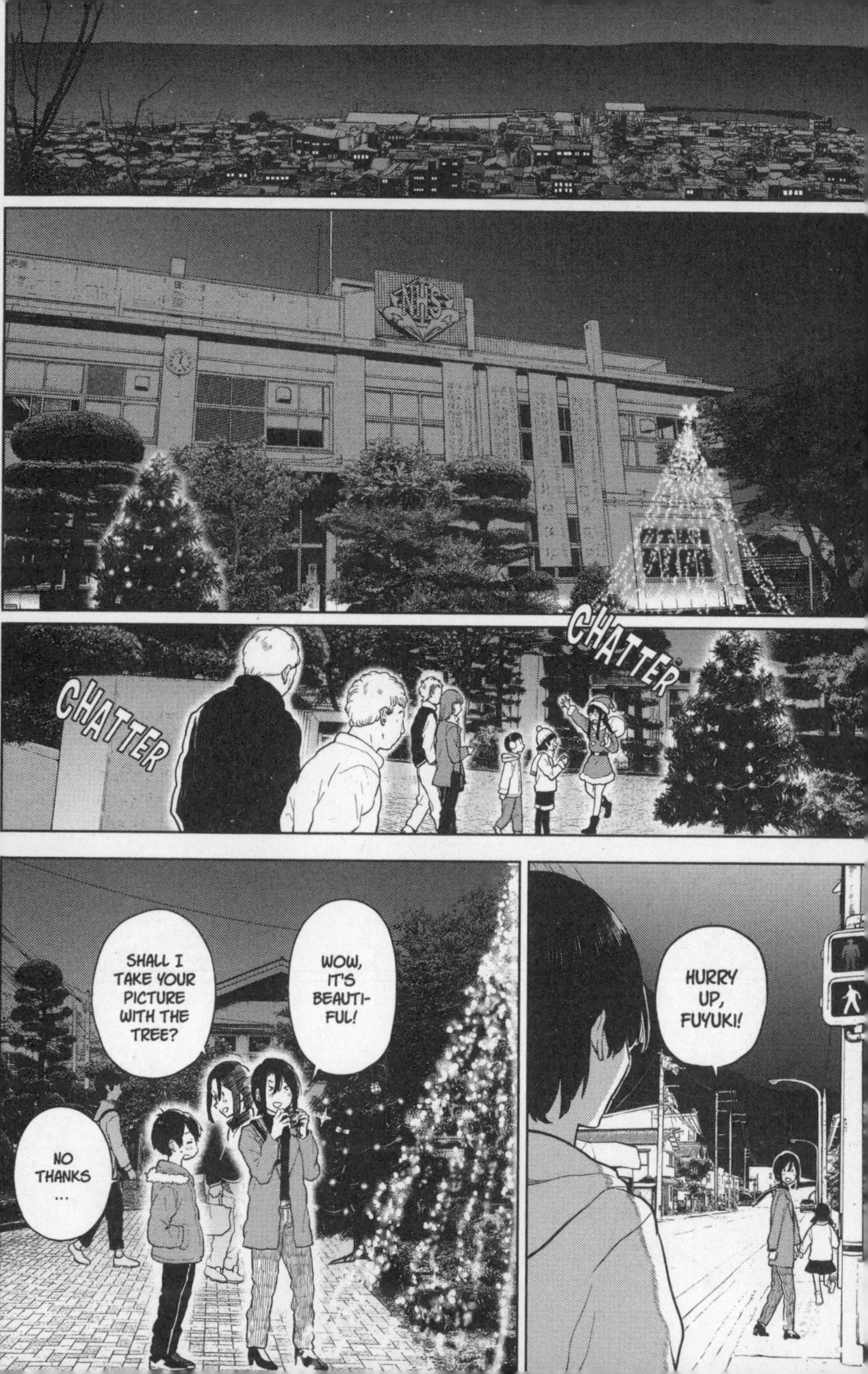
CHATTER
CHATTER
HURRY UP, FUYUKI!
WOW, IT'S BEAUTI-FUL!
SHALL I TAKE YOUR PICTURE WITH THE TREE?
NO THANKS ...

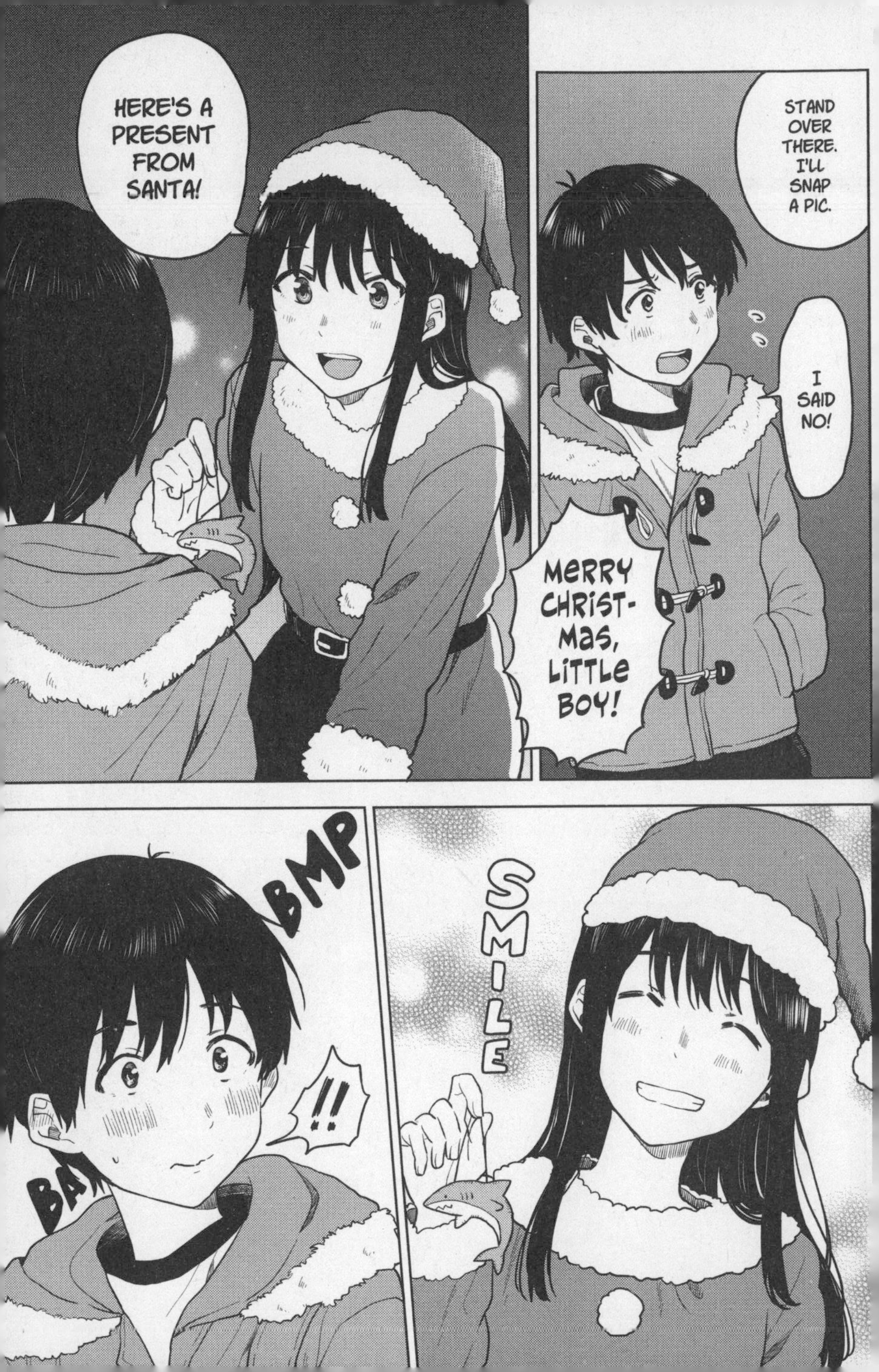
STAND OVER THERE. I'LL SNAP A PIC.
I SAID NO!
HERE'S A PRESENT FROM SANTA!
MERRY CHRIST-MAS, LITTLE BOY!
SMILE
BMP
!!
BA

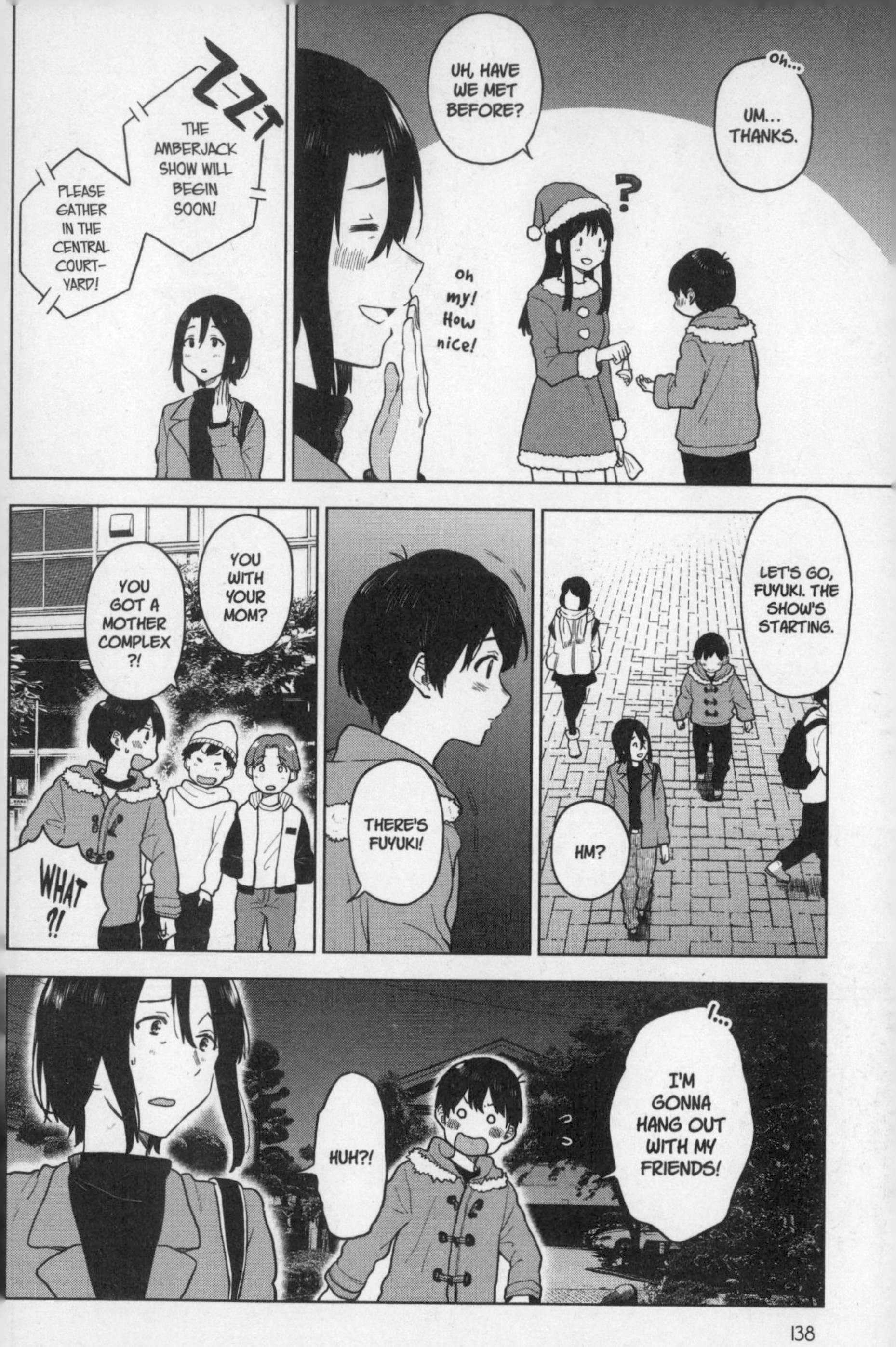
Oh...
UM... THANKS.
?
UH, HAVE WE MET BEFORE?
Oh my! How nice!
Z-Z-T
THE AMBERJACK SHOW WILL BEGIN SOON!
PLEASE GATHER IN THE CENTRAL COURT-YARD!
LET'S GO, FUYUKI. THE SHOW'S STARTING.
HM?
THERE'S FUYUKI!
YOU WITH YOUR MOM?
YOU GOT A MOTHER COMPLEX?!
WHAT?!
I...
I'M GONNA HANG OUT WITH MY FRIENDS!
HUH?!

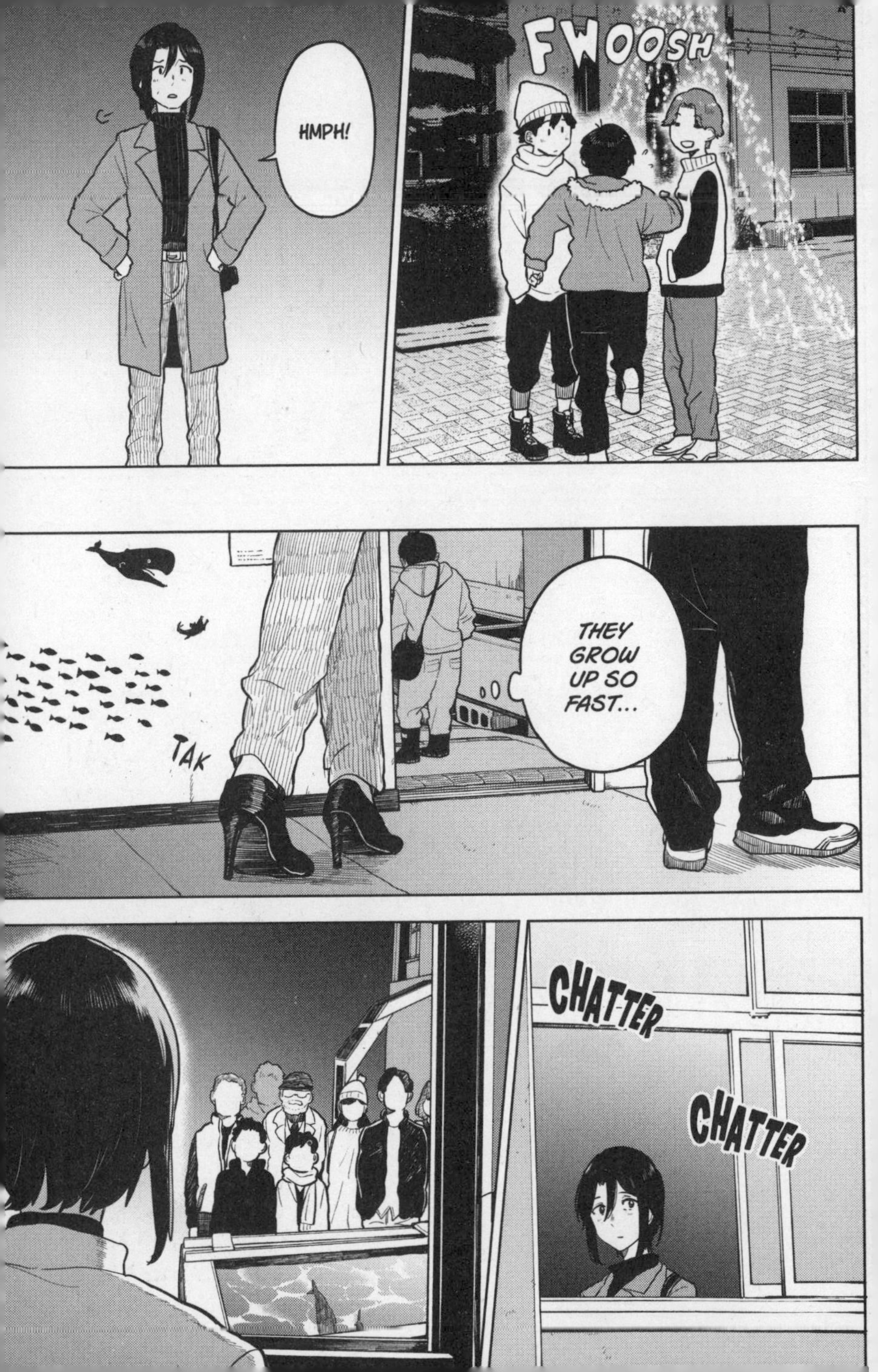
FWOOSH
HMPH!
THEY GROW UP SO FAST...
TAK
CHATTER
CHATTER

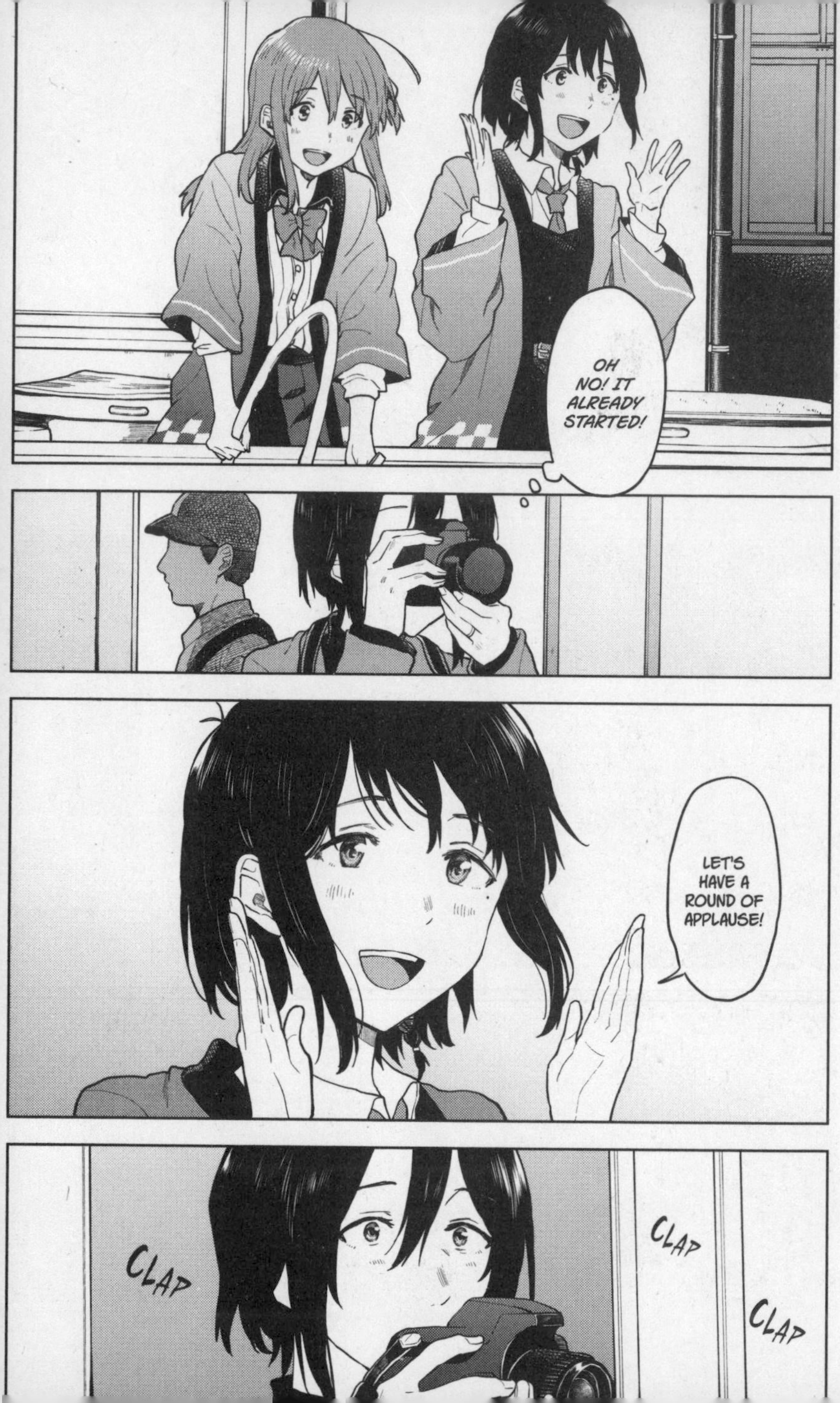
OH NO! IT ALREADY STARTED!
LET'S HAVE A ROUND OF APPLAUSE!
CLAP
CLAP
CLAP

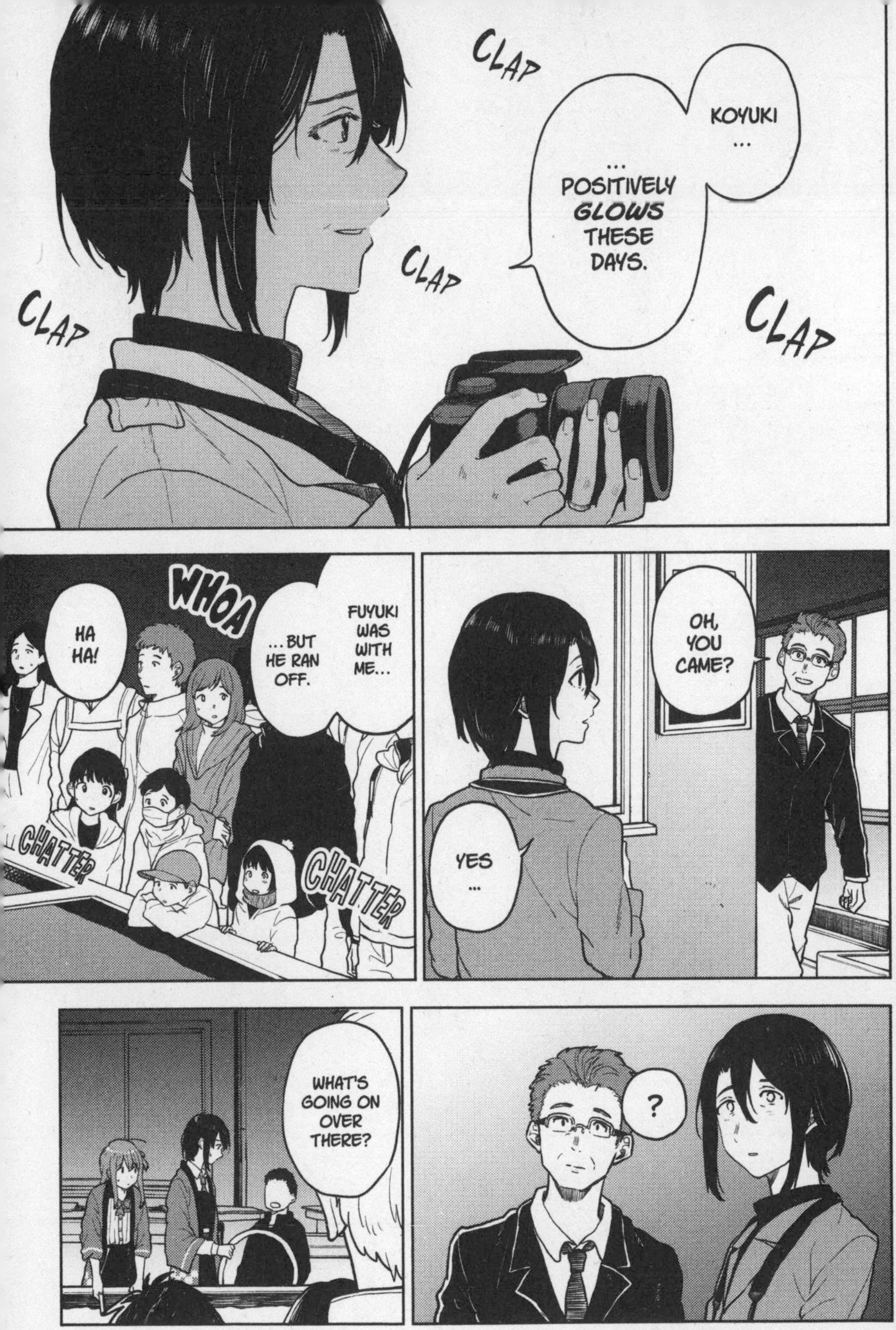
CLAP
KOYUKI ...
... POSITIVELY GLOWS THESE DAYS.
CLAP
CLAP
CLAP
OH, YOU CAME?
YES ...
FUYUKI WAS WITH ME...
...BUT HE RAN OFF.
WHOA
HA HA!
CHATTER
CHATTER
?
WHAT'S GOING ON OVER THERE?

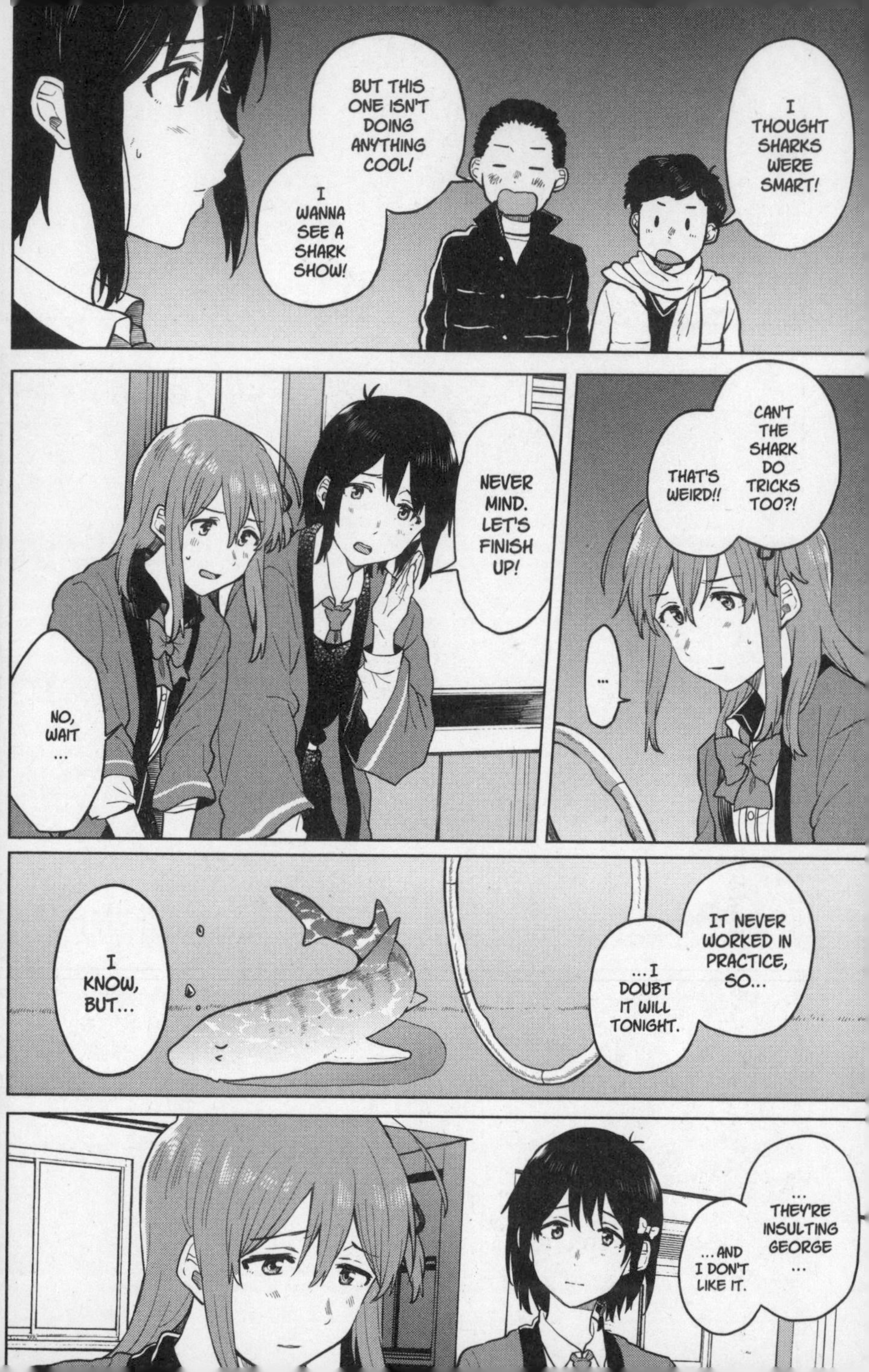
I THOUGHT SHARKS WERE SMART!
BUT THIS ONE ISN'T DOING ANYTHING COOL!
I WANNA SEE A SHARK SHOW!
CAN'T THE SHARK DO TRICKS TOO?!
THAT'S WEIRD!!
...
NEVER MIND. LET'S FINISH UP!
NO, WAIT ...
IT NEVER WORKED IN PRACTICE, SO...
...I DOUBT IT WILL TONIGHT.
I KNOW, BUT...
... THEY'RE INSULTING GEORGE ...
...AND I DON'T LIKE IT.

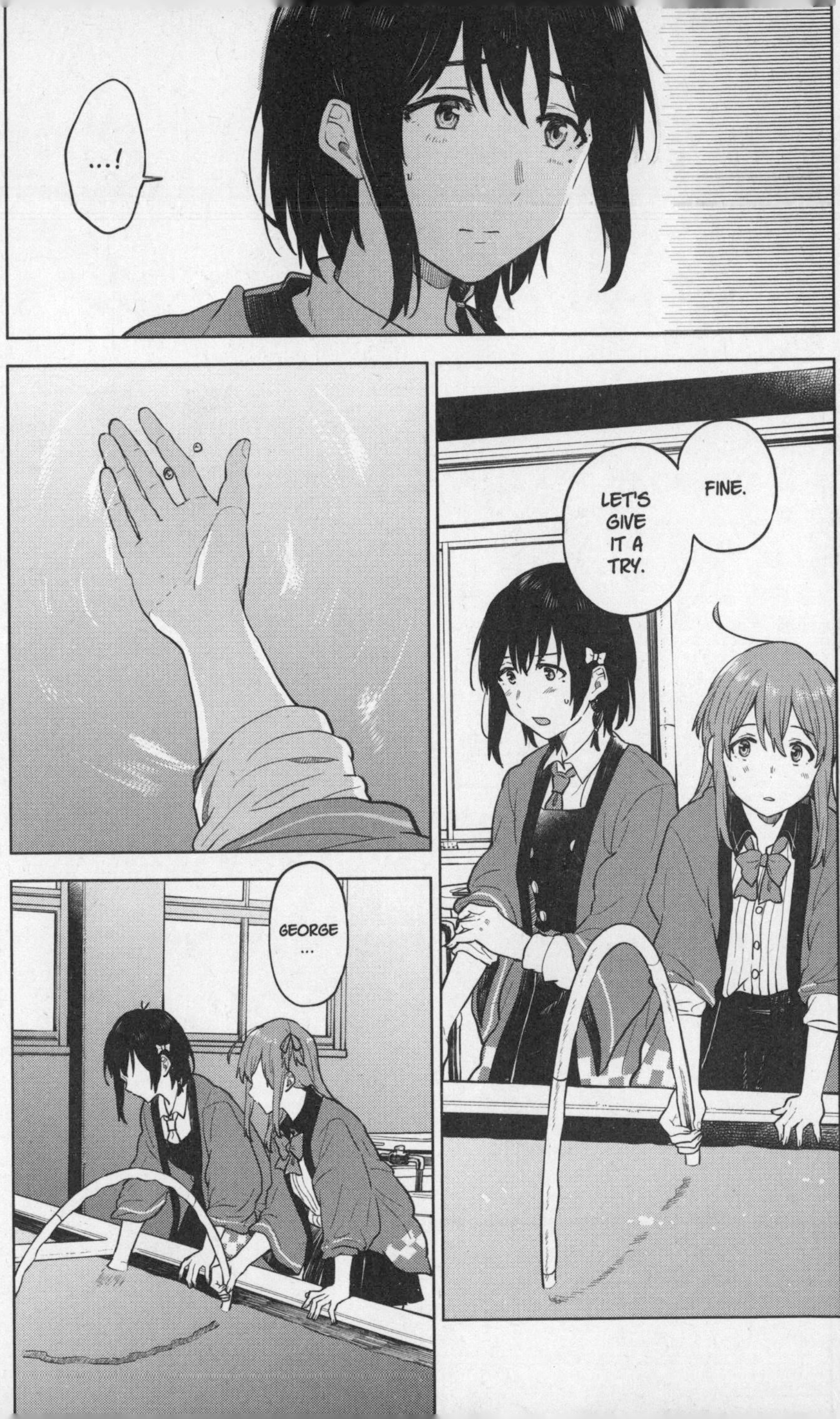
...!
FINE.
LET'S GIVE IT A TRY.
GEORGE ...

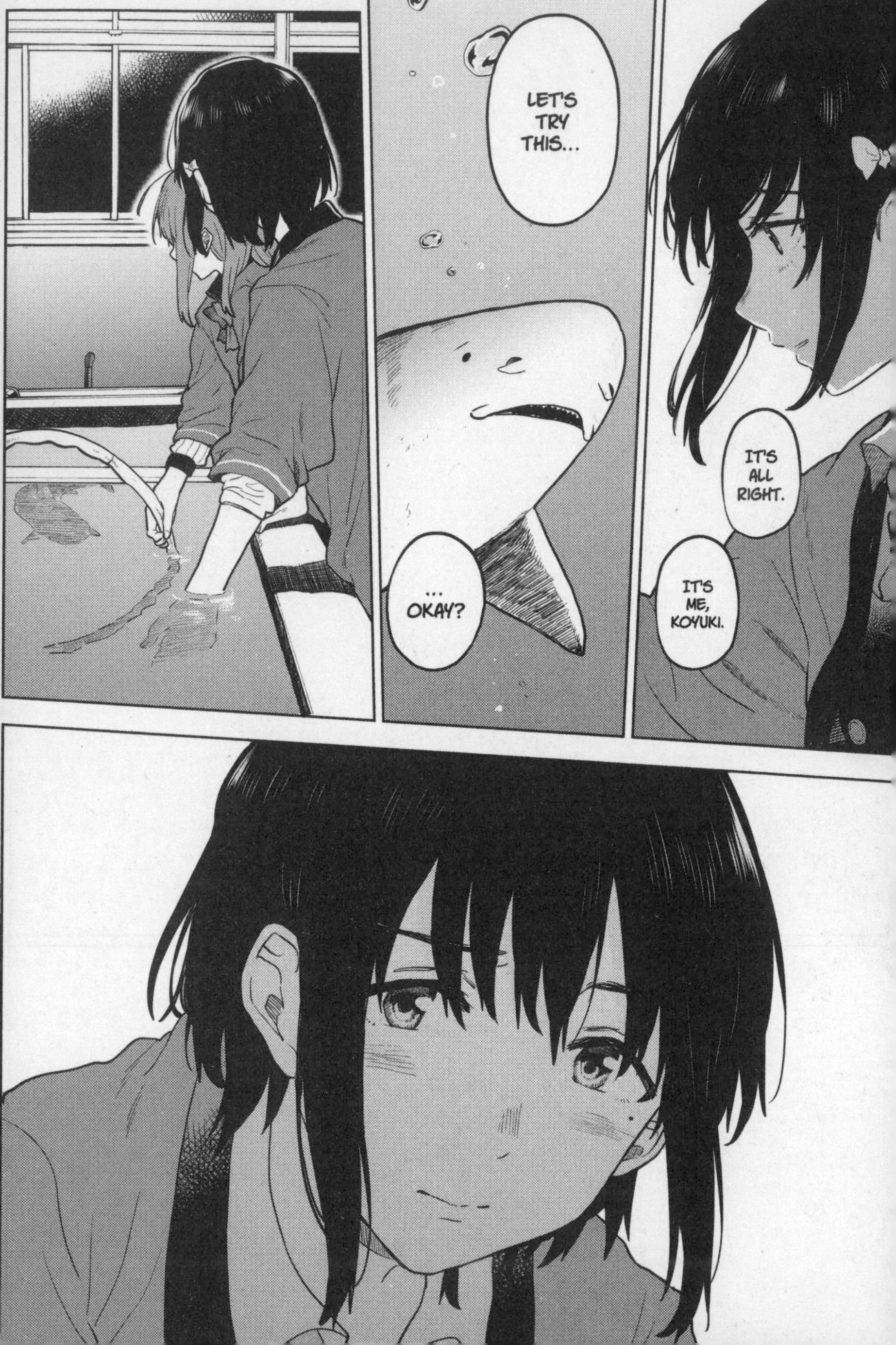
IT'S ALL RIGHT.
IT'S ME, KOYUKI.
LET'S TRY THIS...
... OKAY?

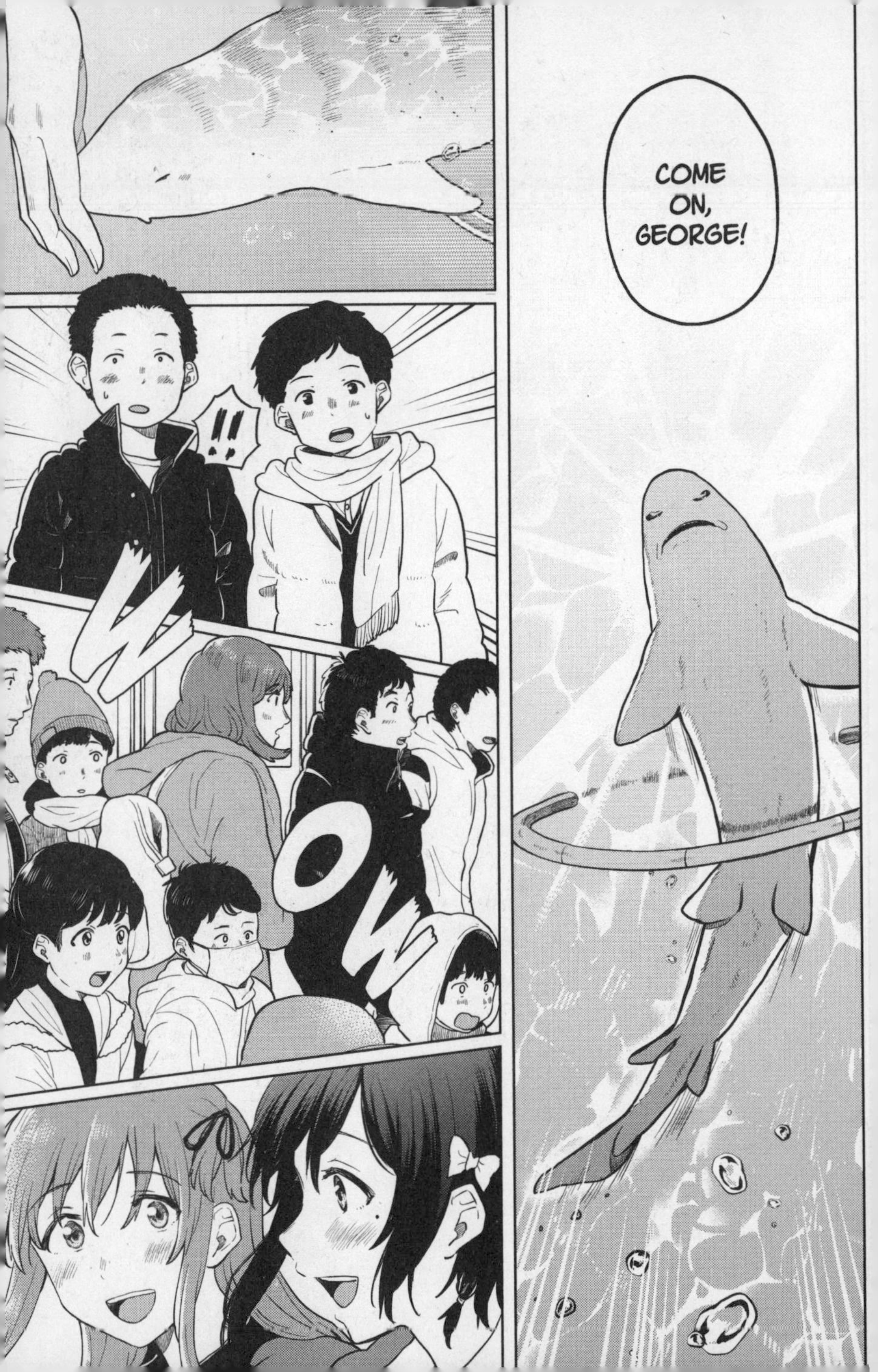
COME ON, GEORGE!
!!
WOW

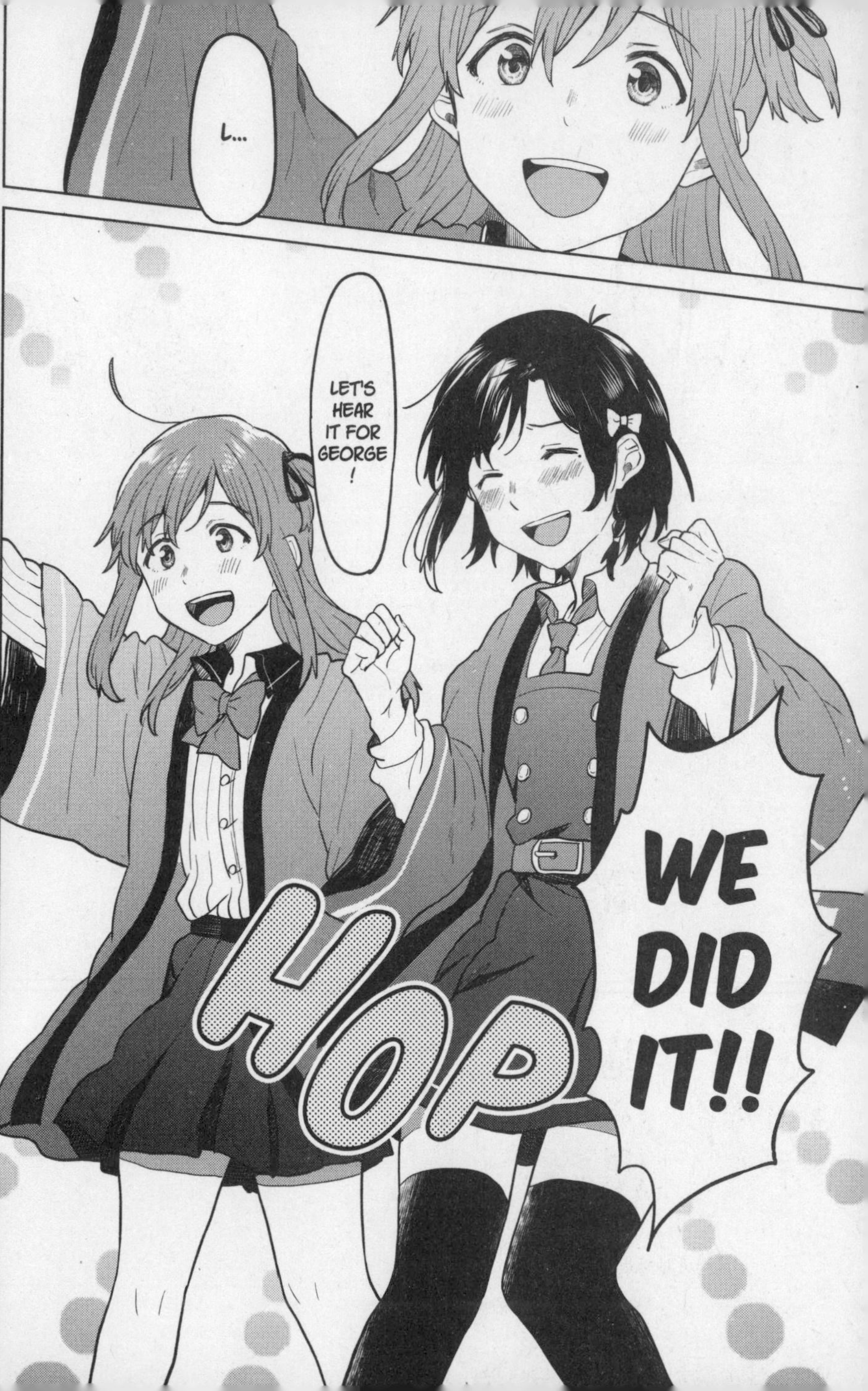
I...
LET'S HEAR IT FOR GEORGE!
WE DID IT!!
HOP

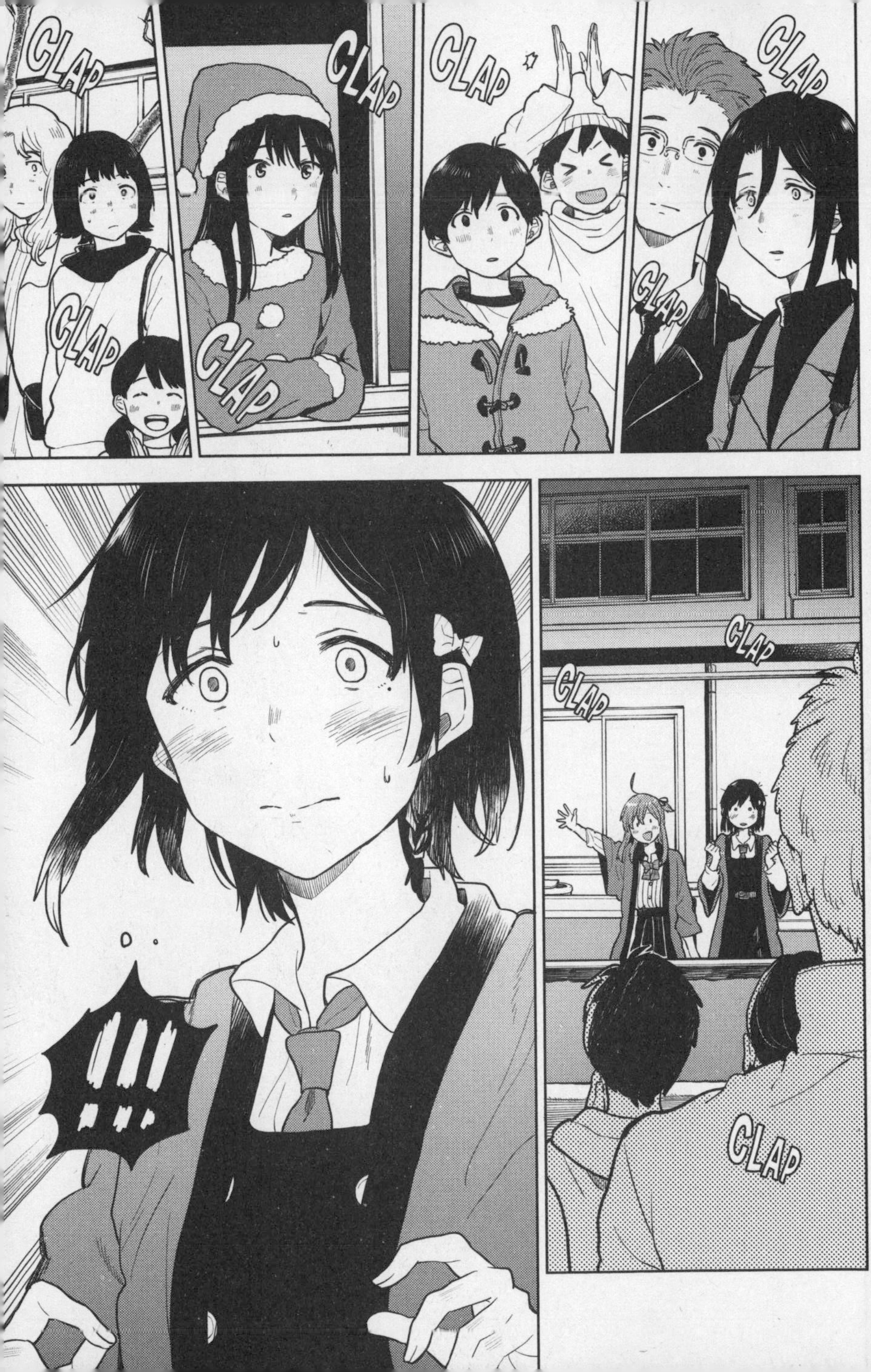
CLAP
CLAP
CLAP
CLAP
CLAP
CLAP
CLAP
CLAP
CLAP
CLAP
CLAP
!!!!

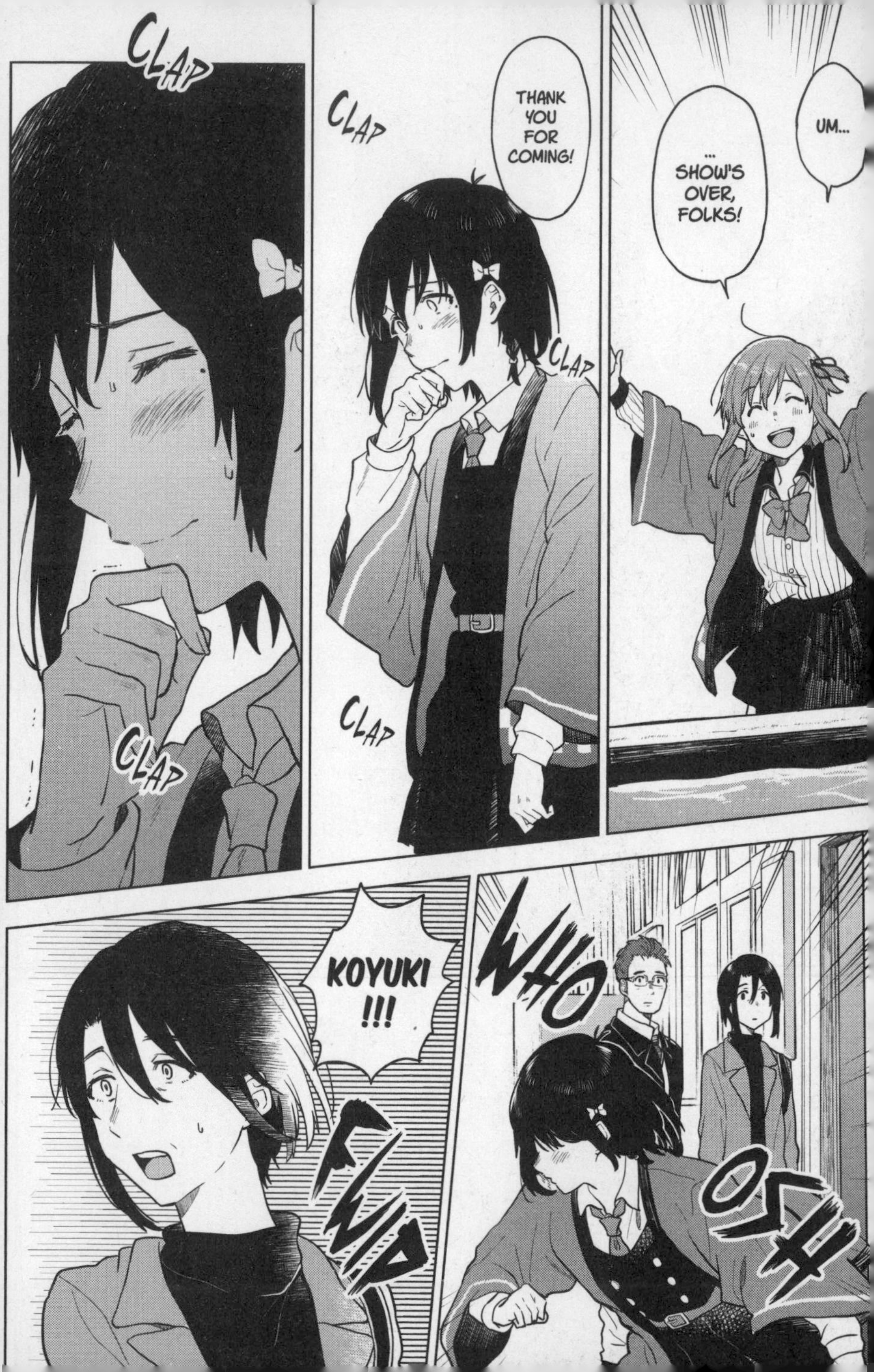
UM...
... SHOW'S OVER, FOLKS!
THANK YOU FOR COMING!
CLAP
CLAP
CLAP
CLAP
CLAP
WHOOSH
KOYUKI !!!
FWIP

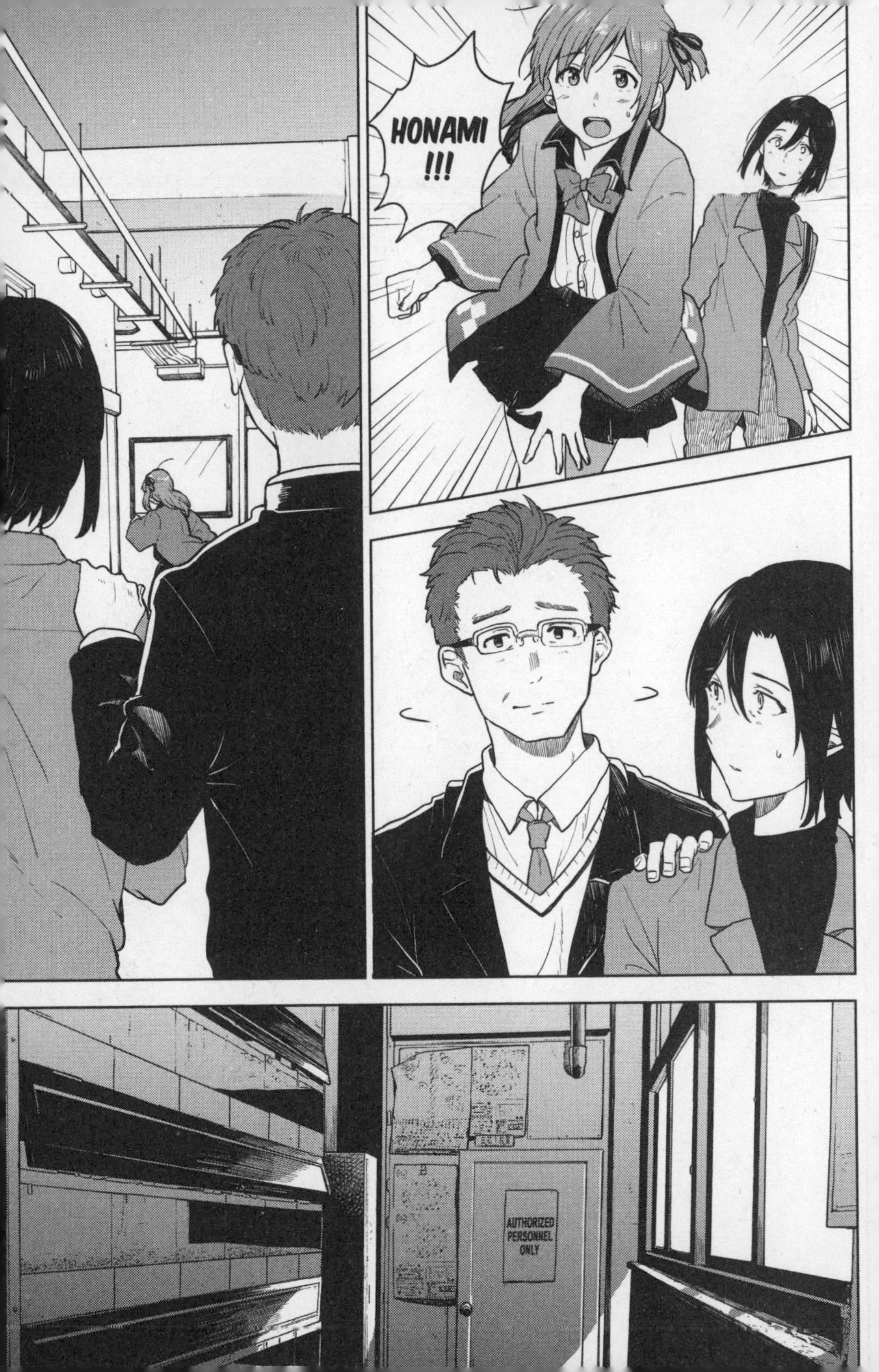
HONAMI !!!
AUTHORIZED PERSONNEL ONLY

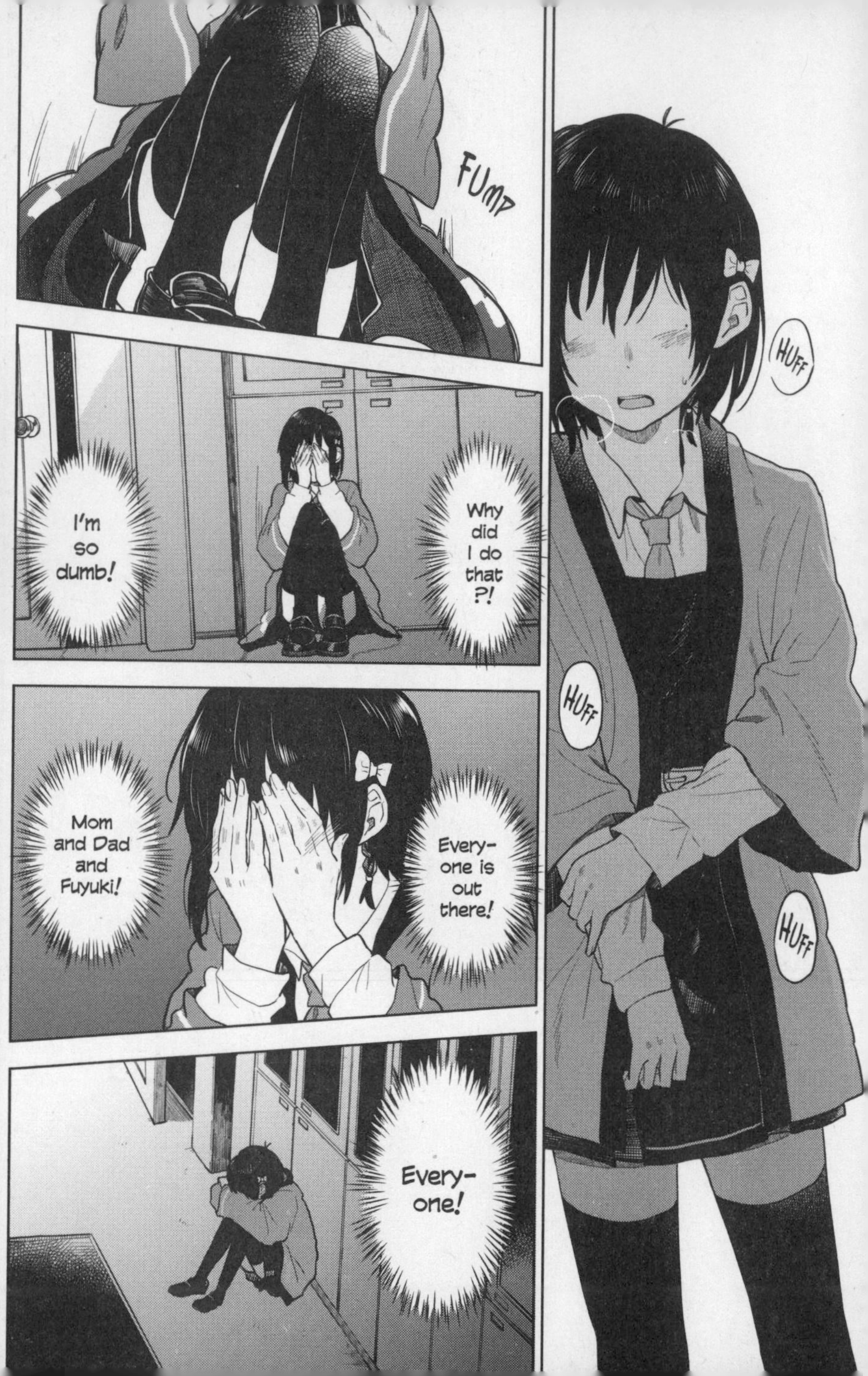
HUFF
HUFF
HUFF
FUMP
Why did I do that?!
I'm so dumb!
Every-one is out there!
Mom and Dad and Fuyuki!
Every-one!

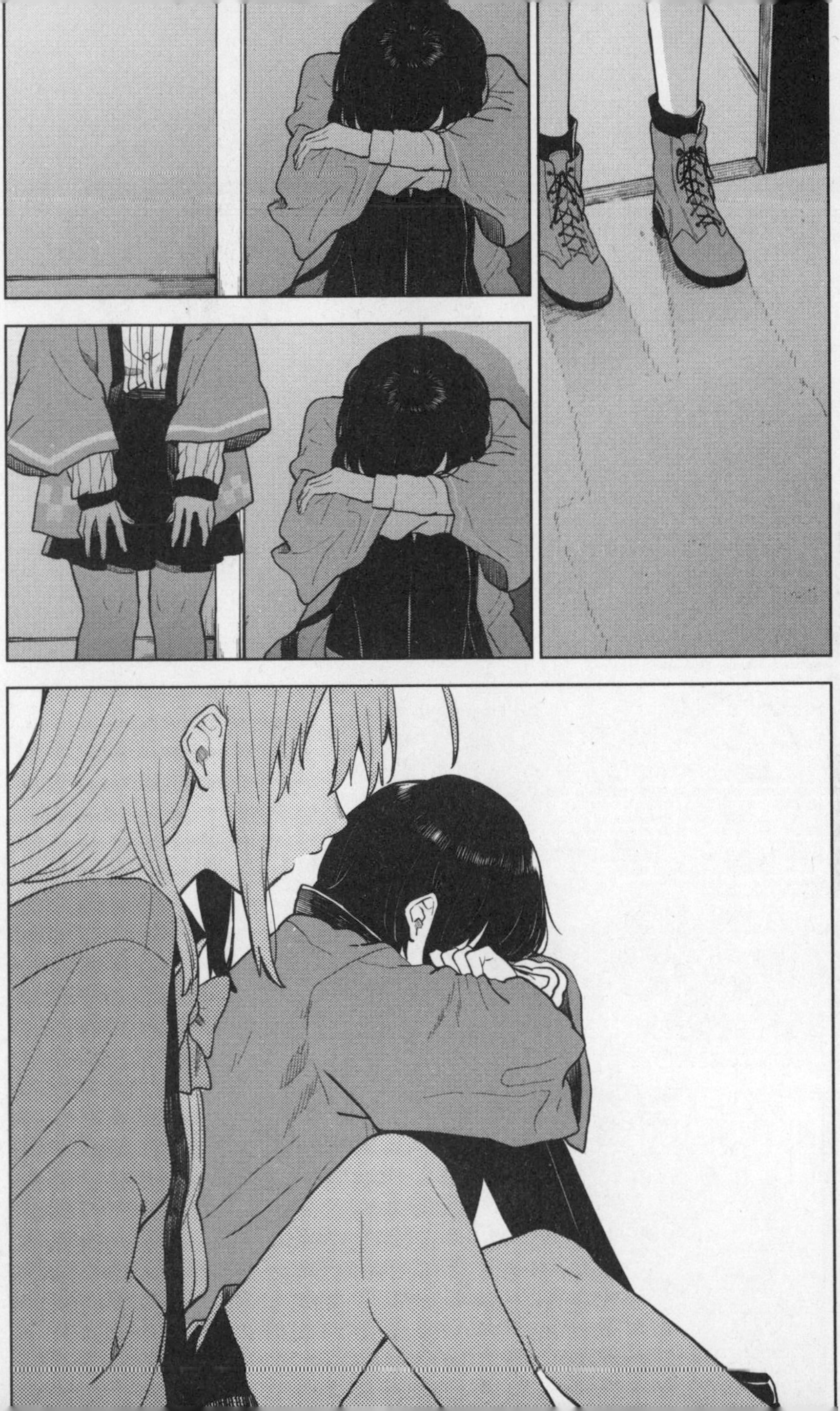

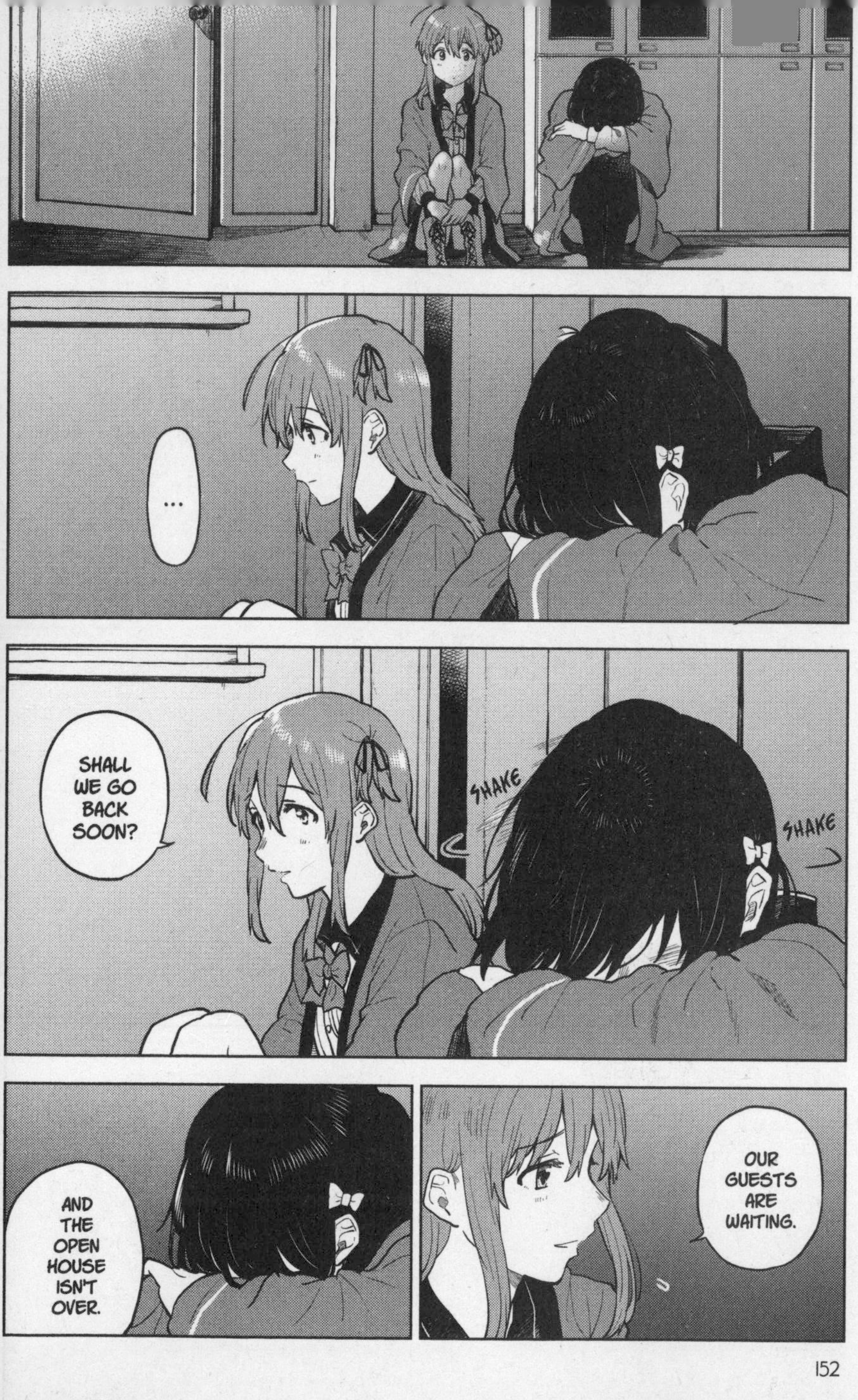
...
SHALL WE GO BACK SOON?
SHAKE
SHAKE
OUR GUESTS ARE WAITING.
AND THE OPEN HOUSE ISN'T OVER.

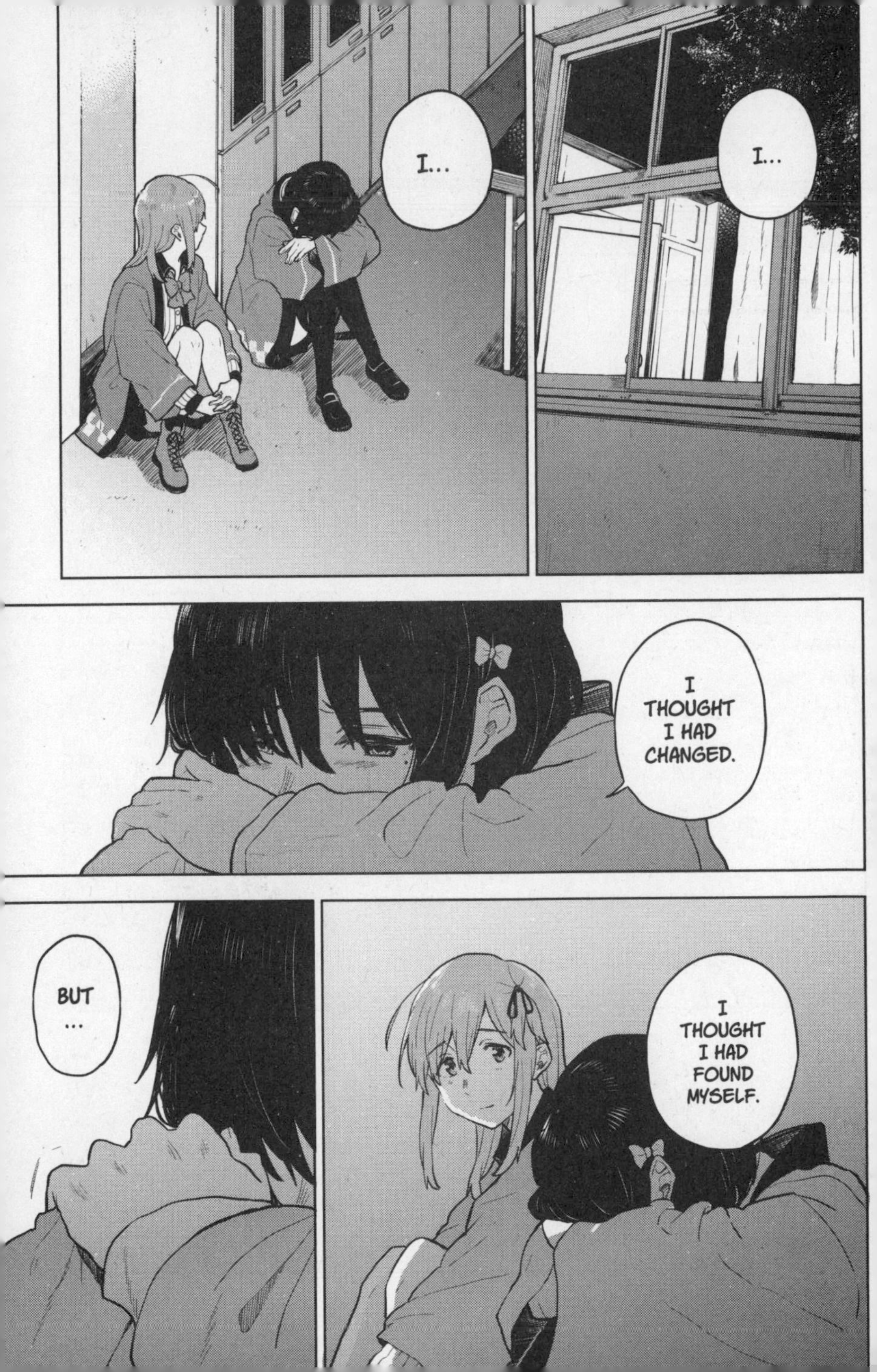
I...
I...
I THOUGHT I HAD CHANGED.
I THOUGHT I HAD FOUND MYSELF.
BUT ...

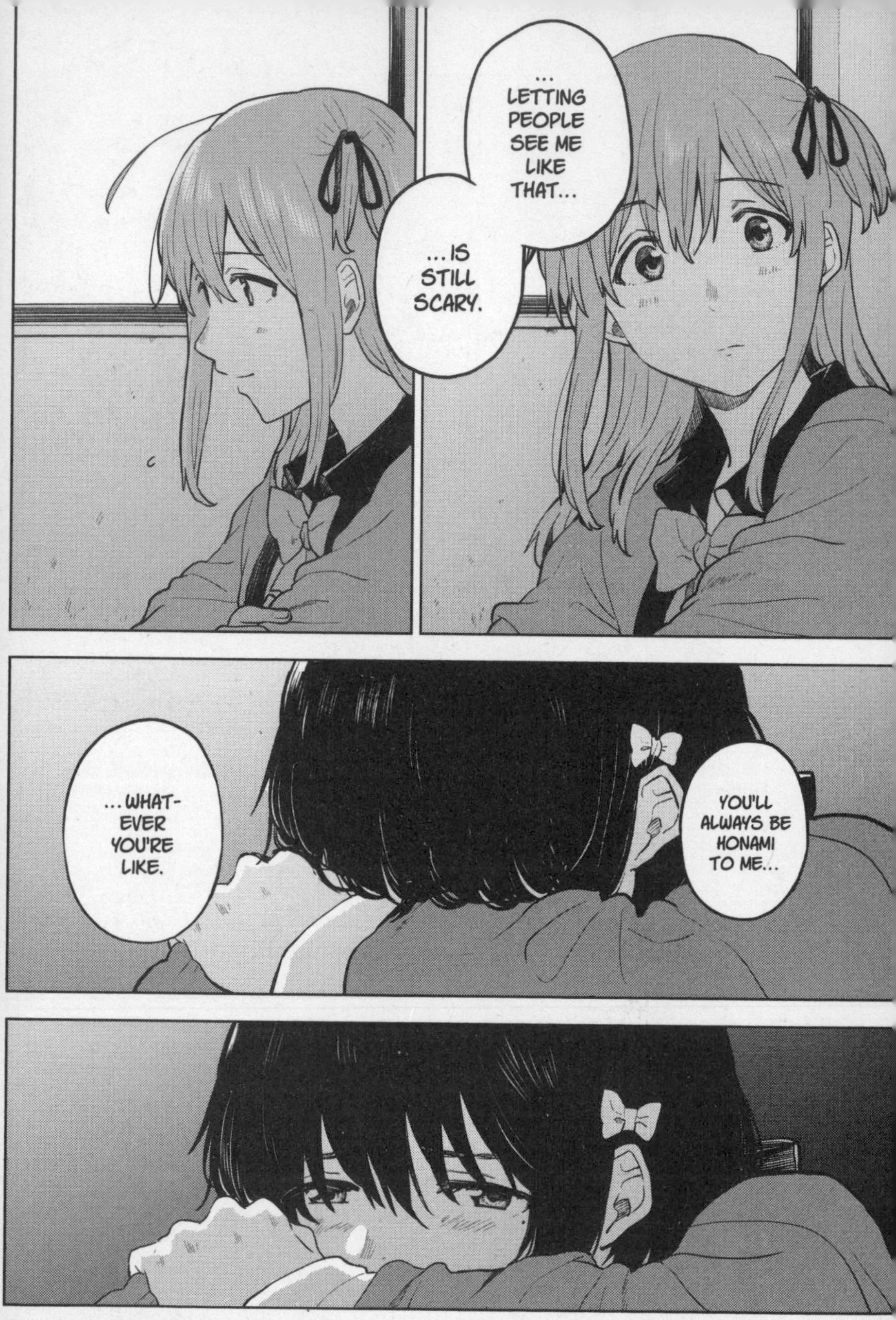
...LETTING PEOPLE SEE ME LIKE THAT...
...IS STILL SCARY.
YOU'LL ALWAYS BE HONAMI TO ME...
...WHAT-EVER YOU'RE LIKE.

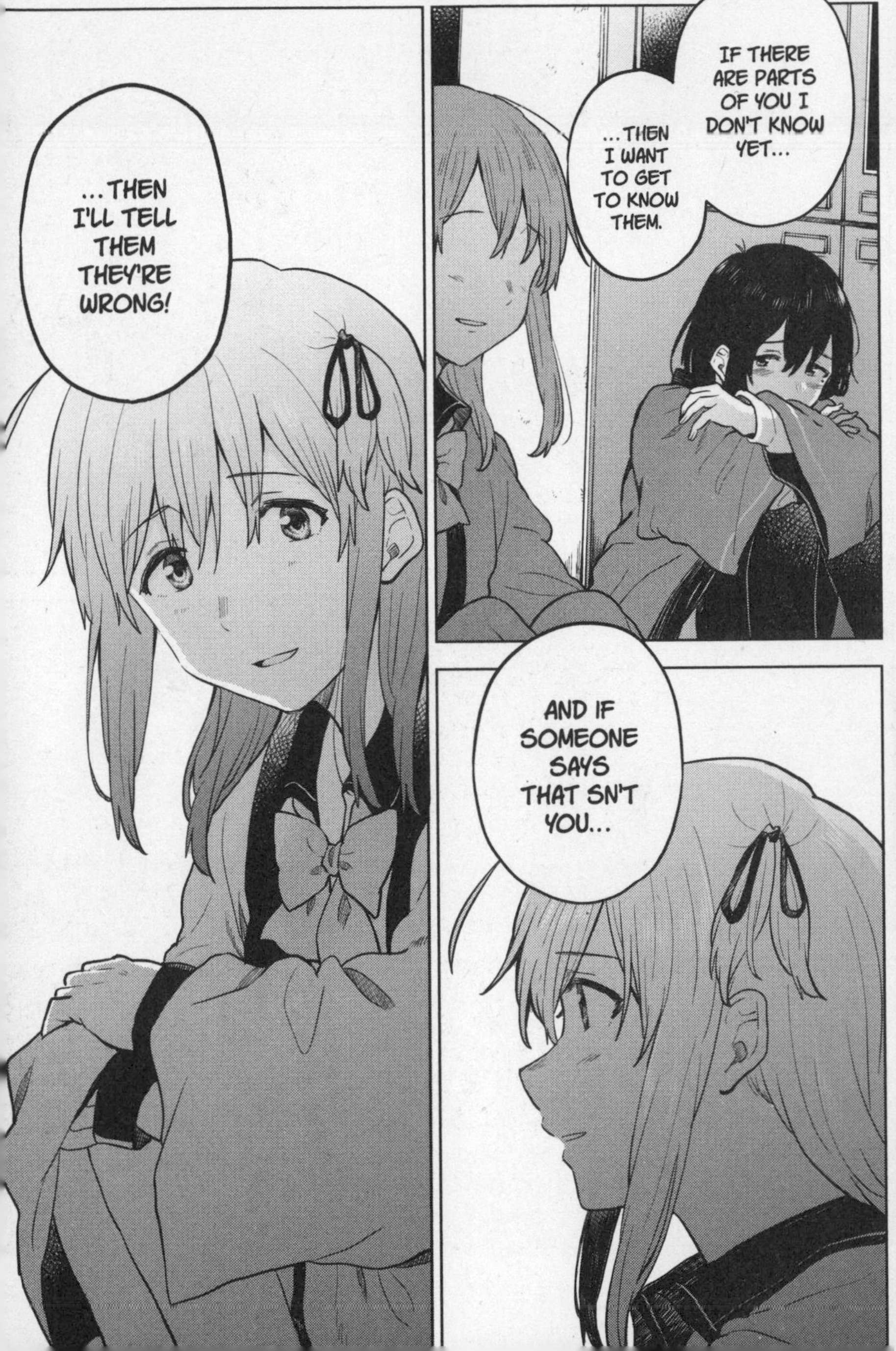
IF THERE ARE PARTS OF YOU I DON'T KNOW YET...
...THEN I WANT TO GET TO KNOW THEM.
AND IF SOMEONE SAYS THAT SN'T YOU...
...THEN I'LL TELL THEM THEY'RE WRONG!

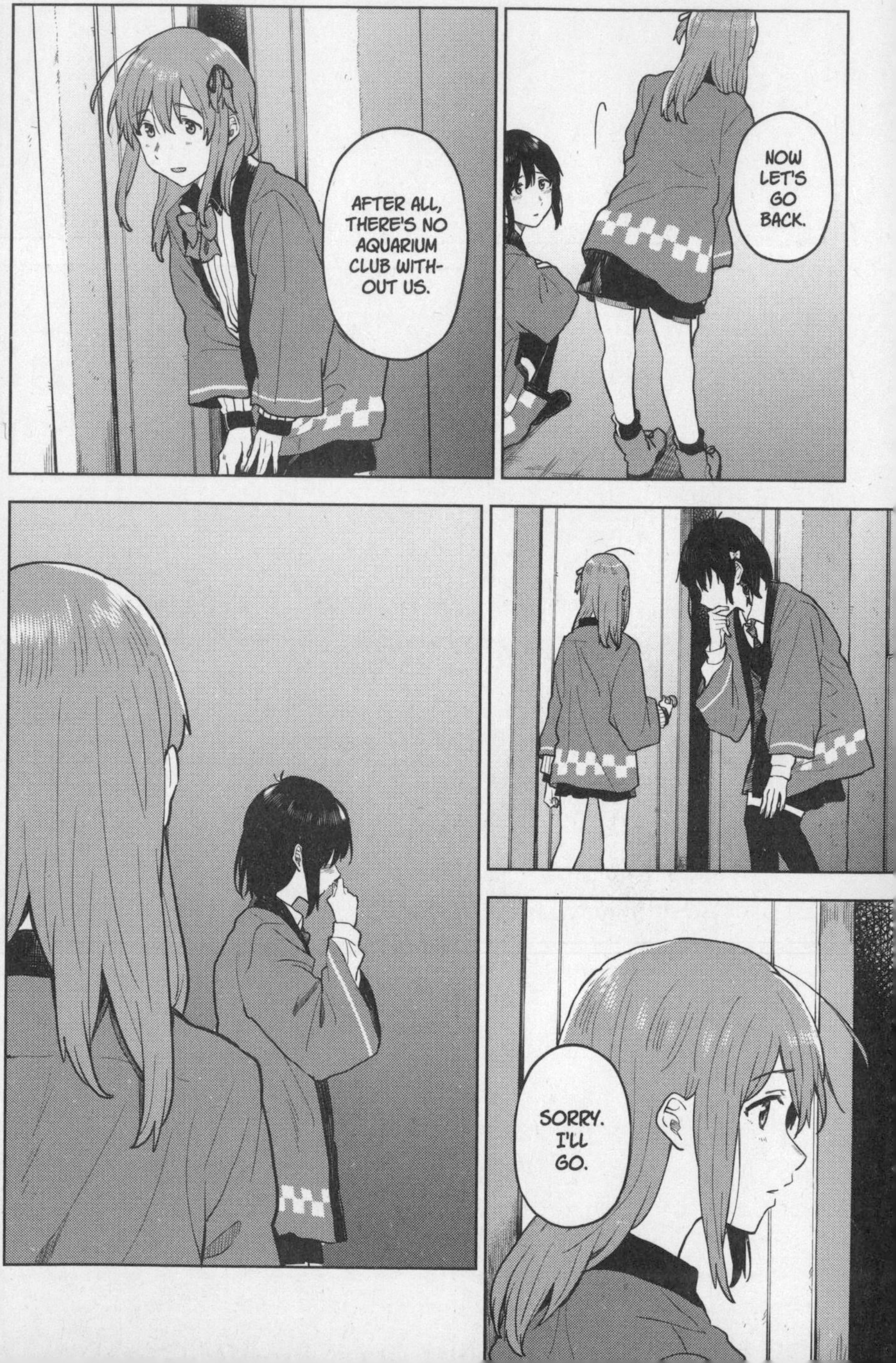
NOW LET'S GO BACK.
AFTER ALL, THERE'S NO AQUARIUM CLUB WITHOUT US.
SORRY. I'LL GO.

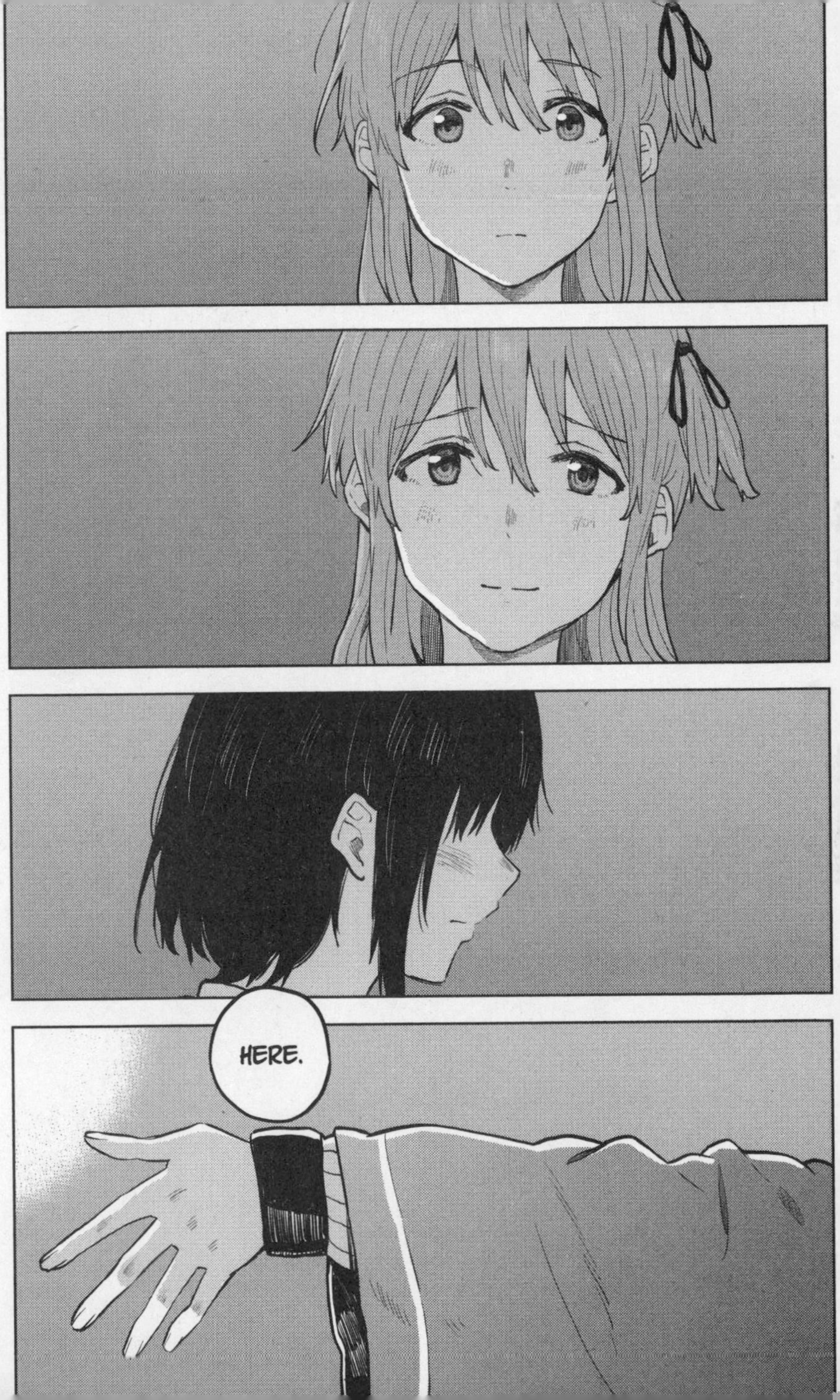
HERE.

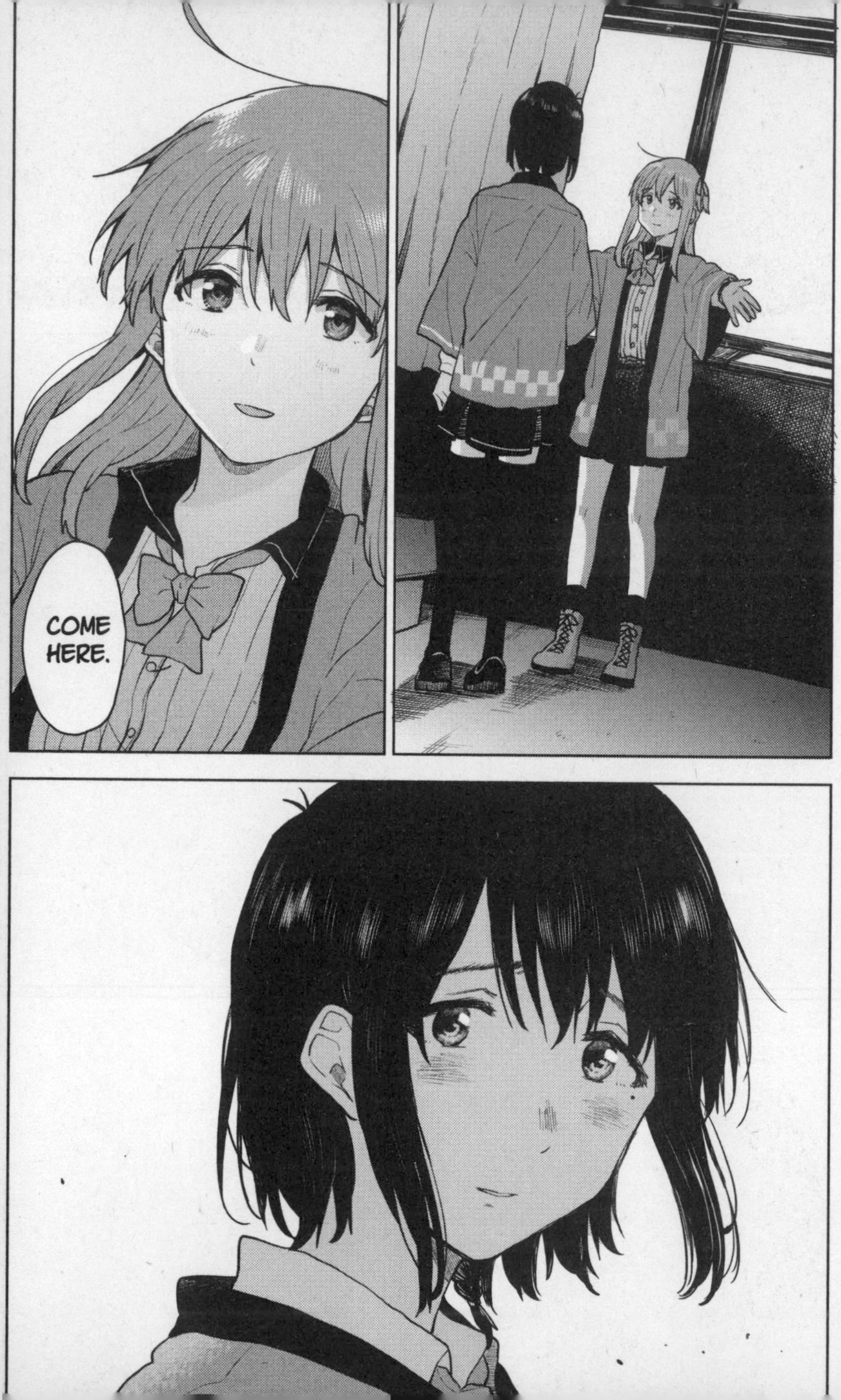
COME HERE.

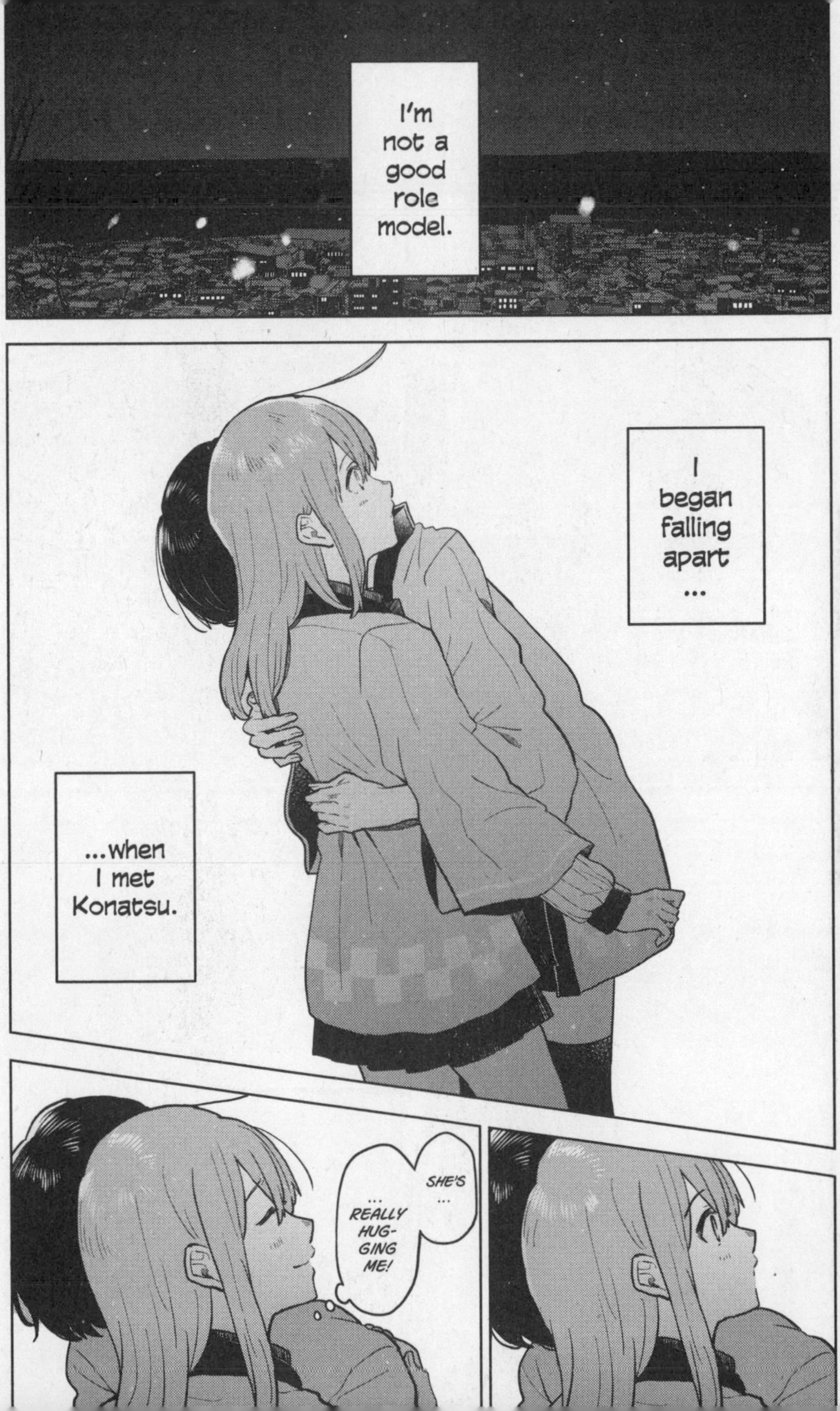
I'm not a good role model.
I began falling apart...
...when I met Konatsu.
SHE'S... ...REALLY HUG-GING ME!

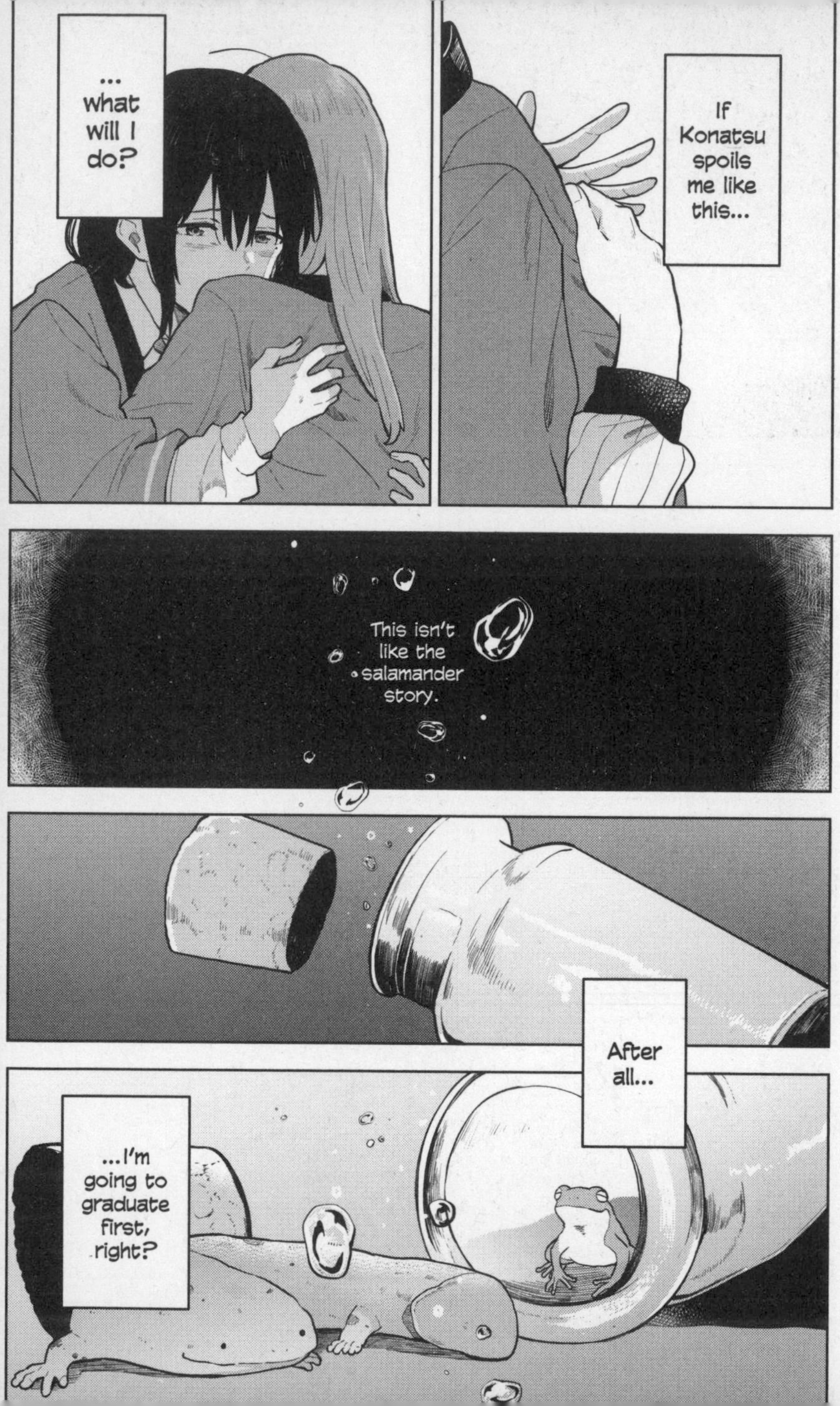
If Konatsu spoils me like this...
...what will I do?
This isn't like the salamander story.
After all...
...I'm going to graduate first, right?

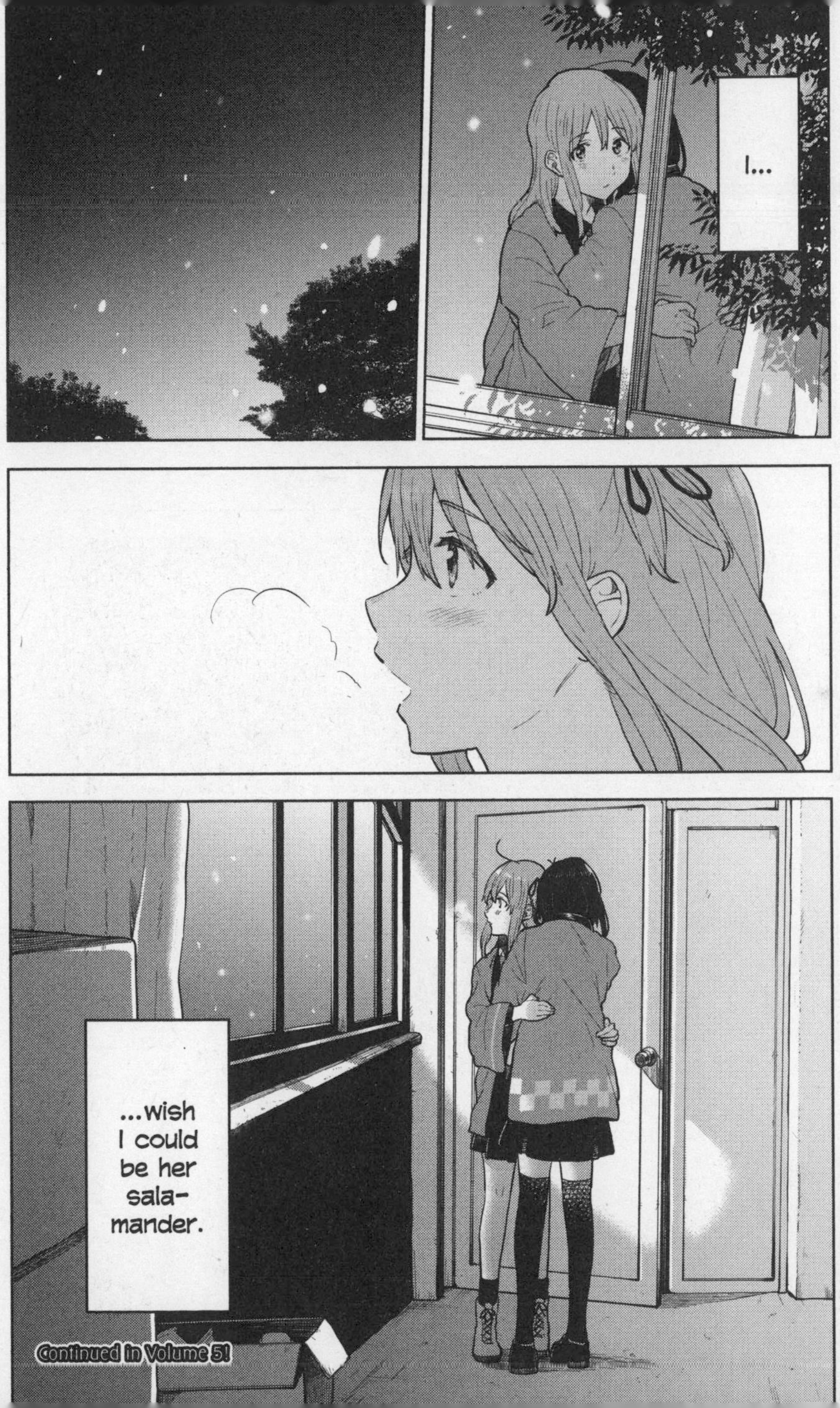
I...
...wish I could be her sala-mander.
Continued in Volume 5!

Afterword

A Tropical Fish Yearns for Snow Vol. 4

Thank you for reading!!

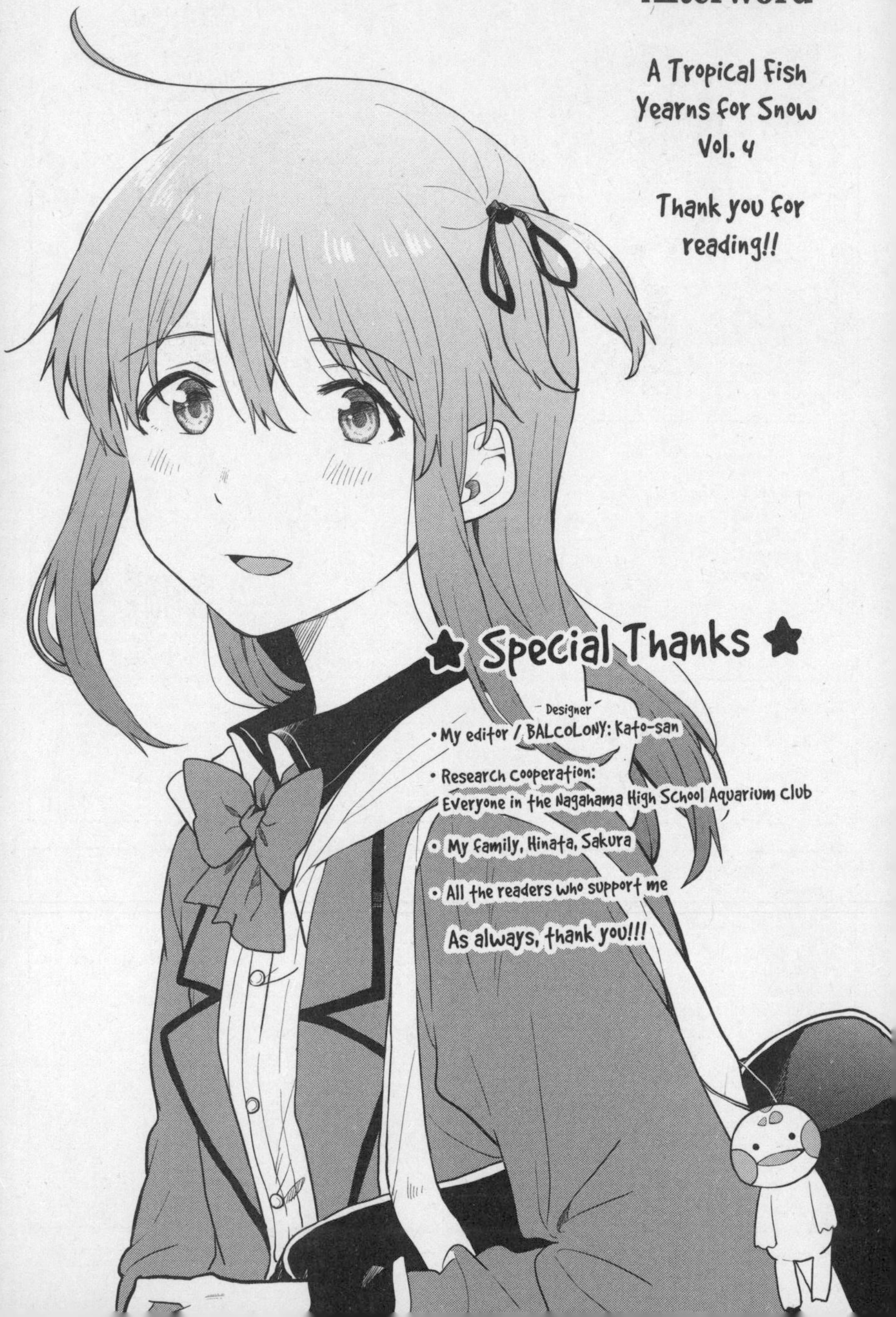

★ Special Thanks ★

- My editor / Designer BALCOLONY: Kato-san
- Research cooperation: Everyone in the Nagahama High School Aquarium club
- My family, Hinata, Sakura
- All the readers who support me

As always, thank you!!!

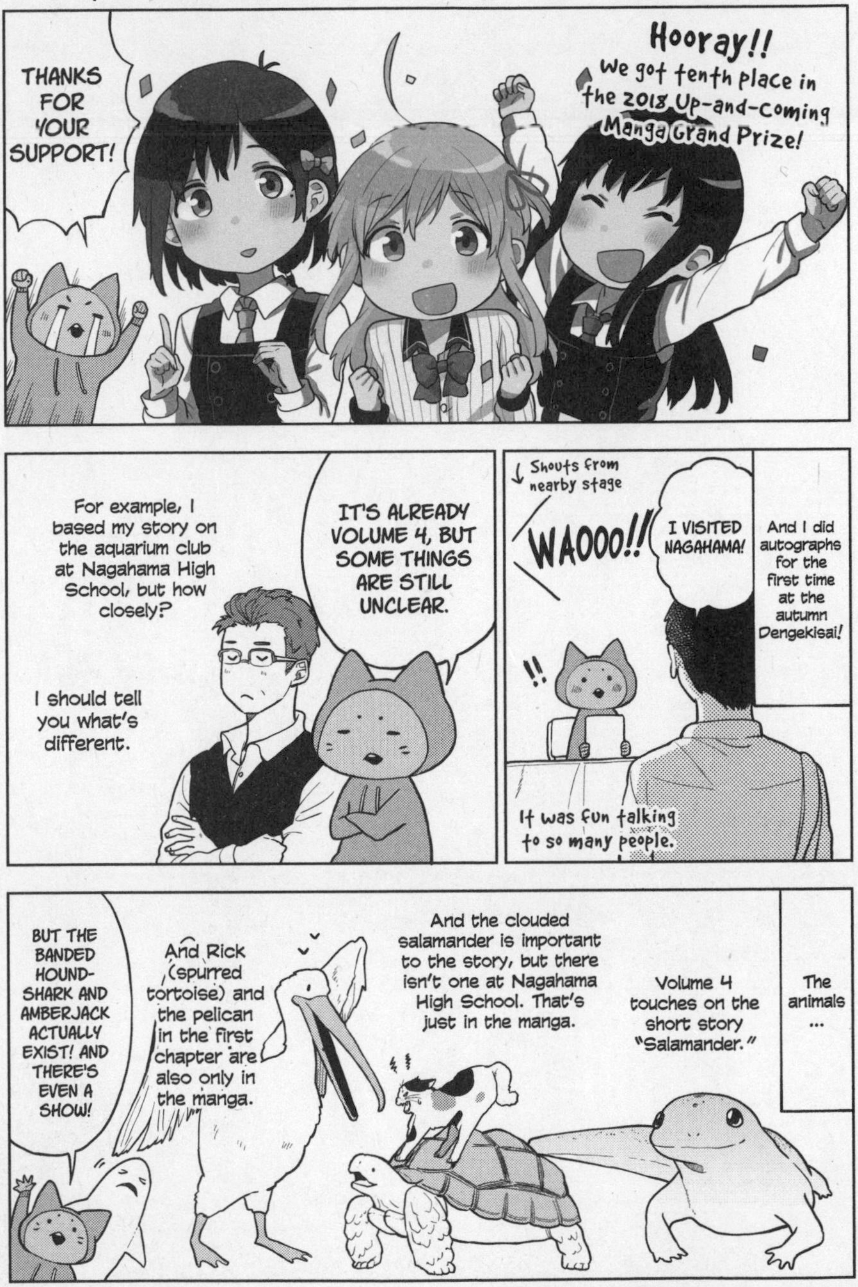
Hooray!! We got tenth place in the 2018 Up-and-Coming Manga Grand Prize!
THANKS FOR YOUR SUPPORT!
And I did autographs for the first time at the autumn Dengekisai!
I VISITED NAGAHAMA!
Shouts from nearby stage
WAOOO!!
!!
It was fun talking to so many people.
IT'S ALREADY VOLUME 4, BUT SOME THINGS ARE STILL UNCLEAR.
For example, I based my story on the aquarium club at Nagahama High School, but how closely?
I should tell you what's different.
The animals ...
Volume 4 touches on the short story "Salamander."
And the clouded salamander is important to the story, but there isn't one at Nagahama High School. That's just in the manga.
And Rick (spurred tortoise) and the pelican in the first chapter are also only in the manga.
BUT THE BANDED HOUND-SHARK AND AMBERJACK ACTUALLY EXIST! AND THERE'S EVEN A SHOW!

★ At present, Nagahama High School has about 2,000 specimens, including tropical fish like clown fish and surgeonfish.

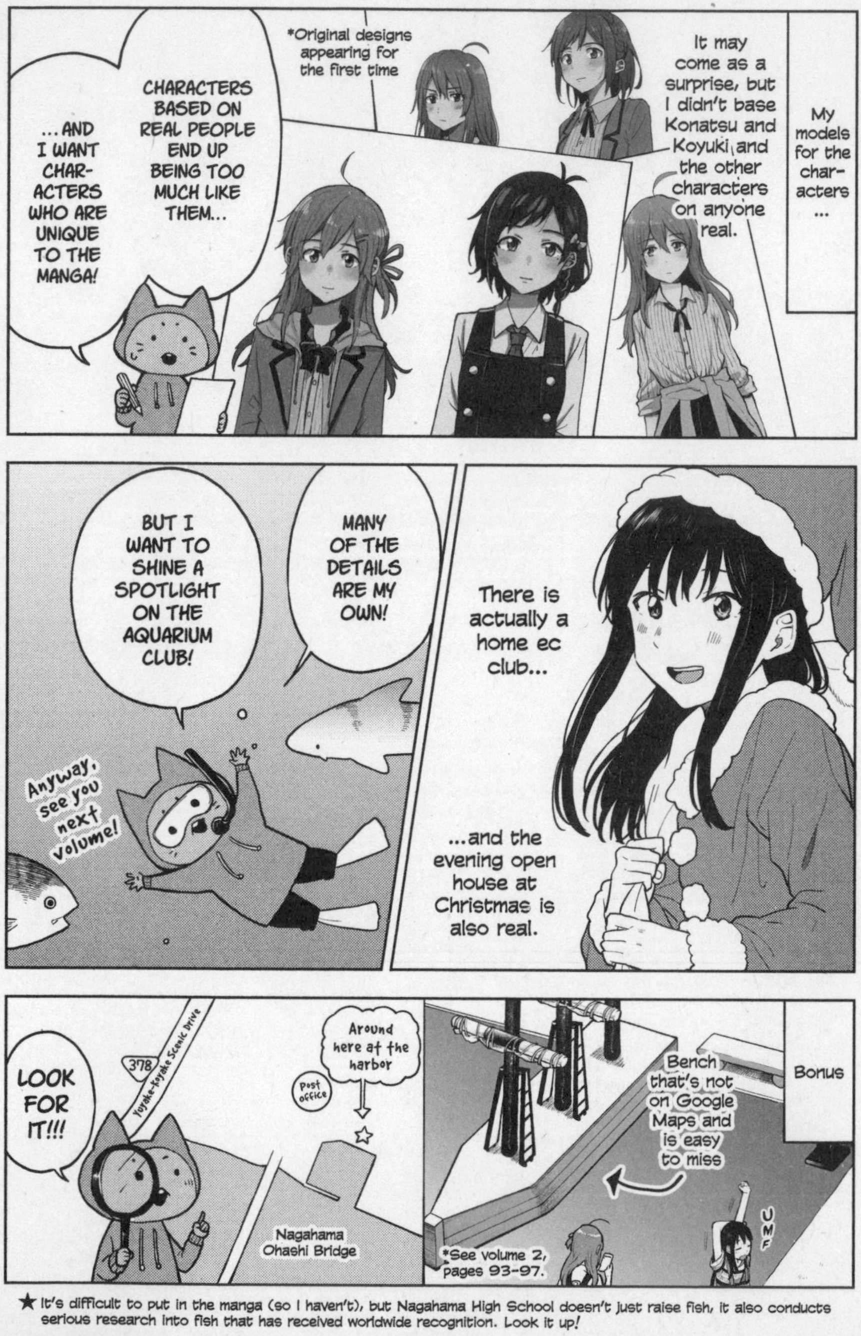
My models for the characters...
It may come as a surprise, but I didn't base Konatsu and Koyuki and the other characters on anyone real.
*Original designs appearing for the first time
CHARACTERS BASED ON REAL PEOPLE END UP BEING TOO MUCH LIKE THEM...
...AND I WANT CHARACTERS WHO ARE UNIQUE TO THE MANGA!
There is actually a home ec club...
...and the evening open house at Christmas is also real.
MANY OF THE DETAILS ARE MY OWN!
BUT I WANT TO SHINE A SPOTLIGHT ON THE AQUARIUM CLUB!
Anyway, see you next volume!
Bonus
Bench that's not on Google Maps and is easy to miss
UMF
*See volume 2, pages 93-97.
Around here at the harbor
Post office
378
Yuyake-Koyake Scenic Drive
Nagahama Ohashi Bridge
LOOK FOR IT!!!

★ It's difficult to put in the manga (so I haven't), but Nagahama High School doesn't just raise fish, it also conducts serious research into fish that has received worldwide recognition. Look it up!

A TROPICAL FISH YEARNS FOR SNOW
Vol. 4
VIZ Media Edition

STORY AND ART BY
MAKOTO HAGINO

English Translation & Adaptation/John Werry
Touch-Up Art & Lettering/Eve Grandt
Design/Yukiko Whitley
Editor/Pancha Diaz

NETTAIGYO WA YUKI NI KOGARERU Vol. 4
©Makoto Hagino 2019
First published in Japan in 2019 by KADOKAWA CORPORATION, Tokyo.
English translation rights arranged with KADOKAWA CORPORATION, Tokyo.

Printed in Canada

Published by VIZ Media, LLC
P.O. Box 77010
San Francisco, CA 94107

10 9 8 7 6 5 4 3 2 1
First printing, August 2020

PARENTAL ADVISORY
A TROPICAL FISH YEARNS FOR SNOW is rated T
for Teen and is recommended for ages 13 and up.

viz.com

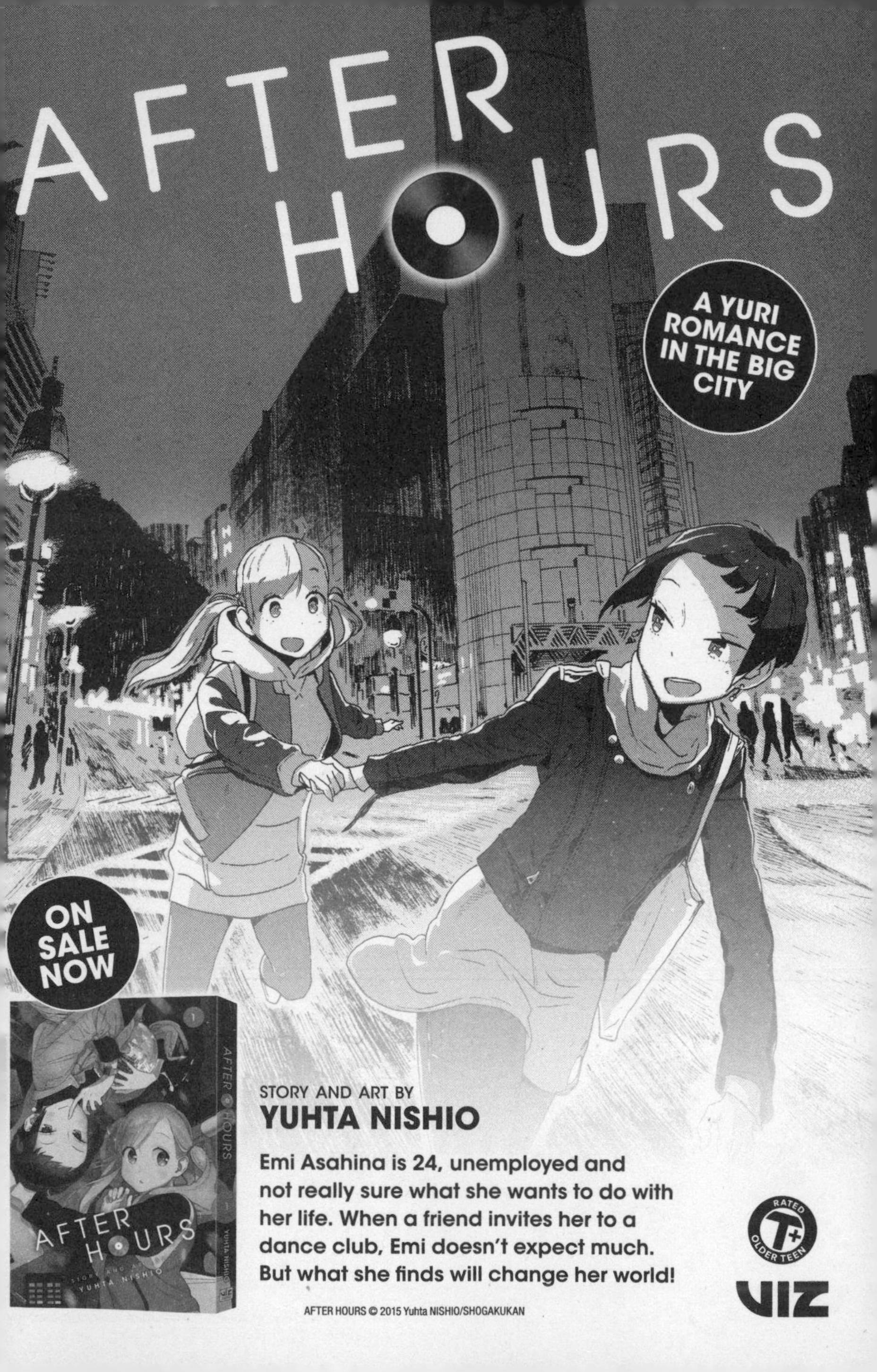
AFTER HOURS
A YURI ROMANCE IN THE BIG CITY
ON SALE NOW
AFTER HOURS
STORY AND ART BY YUHTA NISHIO
1
STORY AND ART BY
YUHTA NISHIO
Emi Asahina is 24, unemployed and not really sure what she wants to do with her life. When a friend invites her to a dance club, Emi doesn't expect much. But what she finds will change her world!
RATED T+ OLDER TEEN
VIZ
AFTER HOURS © 2015 Yuhta NISHIO/SHOGAKUKAN

Sweet *Blue* Flowers

Story and Art by **Takako Shimura**

Akira Okudaira is starting high school and is ready for exciting new experiences. And on the first day of school, she runs into her best friend from kindergarten at the train station! Now Akira and Fumi have the chance to rekindle their friendship, but life has gotten a lot more complicated since they were kids…

Collect the series!

Komi Can't Communicate

Story & Art by Tomohito Oda

The journey to a hundred friends begins with a single conversation.

Socially anxious high school student Shoko Komi's greatest dream is to make some friends, but everyone at school mistakes her crippling social anxiety for cool reserve. With the whole student body keeping its distance and Komi unable to utter a single word, friendship might be forever beyond her reach.

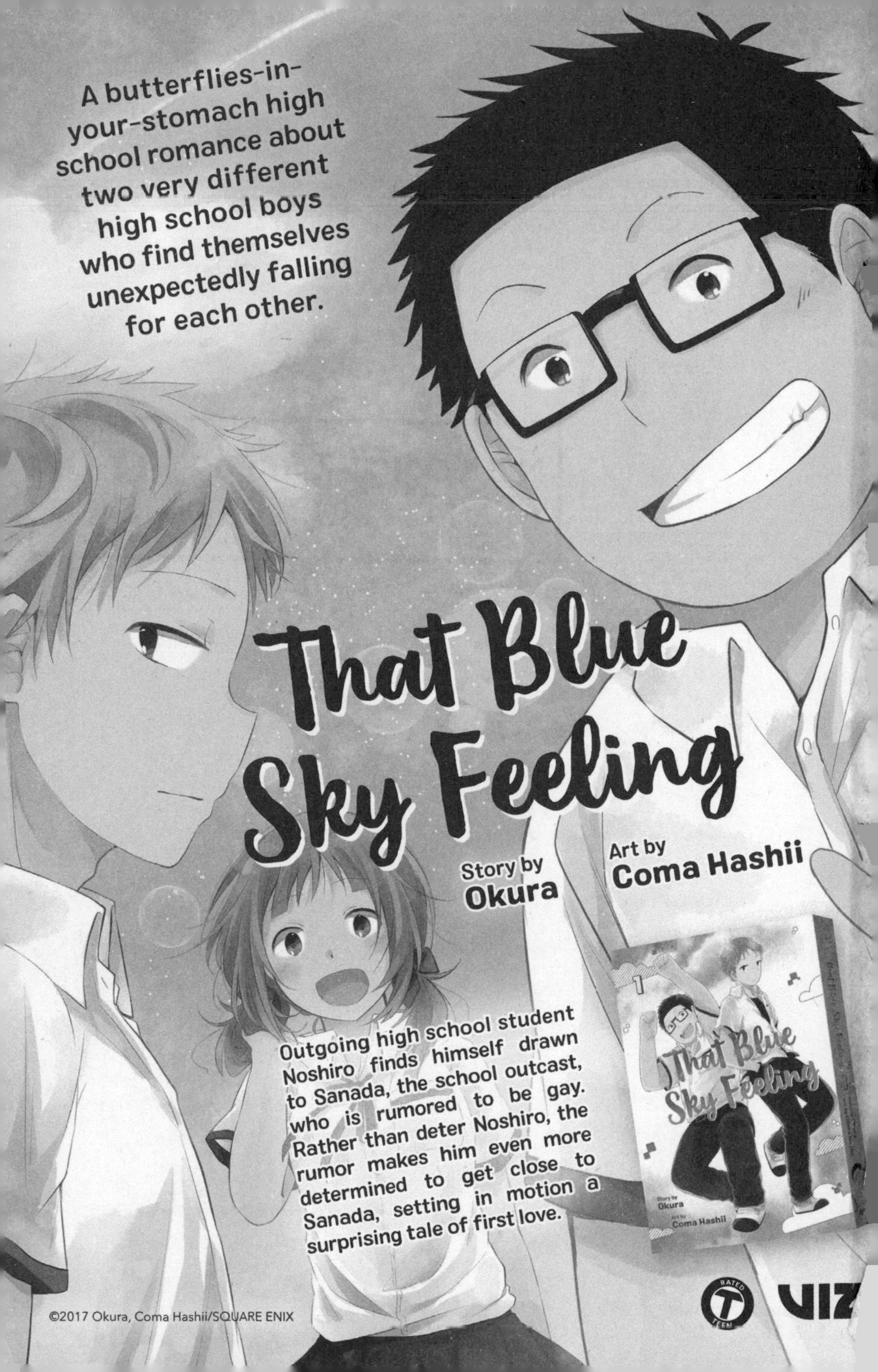
A butterflies-in-your-stomach high school romance about two very different high school boys who find themselves unexpectedly falling for each other.
That Blue Sky Feeling
Story by Okura
Art by Coma Hashii
Outgoing high school student Noshiro finds himself drawn to Sanada, the school outcast, who is rumored to be gay. Rather than deter Noshiro, the rumor makes him even more determined to get close to Sanada, setting in motion a surprising tale of first love.
1
That Blue Sky Feeling
Story by Okura
Art by Coma Hashii
RATED T TEEN
VIZ
©2017 Okura, Coma Hashii/SQUARE ENIX

This is the last page.

A Tropical Fish Yearns for Snow **has been printed in the original Japanese format to preserve the orientation of the artwork.**

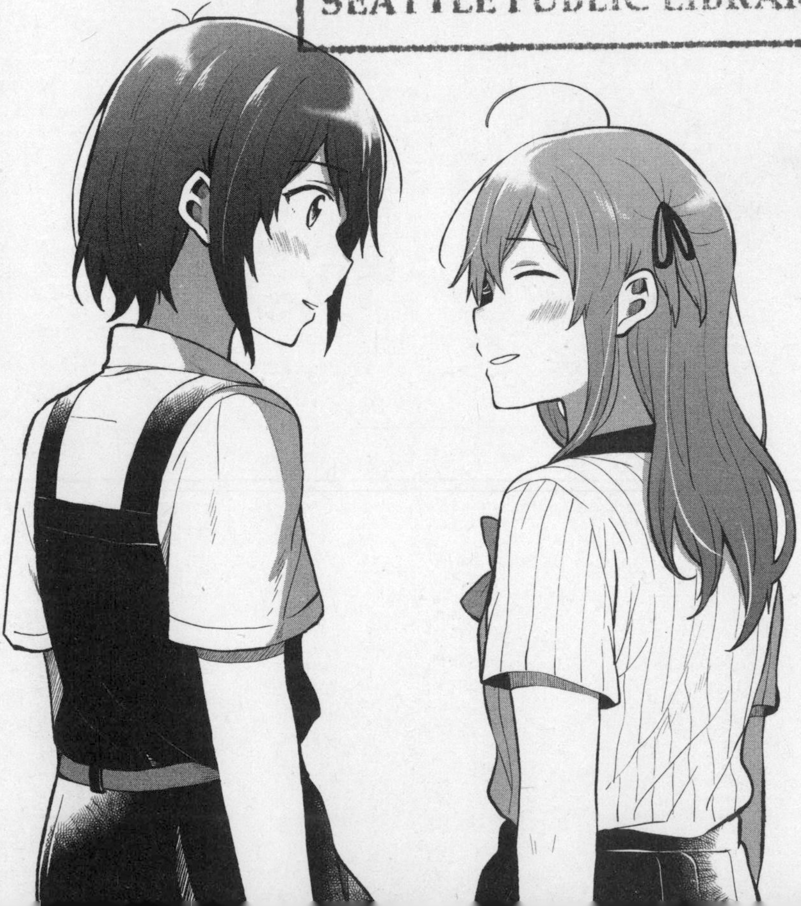

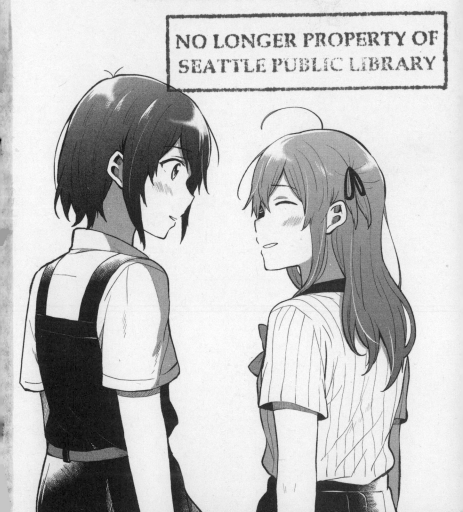